Ancient Myth and Modern Man

GERALD A. LARUE

University of Southern California

Prentice-Hall, Inc., *Englewood Cliffs, New Jersey*

Library of Congress Cataloging in Publication Data

LARUE, GERALD A
  Ancient myth and modern man.

  Bibliography: p.
  1. Mythology. I. Title.
BL311.L32   301.2'1   74-9527
ISBN 0-13-035493-7
ISBN 0-13-035485-6 (pbk.)

© 1975 by *Prentice-Hall, Inc.*, Englewood Cliffs, N.J.

Printed in the United States of America

10   9   8   7   6   5   4   3   2   1

Prentice-Hall International, Inc., *London*
Prentice-Hall of Australia, Pty. Ltd., *Sydney*
Prentice-Hall of Canada, Ltd., *Toronto*
Prentice-Hall of India Private Limited, *New Delhi*
Prentice-Hall of Japan, Inc., *Tokyo*

Contents

Preface

Different approaches to the study of myth have been employed during the past century and a half. Linguists, anthropologists, psychologists, and religionists brought their particular theories to myth, and often what they read into myth was what they discovered in myth. Some sought a primal monomyth or basic myth; others insisted that myths are best understood etiologically, as explanations of why things are the way they are; still others found a link between myth and ritual. Diffusionist theories account for shared features and provide hypotheses to explain the transmission of myths from group to group.

There are dangers of oversimplification in the use of any single approach to the study of mythology and in the search for an underlying theme to unite all mythic expressions.[1] Differences are obscured in the interest of stressing commonality. While diffusionist theories account for certain similarities, individual groups developed their own interpretations of common concepts, and some groups clearly produced their own myths. A brief review of some of the schools of mythological interpretation that have developed during the past 150 years demonstrates the need for caution before accepting the theories of one school over another and underscores the importance of reading the myths themselves, even in translation.

Modern study of ancient myth can be said to have begun with the work of Jacob and Wilhelm Grimm. In *Kinder- und Hausmärchen* (1812) they defined myths as "stories of the gods," and in *Deutsche Mythologie* (1835) they demonstrated that oral and written traditions were waiting collecting and collating among German peasants and other such groups, if only scholars would set aside their prejudices. Some scholars responded to the challenge. In 1846 William Thoms coined the term *folk-lore* to designate the study of traditions current among "common people."[2] For others the study of myth remained as it had been: the recounting of interesting and fanciful tales of the savage past.

During the last half of the nineteenth century, the conflict between two differing schools—linguistic and anthropological—stirred interest in the study of myth. Max Müller, employing a linguistic approach, argued that all Aryan myths went back to Sanskrit originals which were solar myths.[3] Before he died in 1900, his considerable writings had read solar mythologies into such diverse hero stories as those of Herakles, Perseus, Theseus, Oedipus, Samson, Beowulf, King Arthur, Cinderella, and Hansel and Gretel. According to Müller, a single plot underlay all myths and fairy tales: the struggle between light and darkness, the sun and the powers of night. The sun hero battled armies, monsters, ogres, and witches and suffered in the nether regions, just as the sun toiled across the heavens opposed by clouds and tempests. The precious gold found at the end of the struggle was golden sunshine. The magic weapons—spears, swords, and arrows—were shafts of darting sunlight. Müller's linguistic associates used fire, rain, snow, and the moon in their interpretations.

The early anthropological school, led by Andrew Lang, attacked the Linguists with scholarly argument and ridicule. Lang's theories rested on anthropological and ethnological research. Following the Grimm brothers' lead, Lang investigated village festivals, agricultural rites, and household beliefs, convinced that he could find in such folklore the archaic survivals of early myths. He was interested in reports from missionaries, travelers, and colonials about "savage myths" and barbaric customs they had observed in remote areas of the world. He was puzzled by the barbarous elements in the myths of the otherwise civilized Greeks. On the basis of anthropological studies by E. B. Tylor, and influenced by the Darwinian theory of biological evolution, which he transferred to anthropology and folklore, Lang understood Greek myths as containing remnants of earlier cultural patterns wherein cannibalism and human sacrifice prevailed. On the basis of a theory of unilinear cultural evolution, he traced stages of development from the simian to the polished sophisticate and predicted that the primitives of his day would be the Victorians of the future.

Shortly afterward, the psychoanalytic school brought its theories to the study of mythology, just as linguists and anthropologists had brought their preformulated hypotheses. Freud's analysis replaced Sanskrit with the unconscious, the conquest of light over dark with the victory of the conscious over the unconscious, and the toiling sun and the dark night with the phallus and the womb.[4] Through psychoanalysis, the hero was identified as a child rebelling against his parents; the hostile parents projected back the child's animosity and exposed him in a chest or ark in the water.[5] Myths, dreams, and fairy tales related a genital saga. The story of Red Riding Hood was interpreted as a tale of women who hate men and sex, the wolf with the living grandmother in his belly revealing pregnancy envy.[6]

Carl Jung and his followers developed a hypothesis of the collective unconscious and archetypal myths.[7] The collective unconscious, which

Jung believed exists in addition to immediate personal consciousness, is the universal, impersonal inheritance of all people which consists of archetypes or forms which can become conscious only on a secondary basis. Jung insisted that the theory rests on an empirical foundation. Although many scholars would admit that there are elements of fact in the hypothesis, it is too inclusive to be acceptable.

There may be some who would still like to make myth the equivalent or the forerunner of philosophy. This argument has been refuted too many times to be dealt with here. Obviously, myth and philosophy can exist in the same cultural milieu.[8] Mythology defined as "stories of the gods" is closer to theology, and what Westerners call "mythology" when they approach beliefs of other peoples is labeled "theology" when they discuss their own belief systems. Obviously, theology is preferable to mythology because one's own beliefs are always superior to those of others—else why retain them?

Some people prefer to think of myth in terms of a world-view—a *Weltanschauung*—because to define myth in terms of divine beings would eliminate certain forms of Buddhism from consideration, as well as certain scientific world-views that are not supernaturalistic. Although mythic thought may be incorporated in a world-view, myth and *Weltanschauung* are not equivalent terms. To eliminate the role of divinities as essential components of myth would result in demythologizing the literature (see below).

Mythological typologies raise too many questions for use in discussions in this book. Kees Bolle has pointed out that distinctions between some categories are blurred.[9] For example, cosmogonic myth treats of cosmic origins, cosmological myth explains the development of qualities or facets of the cosmos, and etiological myth interprets geological formations or the origins of unusual plants. In this book I have not used these detailed distinctions, and I have used *cosmogonic* and *cosmological* as interchangeable terms.

Biblical scholars tend to view Hermann Gunkel as the father of biblical form-criticism.[10] In applying the Grimm brothers' definition to the Old Testament, Gunkel found only truncated or faded myths. Gunkel believed that the Grimms' definition presupposed polytheism, and since Old Testament thought centers in the acts of a single deity, there could be no true myth in the Old Testament.[11] The definition used in this book is more inclusive than Gunkel's (see pp. 4f), embracing monotheism as well as polytheism. Thus it does not protect the Bible from mythological analysis.

In recent years some biblical scholars have sought to demythologize the New Testament, to remove outmoded world-views and to discern and preserve the deeper meaning of the Christian scriptures.[12] Such demythologizing operates within a continuing Christian mythological-theological framework by affirming the reality of the interaction of God with the world and by ascribing unique status to Jesus as Messiah and revealer of the divine will. This approach accepts modern scientific world-views but holds that they are inadequate and do not comprehend the entire reality of the cosmos and of life, which requires recognition of the hidden, undiscerned presence of the deity operating in the world.[13]

To demythologize—completely—is to desacralize or to secularize. Mythic history without claims of what the gods did or did not do becomes secular history. Cosmological myths without divine participants are no more than human projections concerning the nature of the world and the universe, secular statements that may be more or less scientifically accurate. Societal myths without the authority of god figures are secular statements establishing social boundaries. Hero stories without gods are simply hero stories—no more, no less. Myths about death and dying and myths of the end of the age become statements about death and the future when the divinities are removed. Without the gods, the myths are no longer myths.

Can humans live without myths? Of course, if the classical definition established by the brothers Grimm is used. Substitutes are developed: philosophies of life, existential interpretations of life and living, secular humanistic approaches to existence. These nonmythic expressions, while they may embrace many of the same values as mythic statements, recognize these values as originating in human interaction rather than from divine pronouncements. There is no way to determine who accepts a mythological interpretation of life and who is a secularist on the basis of people's behavior in human situations. But this discussion has led to the content of the book, where the issues will be expanded and the power of myth explored.

The best and most accessible source of ancient Near Eastern texts is the third edition of *Ancient Near Eastern Texts Relating to the Old Testament* (abbreviated *ANET*), edited by James B. Pritchard.[14] Although I follow the general format and occasionally some of the language of *ANET,* my translations are freer but hopefully still true to the ancient sources.

Of course, I am solely responsible for the contents of this book, but many persons have contributed to it: teachers, colleagues, students, and friends. During one exciting summer in Berkeley, Theodor H. Gaster stirred my thinking and expanded horizons in ways that continue to affect me. David Martin, of the School of Public Health of the University of Texas at Houston, and Herman Harvey, Dean of the College of Art and Design in Los Angeles, are friends with whom I have shared experiences, challenging ideas, trust, and unabashed acceptance. Bronwyn Emery, Marilyn Rutgers, Lucinda Simpson, Melinda Woodrich, Robin Wallace

Conerly, Carol Goidich, Ed Ostermeyer, Harriet F. Smith, Judy Simonis, and my sons Gerry and David have loved and shared and helped me grow. Most of all, Gayle E. Shadduck has sustained me during dark moments with loyalty, love, and support and has contributed more than time and typing to the development of the concepts within this book.

David Friedman, Professor of Biblical Studies at the University of Michigan, and Leonard Thompson, Professor of Religion at Lawrence University, read the manuscript in its early stage and offered helpful criticisms and comments. Carolyn Davidson of Prentice-Hall, my production editor, worked with the manuscript in its final stages, becoming in the process a friend and colleague.

NOTES

[1]For a discussion, see Stith Thompson, "Myth and Folktales," in Thomas A. Debeok, ed., *Myth, A Symposium* (Bloomington: Indiana University Press, 1955, 1965), pp. 169–80.

[2]William Thoms, in *The Athenaeum*, 1846, p. 862.

[3]For a concise but inclusive summary, see Richard M. Dorson, "The Eclipse of Solar Mythology," in Debeok, ed., *Myth, A Symposium*, pp. 25–63.

[4]Sigmund Freud, *The Interpretation of Dreams* (London: Allen & Unwin, 1955; Basic Books paperback ed., 1965).

[5]Otto Rank, *The Myth of the Birth of the Hero and Other Writings* (New York: Vintage, 1959).

[6]Eric Fromm, *The Forgotten Language, An Introduction to the Understanding of Dreams, Fairy Tales and Myths* (New York: Grove Press, 1957; paperback reprint of 1951 ed.).

[7]*The Collected Works of C. G. Jung*, Bollingen Series XX, Vol. 9, Part 1, trans. R. F. C. Hull (Princeton, N.J.: Princeton University Press, 1959), pp. 87–110.

[8]See Henri Frankfort, *Before Philosophy*, Ch. 1 (Baltimore: Penguin Books, 1949); Kees W. Bolle, *The Freedom of Man in Myth* (Nashville: Vanderbilt University Press, 1968), pp. 28ff.

[9]Bolle, *The Freedom of Man in Myth*, pp. 10ff.

[10]Gene M. Tucker, *Form Criticism of the Old Testament* (Philadelphia: Fortress Press, 1971), pp. 4f.

[11]Hermann Gunkel, *The Legends of Genesis*, trans. W. H. Carruth (New York: Schocken Books, 1964; first pub. in 1901).

[12]Rudolf Bultmann, *Jesus Christ and Mythology* (New York: Charles Scribner's, 1958), pp. 18, 35.

[13]Ibid., p. 65.

[14]James B. Pritchard, ed., *Ancient Near Eastern Texts Relating to the Old Testament*, 3rd ed. with Supplement (Princeton, N.J.: Princeton University Press, 1969).

one

Concerning Myth

Ancient man and his gods are dead and nearly forgotten, but their influence lingers. Myths—accounts of divine beings and their activities—formulated in the Near East two thousand to five thousand years ago continue to affect and in some degree to structure our individual and collective lives. The long dead give directions for life and living. Present-day attitudes are affected by what people believed thousands of years ago, and most of us are so conditioned to accept our mythic environment that we fail to be aware of it.

We inherit the structure of our society; it is predetermined when we arrive on the human scene. As we grow into it, it continues to develop and change. To some extent, each of us contributes to the form it is taking and will take. What we accept and live by becomes our life-style and contributes to maintaining the status quo. What we refuse or rebel against may produce reactions that tend either to harden the life-set of society or to help develop new societal values. No one fails to make a contribution; no one is uninvolved.

For the most part, the mythic antecedents of what we inherit are lost in the complex patterns of the past. We cannot always know what persons or groups became catalysts of change or stabilizing influences. Historical lines are broken; the lacunae are enormous. Nevertheless, the discovery of ancient literature has enabled us to glimpse some facets of ancient life and to apprehend some insights which, amazingly enough, are very much part of the modern scene. Perhaps we learn only that we are what we have always been throughout time—human. Perhaps we discover that we have inherited attitudes and patterns from those who lived five thousand and more years ago. Some of us may rejoice in this heritage; believing that the societal patterns that have evolved over thousands of years are the "right" ways, norms that have proven themselves through much testing and use. On the other hand, some of us may be irritated that we have been programmed by the past and by those who accept ancient attitudes. We may feel that we are different, that we should be free to express varying life-

styles and attitudes without threatening those who disagree and without
experiencing social pressure to conform. We cannot be sure that variable
life-styles will be tolerated in the future, or that viable choices will be
available, or that individuals and groups will be able to develop new
patterns for living.

This book deals with myths that developed in ancient Near Eastern
centers of civilization: Egypt and Mesopotamia, and the territories immediately adjacent to them, particularly Israel. From these centers through
thousands of years mythic implications have streamed, often in altered
form, through Judaism and Christianity into the modern world, impacting,
at times subtly, on our lives. If the book appears to emphasize biblical
mythology disproportionately, it is because biblical myths have most
affected the Western world. The continuum is, therefore, not to be discerned in the mysterious forms of Jungian archetypes, interesting though
the Jungian hypothesis may be, but in the dynamic acceptance and promotion of mythic concepts by both church and state.[1]

In this book we will look at the ancient past and at modern man and
note patterns of thinking about and responding to life that have been with
us for millennia. We will suggest some potential developments and comment on what appears to be happening now and what present events may
portend for the future. The tension between stability and flux should
become obvious.

Some may argue that Greco-Roman mythology might also be included,
for Mediterranean thought has contributed in many ways to the life and
attitudes of the Western world. There are reasons for limiting the subject
to the ancient Near East. First, there is slender but growing evidence that
certain facets of Mediterranean mythic thought originated in Mesopotamia and Egypt. What was borrowed was, of course, transformed as it
merged with and was absorbed into the Greco-Roman world, but thematic
strains and implications often remained. It is well to remember, as Cyrus
Gordon has pointed out, that during the second millenium B.C. there was
active interchange of information in the Near Eastern world, and we
should not be surprised to discover that from the older and long-estab-
lished civilizations of Mesopotamia and Egypt, mythological concepts
flowed into the Mediterranean world.[2] To attempt to trace the myths that
moved from the ancient Near East into the Mediterranean world, to follow
the changes in the myths as they entered new environments and as divinities merged into existing pantheons, is far beyond the scope of this book.[3]
Nor will we try to trace the changes that took place, for example, in the
Isis myth as it was observed in the Roman world up to about the fourth
century A.D. Such discussions would divert us from our intent, which is to
consider the impact of ancient Near Eastern myth on modern society.

Second, despite numerous references in Western literature to Greco-Roman themes and despite the distinct contributions of the Greco-Roman world to our civilization, the Mediterranean world has not had the continuing substantial influence of the ancient Near East on Western life-style and thought. Ancient Near Eastern thought continues to affect our society, often in vastly altered form, through Judaism and Christianity, and its effect is actively promoted by synagogue and church. Although New Testament literature was produced in the midst of and was affected by Mediterranean mythology, its mainstream is Hebrew-Jewish and Near Eastern. To attempt to relate Greco-Roman mythology to the New Testament and the Christian church would expand this book far beyond its intended purpose and would perhaps cloud some of the issues and confuse the content. Thus, without denying the significance of Mediterranean mythology, we will not include it here.

Nor will Far Eastern myths be introduced. The area is far too broad and its influence on Western society both recent and limited. In fact, only within the present century has Eastern mythic thought had any broad impact on Western thought and life-style.

Because there are interrelationship of concepts and parallel thought patterns among the nations of the ancient Near East, it should not be assumed that their mythic ideas and implications were necessarily identical. Each nation developed distinct mythic patterns, involving its own gods, life-styles, worship patterns, legal systems, and communal norms. If ideas were borrowed, they were modified to fit new settings. If hymns were borrowed and the names of the gods invoked in the hymn changed, new implications were given to the songs by their very setting in a different culture and a different cultus. For example, the parallels between the hymn to the sun by Akhenaton of Egypt and Psalm 104 may indicate that a Hebrew writer borrowed ideas and perhaps words from the Egyptian composition. In the Hebraic setting and in Hebrew worship, the hymn became something new and different. To borrow ideas and phrases is not necessarily the same as to accept mythic concepts. Each religion was unique, neither better nor worse (if evaluative adjectives are important) than the others. Cultic worship was related to basic human responses to life and living, to the known and the unknown in the cosmos, and to man's need for both physical and psychic survival. Nor does the borrowing of an idea render it less effective or less meaningful. In a new context, the borrowed phrase or image becomes an original expression. Past connotations may linger, but they are altered by their new setting. On the other hand, similarities and parallels suggest that many aspects of mythic thought were common property among the peoples of the ancient Near East: ideas were disseminated, diffused, and melded into the cultures that preserved them.

While it is important to note similarities, it is equally important to be aware of differences. Differences do not make one myth better than another; the responsibility for value judgment rests with individuals, who respond from unique personal backgrounds. Westerners raised in the tradition of monotheism tend not to be attracted to the polytheistic myths of the ancient Near East. Yet our Western culture includes groups that recognize angels and demons, a supreme deity and a devil, and the influence of saints, and some groups' creeds concern a tripartite god—all of which might be interpreted as polytheism or monolatry.[4] Because we insist on a monotheistic mythic statement, however, the idea of monotheism has been broadened for Judaism, Christianity, and Islam to include a variety of minor divine or semidivine figures, without impairing the one-god idea.

We are so much a part of our modern mythic environment that we usually fail to perceive it. It has, in a sense, environed us and it has become a projection of the self, just as it has helped to shape the self. We and our mythic environment are one. Only when we alienate ourselves from the mythic strands within and around us are we able to see (and then, perhaps, imperfectly) the shaping influence of ancient myth on our lives. But to stand outside ourselves is difficult. We are prisoners of our time, limited by the pressures of current opinions and communal standards. There is tension between those who feel inhibited by prescribed boundaries and those who feel secure and satisfied living within established norms. Most societies experience a constant shifting and altering of standards, depending on the attitudes of the group in power and the pressure exerted by the dissenting minority. Only in extreme instances and in times of violent revolt are boundaries completely demolished. Perhaps by examining ancient mythic patterns and by realizing their conditioning effect on the individual and society, we will be able to some degree to remove ourselves intellectually from our personal mythic involvement and to become aware of and evaluate our mythic heritage and the mythic tensions present in society and in ourselves.

DEFINITION

The word *myth* is, as Henry A. Murray put it, a "chameleonic term."[5] In modern vernacular, myth is often confused with fairy tales, with imaginative or fantastic writings, with that which is not quite real or believable, and even with that which is false. News writers comment on "the myth" of one nation's missile superiority or "the myth" of the death of a national leader who has dropped from public view. *Myth* thereby becomes a disparaging term prompting the dismissal of the reliability of a statement or subject. In this book, myth will be treated differently, our emphasis being the impact of ancient mythic themes in the past and on modern life.

The English term *myth* is derived from the Greek *muthos,* meaning "word" or "speech," "the thing spoken," "the tale told"—perhaps any information transmitted verbally including both truth and falsehood. Ancient myths deal primarily with the activities of one or more divine beings —gods, goddesses, and other superhuman beings—and their relationships with one another, with humans and other earth creatures, and with the cosmos. At first, myths were transmitted orally, but the ancient myths that we know now were preserved in written form. Thus, we could define myth as a literary vehicle or kind of literature involving divine beings. Such a definition embraces systems belief from monotheism to polytheism, from animism to demonology. It is not limited to what gods and goddesses do in their own realms, but also embraces what they do in the world of men. However, we need more than a simple definition to understand the nature of myth.

MYTHIC BEGINNINGS

Any comment on the origin of myths is conjectural. Some sources are at least 4,000 years old, and because these ancient documents display sophistication, maturity of observation, reflection, insight, and organization, we can surmise that behind the written forms lie long periods of oral tradition. The written documents contain allusions to mythic themes concerning which we have no information and which in the records seem to be in the process of being discarded. Therefore, we must conclude that before the third millennium B.C., man had been involved in mythopoeic thought and that he possessed myths that are not now known to us.

Within a given culture, variations in mythic interpretations indicate that although a myth once recorded in written form might tend to resist alteration, nevertheless a process of continuing interpretation was at work through the centuries. New insights, experiences, and sociopolitical developments called for reinterpretation of old concepts. Nor did there seem to be any resistance to recognizing simultaneously several mythic interpretations of one theme. Today, scientists hold differing theories of cosmological origin, and Christians and Jews accept the existence of varying patterns of worship and belief in different denominations. That variant myths could coexist in a culture warns against treating myths as fixed creedal statements, even though at times a myth might embody such a statement. Myths were believed and they were meant to be believed. They were accepted as a reasonable and authoritative explanation of why the world is as it is.

Part of our intention in this book is to discern—almost intuitively, at times—what myths conveyed to those who recited or listened to them or participated in or observed the dramatic presentation of the myths. How did the myth itself and the issues it touched (often only by implication) affect society and the individual? What did it say about the cosmos and man's place within it? And how do the myth and mythic implications affect Western society?

Of course, such an inquiry presents basic problems. We have no way of knowing how ancient man (or modern man) internalized myths. Unstructured discussions with individuals and groups concerning the implications for the individual of modern mythic themes have revealed a variety of responses. Even within an established group, such as a family, a Sunday school class, or a neighborhood, a given myth has different implications for each individual. Such an observation warns against generalizations; everyone did not and does not react alike to mythic concepts. For example, in ancient Egypt, the pharaoh was mythically defined as a god. The stability of the government rested in part on general acknowledgment of this concept. But some Egyptians did not believe that the pharaoh was divine and did not hesitate to plot mischief against him. Thus, we can say only that certain Egyptian myths proclaimed the divinity of the monarch and that most people appear to have accepted the teaching.

Another problem is that we have only the written texts that were in ancient times recorded by an elite, literate priesthood. The average man could not read or write and did not have access to the sacred library. We suppose, therefore, that minstrels and local storytellers memorized what they could not read and sang and recited the accounts in villages throughout the land. We have no way of knowing how individuals responded to the noncultic presentation of the myths, nor can we know what effect the myths may have had on life in families and local communities. Perhaps we can draw an analogy with the illiterate, seminomadic Arabs and Bedouin who quote passages from the Quran and know numerous anecdotal teaching stories about the patriarchs that are not found in the Quran. These people do not always have a local storyteller, but listen instead to transistorized portable battery radios broadcasting cultic interpretations from Cairo and other religious centers, and discuss what they have heard around campfires in the evening. Some have made pilgrimages to holy places. The oral tradition, whether shared by tribal members or acquired by radio, plays an important role in informing nonreaders about Muslim belief and culture.

MYTH AND PSYCHIC SURVIVAL

There is a happenstance dimension to being alive. No one can determine where or when he will be born, who his parents will be and what their status, or what his physical, mental, and psychical makeup will be. Few individuals have anything to do with determining the time, nature, or mode of their death. Even between birth and death, much of life is determined by factors over which the individual has little control and about which he has little understanding. Why does disease attack one family and not another? Why does fortune seem to smile on everything one individual undertakes, while misfortune strikes every effort of another? What does it mean to be alive? Myth is intimately related to attitudes toward life, death, survival, and, most of all, "meaning."

We can define life in a number of ways. For example, we might use terms developed by biological scientist, but DNA (deoxyribonucleic acid) structures do not convey much about what it means to be human. We might resort to evolutionary terminology and discuss the various *homo* types known from anthropological studies, but life and living encompass more than biological or evolutionary theories or categories.

To live as a human involves more than the acquisition of sufficient food, adequate shelter and clothing, and the continuation of the species. There is a psychic dimension to human survival that presses man to make some sort of sense out of his universe beyond merely accepting it, that impels him to articulate a statement about himself and reach some understanding of himself and his place in time and space. Without such formulations, he would simply be another animal, devoid of the distinguishing human traits of pondering, of creating patterns, of reaching out in new ways to explore new dimensions. Because he is unique within the animal kingdom, man does reflect on his observations and experiences, seeking to understand himself and his relationship to his world. Without answers to his questions, he is frustrated. Psychological research has demonstrated the results of frustration. When carefully developed patterns of behavior are reduced to a level where they no longer function and when it is therefore impossible to know how to respond or make a choice, varying reactions occur, including flight or withdrawal, subsidence into a comatose state, and even death. There may be a search for alternative patterns, or a recognition of the impossibility of the situation and a passive acceptance of this meaningless state as the norm, or continuing fruitless and often frenetic attempts to overcome. Such behavioral patterns are recognizable in our society. Even people who appear to be well-adapted and "normal" might be compared with the rather pathetic King Sisyphus in Albert Camus' treatment of the

Sisyphus myth, fated to follow the stupid routine of rolling a boulder up to the crest of a hill, only to have it roll down again each time. At the end of the essay, Camus is compelled to note, "One must imagine Sisyphus happy."[6]

At some time in prehistory, man began to try to untangle the web of his experiences and the basic polarities of his life: birth and death, health and illness, security and destruction. Seasons changed without explanation. Clouds gathered and obscured the sun and rain hammered the earth, transforming it into a quagmire, raising the level of ponds and rivers, and washing away fragile, man-made structures. Winds ripped out mighty trees that had seemed to be firmly rooted in the earth. Lightning started fires. There were days of pleasant, warm sunshine when fresh-running streams kept to their channels. There was abundant food. Then all would change. The sun became an enemy. Water sources dried up and food grew scarce. Life forces seemed malicious and malignant, releasing food grudgingly. Why did these changes occur?

In his community, a person who had been well would suddenly become ill and die. Another individual became ill but recovered. Why? Unique experiences added to the confusion. On one occasion, a root seemed to reach up and trip a man, causing him to fall and be bruised. A rock fell from the wall of a ravine and broke a man's leg. An angry wild beast or an enemy attacked, causing injury. Why did such events happen?

Conjectural? Of course! But somewhere in the forgotten past, perhaps because of uncanny or mysterious encounters, mythic patterns began to emerge as one answer to the need for psychic survival. There were simply too many inexplicable issues and too many puzzling happenings. Man knew he was a part of his world. The dramatic alterations in natural patterns that occurred regularly and the continuing changes in life patterns in the growth cycles of the earth, of which he knew himself to be a part, were assimilated into his thought patterns. He adjusted his interpretive time sequences to the natural and seasonal patterns he witnessed and experienced in his topocosm. Myths provided answers. When the problems seemed too complex for human explanation, man simply acknowledged the mystery of divine ways. For example, the Sumerian hymn exalting Enlil, the chief god of the city of Nippur, confessed the human dilemma in seeking to understand Enlil's ways. The poet described the god's actions as "tangled threads" defying separation.[7] Thus, even when they provided no specific answer to problems, myths enabled humans to cope with their world, by one explanation or another bringing order into their complex environment.

Myth postulated beginnings. Almost all the ancient Near Eastern creation myths began with primeval chaos. Myth described patterns and brought meaning out of the chaos. The world was described as originating through acts of divine beings. Seasonal patterns were explained as ordained by gods. Variations in these patterns were attributed to the whims, the anger, or the goodwill of gods who were invested with human moods and temperaments.

Speculation on mythic origins may encourage dismissal of myth as the product of man's fears, forebodings, and imaginings. There may be some validity in describing mythic explanations as obsessive defense mechanisms or survival techniques; there is a certain security in labels and mythic interpretations that never really confront the basic question, How does the myth-maker know or ensure the validity of his answer?

It would be illogical to argue that on a certain day a man or men decided to create a myth to account for the cosmos. So far as we can tell, myths developed from experience and observation. Mythic themes had fluidity and could be altered to fit new experiences or different attitudes or responses to experience. And, as we have observed, it was possible for differing mythic interpretations to exist side by side in a single culture.

Myth is not to be understood as philosophy in the sense of detached reflection or a search for "truth," nor as basic science in that it grew out of repeated experiences and observations. Rather, myth must be viewed as literature that developed out of a concern for survival and the desire to understand the implications of what it means to be human.

Myth may be understood as the human effort to discriminate between an understanding of life, not as bare existence, but as the relationship between the totality of body, mind, spirit, and the world—the effort to achieve harmonious relationships (peace) within the totality of one's environment. Through myth, man is able to give order and structure to his world and perhaps bring meaning or purpose to an existence that otherwise may appear meaningless. By mythically defining and structuring his world, man provides himself with an appreciation and understanding of areas outside human control which affect human well-being and destiny. The structure or order may in itself be interpreted as a kind of status quo into which myth gives insight. The myth explains why life is as it is and what man's significance is, and provides an understanding that to be human, to be alive, and to have purpose is to move beyond the bounds of animal existence. Myth supports existing social structure, patterns of belief and conduct and the current interpretation of the world. At the same time, myth tends to program attitudes of individuals and groups to encourage an uncritical acceptance of the established norms of the particular society.

MYTH AND CULT

Myth can also be understood in terms of man's response to or awareness of power outside and beyond himself—to the wholly "other," to what

Rudolph Otto has termed the "numinous experience" or what William James has called the "religious experience." Contact with, confrontation by, or experience of that which lies outside what is considered normal human experience might provoke one or more of several reactions, including curiosity, ecstasy, awe, uneasiness, fear, and terror. The responses might be attraction or repulsion, fascination or avoidance.

Today, an uncanny experience of that which lies outside the norm might prompt lengthy scientific probing, scholarly papers and books, and an appeal for a government grant to underwrite further investigation. For example, reported sightings of unidentified flying objects and mysterious lights in the night sky engendered theories of visits to this planet by extraterrestrial and perhaps supernatural beings and triggered the writing of articles and books and the investment of money and time in investigation. The approach was an "objective" attempt to determine what lay behind the report, and at this point mythic interpretation came into conflict with scientific methodology—a tension-creating confrontation that we will meet again elsewhere in this book.

In earlier times the response to strange phenomena was less objective, because, so far as we can tell, people in the ancient Near East did not consider the world from the point of view of "I–it" relationships, but rather on "I–thou" terms. An I–it attitude treats the objective world as made of things or objects that may be manipulated and exploited for man's benefit. Man analyzes the soil in his fields and sows seed that will produce the maximum yield and profit in that soil. As soil energy is depleted, he uses various fertilizers to rejuvenate the land, or rotates crops so that one crop replaces nutrients lost through previous plantings of another. Man eliminates harmful insects with poisons. If poisons harmful to man remain in the agricultural produce, the I–it attitude may be extended and the concern fixed on immediate profits for the producer rather than on the long-range effects of the insecticides on humans and other animals.

In ancient times, a different attitude prevailed. The world was infected with personality. The soil, the seed, and the crops were all part of the topocosm[8] in which man lived—a world composed not of self and external things, but of personalities and divine beings. Gods were everywhere. Seasons did not come and go because of the tilt of the earth and its rotation about the sun. The life-giving rain was not the result of the interactions of air currents, clouds, and high and low pressure areas. Rivers did not rise because of heavy rains in the regions of the headwaters. The increase of crop-devouring insects did not call for spraying with insecticides (which were, of course, unknown). All of life was seen in terms of relationships. Seasons came and went because ancient mythic patterns were repeated in a cyclic rhythm. As seasonal gods had risen and fallen in power and influence "in the beginning," that rise and fall was cyclically and seasonally reflected. Rain came because the fertility god was ascendant and was pleased to send down life-giving waters. Rivers rose and fell according to the moods of the river god, and the swell of waters could be beneficent or malevolent. Hordes of insects might be interpreted as punishment from the gods or as an invasion by demonic powers. In every case, relationships with personalities were involved, and human survival depended on maintaining right relationships—peace within the human place-world. The omnipresent forces or powers that could bring destruction and chaos could not be ignored. To maintain order within the topocosm, certain rites, observances, attitudes, and patterns of behavior, ordained by the gods, were necessary. But how was man to comprehend the gods' wishes? The answer came through *theophanic* or *revelation myths.*

The combination of the experience of uncanny power and the I–thou attitude gave rise to a basic mythic theme: that something other than human had revealed itself and communicated with man. The revelation might come through a physical experience. The Stone Age hunter whose leg was broken when a rock mysteriously dislodged itself from an overhanging cliff and fell on him, might sense within the stone malevolent forces that needed to be avoided or appeased. If the rock had instead flushed a covey of partridge from the brush, and the hunter had killed several by throwing sticks or stones, he might interpret the action of the rock as expressive of a benevolent power and take the rock back to his camp. From then on, before going on a hunt, he might address the rock, seeking its power, or he might carry a fragment of it with him to increase his fortune. In either case, the rock had a personality. It could be viewed as the abode of some spirit (*animism*) or simply as possessing power in and of itself (*animatism*). Much later, when man began to carve images of his gods from wood and to overlay the statues with costly metals, jewels, and fabrics, the awareness that the image held and transmitted power was not lost. Image makers belonged to a special class of artisan, and those who attended the god figures were priests.

The revelation might be visual or visual and auditory, or it might come in a dream. Moses on Mount Horeb "saw" a burning bush and "heard" the voice of the god who manifested himself in this form (Exod. 3:1–6). Jacob used a stone for a pillow and experienced a revelation in a dream. On awakening, he anointed the rock with oil and called the place Bethel—the house of god or a god (Gen. 28:10–22; see also Gen. 35:1–8). The locale of the experience became a holy place. The account of the experience became the basis for myth. The personalizing of the power gave rise to what the god "said." The revelation enabled man to understand what the god demanded of him, what were the rules and regulations for societal life, and in some instances what was the meaning and purpose of human life.

Revelatory myths often provided the basis on which divine-human relationships were explained. Alliances were formed with the forces feared by humans, with divine powers that threatened, affected, and controlled the environment and determined the quality of human existence. Revelation myths gave instruction about the ways in which the god-power worked in the cosmos and informed believers about proper modes of response. Thus, the divine will is given to Jews by revelations experienced by Moses, to Christians through revelations provided by Jesus, and to Muslims through revelations received by Mohammed. Rituals, as we shall see, were enabling techniques, assisting individuals to come to grips with the cosmos. The organized cult provided for the dramatization of cosmic beginnings and the symbolic reenactment of revelatory moments. The rites served to educate, to control, and to appease.

The gap between the concepts of the sanctification of a place or an object and the acceptance of accounts as true revelations of the will or words of the local deity may not be very great. By the time the texts of the myths were written, ancient Near Eastern society had been organized into villages, towns, cities, and nations. The myths reflect the organizational patterns and sanction them. What myths may have existed in earlier times and different social circumstances cannot be known. The preservation of the myths, the ritual enactments, the determination of times and seasons for observing the myths, and the interpretation of the myth were centered in the temple, its cultic rituals, and its cultus or personnel. Therefore, it is not surprising to find that Hammurabi's law code, which was backed by Shamash, the sun god and lord of justice, reflects societal structure. Some men were slaves, others freemen, others nobility, and one was king. The social structure was divinely ordained, man knew that his social status was a given. Only by following certain procedures could a person move into a new status—and perhaps he could never change. The laws governing human relationships were also divinely sustained. To violate social mores was to violate the will of the god. In the same way, the Mosaic code regulating food, society, mores, and values was god-given. The laws told the Jew who he was and what he must do to maintain his relationship with his god, Yahweh.

The ancient temple was related directly to the government. Even though there are vestigial elements of this relationship in current society, it would be a mistake to think of temples in terms of present-day churches or synagogues. Today, religious groups often maintain offices in the capital city, and legislators know it is wise to check proposals before presenting them publically, to avoid offending the religious sensibilities of such groups. Church groups may employ lobbyists. When the president of the United States is inaugurated, prayers are given by representatives of Jewish, Roman Catholic, Eastern Orthodox, and Protestant communities. In

England, there is a close bond between the Church of England and the Parliament. The Vatican has official representatives in many of the government centers of the world. In the ancient Near East the ties were more direct. The temple was related to the government. Responsibilities of the priest included duties now assumed by public officials. Modern-day administrators have councils to advise them. In the ancient Near East, every court retained cultic personnel as experts or specialists who received guiding oracles from the gods, foretold the outcome of events, interpreted happenings, and helped to maintain good relationships with the gods. For example, a seventh century B.C. Assyrian text records King Esarhaddon's oracle from the goddess Ishtar, guaranteeing divine support and blessing, long life, and victory over enemies whom the goddess offered to crush with her own hands.[9] Matters of public health, now under the administration of health departments, were of concern to the priests who, despite the presence of physicians, were called on to diagnose illnesses and prescribe cures or quarantines (see Lev. 13–14). Some priests served as tax collectors, administrators of flocks and herds, or agricultural overseers. The temple was, therefore, more than a center for worship; it was closely linked to the government of the community, state, or nation.

The temple building was not a gathering place for worshippers. Temples were cultic structures, often located on hallowed ground where there had been a theophany or some manifestation of the holy. The buildings testified to the magnificence and power of the gods; symbols and design manifested the obscure forces that motivated all existence. They marked places where events fundamental to the welfare of human society had occurred or where profound encounters with a god had taken place. For example, the temple at Heliopolis, Egypt, was said to sit on the cosmic hill which first emerged from the waters of chaos. In Bethlehem, the Church of the Nativity is supposed to stand on the very place where Jesus was born, and the Church of the Holy Sepulcher in Jerusalem is said to encompass the site of the crucifixion as well as Jesus' burial place. Beneath the golden dome of the Harem esh-Sharif (the so-called Mosque of Omar) in Jerusalem is an outcropping of rock which is supposed to be the site of Abraham's near-sacrifice of Isaac (Gen. 22:1–14), which later became part of Solomon's temple and still later was identified as the place from which the prophet Mohammed ascended into heaven. Holy places were separated from common or profane areas by protective walls. The temples were often understood to be earthly replicas of the heavenly abodes of the gods. They were not assembly rooms.

In the innermost recesses of the sacred precincts, the *cella,* was the statue of the god or some other sacred symbol or object. Other rooms provided areas for special rituals performed by the priests; storehouses for the accumulated wealth of the deity, cultic paraphernalia, stores, and supplies; and

accommodations for priests and temple personnel. Special tasks were performed by sanctified clergy including priests and priestesses, singers and
dancers, musicians and keepers of sacred fire, those who washed and
dressed the statues, and those who cleaned the precincts and kept the
accounts. All were servants of the god. Perhaps the best modern analogy
would be the vast army of clergy associated with the Vatican. Cult functionaries and sometimes certain other highly placed officials, such as a
monarch, performed rites in the presence of the images of the gods. Public
ceremonies were held in the courtyards, or perhaps around an altar of
sacrifice.

The cult bore witness to the manifestation of the divine, to some revelation by the gods, to a moment in the past when the sacred had come into
direct contact with the profane or common. Whether the event actually
had occurred historically and whether the cultic interpretation was precisely in accord with what had happened was really immaterial; these are
problems raised by modern scientific historians. It was assumed that the
cult myth recorded a reality. That assumption and the rites and expressions
associated with it, plus the responses evoked in the worshipers, were and
are more important than the historical data. The reality was and is what
happened to participants in cultic rites. For a divine-human encounter
reported to have occurred in the past to have relevance for the present, the
event had to be transmitted and interpreted. The gods had revealed themselves or their will then, and that past event had meaning and significance
for those who lived now. The cult made real the essence of the myth,
demonstrating that what had happened in the remote past had bearing on
the immediate present.

The cult was more than an interpretive structure. It also represented
continuing interaction with the gods. If the gods were offended the cultus
provided ways for appeasing an angry god. Gods made demands on their
worshipers, and the cult was the instrument for meeting those demands.
When drought, plague, or defeat by enemies occurred, cultic personnel
interpreted the meaning of the disaster and provided rites for alleviating
the situation.

Through the cult the ordinary mortal drew near to the sacred, approached the theophanic experience granted to hero figures of the past, and
came into proximity of the awful mystery of existence. Public celebrations
provided the opportunity to express inner responses of wonder, awe, fascination, and fear, to thank the gods or to plead with them on behalf of the
nation or community, and to be stirred through pageantry to new depths
of wonder and new heights of exaltation.

Cultic rites tended to support and strengthen the existing social structure. Some myths implicitly and others explicitly indicate that the societal

patterns were ordained, approved, and sustained by the gods. Any infraction of social norms or attempt to disrupt social patterns was treated not only as a crime against society, but as a violation of the will of the gods. Each time a myth was recited or enacted, societal implications were reinforced. Cultic performances left no opportunity for the group or the individual to debate the theses of the myth. The ritual validated the distinctive patterns and values of the society and stimulated the participants to greater compliance with the social norms as expressions of the divine will. In this sense, the purpose of the myth was to transmit patterns of belief; to dramatize the superiority of a people, a culture, or a faith; and to provide instruction in living by answering basic questions about living, by reinforcing existing patterns, and by explaining the validity of existing social structures.

Each time a priest or prophet gave an oracle, the concept of revelation by the god was reinforced. The oracles expressed the will of the god concerning specific issues, and the revelation generally sustained known and previously expressed divine attitudes.

MYTH AND RITUAL

Some ancient Near Eastern myths are related to festivals that inaugurate a new year or celebrate the seasons, the plentitude of the harvest, and the like. Rituals performed by priests, other cult functionaries, and worshipers on these occasions were often the physical response to or the enactment of the words of the myth. For example, when the prophets of Ba'al, the Canaanite deity of rain and fertility, performed their limping dance around the altar on Mount Carmel and gashed themselves (1 Kings 18), they were apparently enacting mourning rites for the dead god similar to those described in the myth of Ba'al found at Ugarit. A twelfth century B.C. text recovered at Abydos recounts the reenactment of portions of the Osirian myth by Ii-kher-nofret, a high officer of the court, and it is clear that a dramatic ritual symbolically recreated the events described in the myth.[10]

Mythic concepts often lay behind other rituals. During the first half of the second millennium B.C., when a Mesopotamian worshiper involved in a night divination ceremony offered a lamb and called on the night gods for response, back of his actions lay mythic presuppositions about the reality of those divinities to whom he appealed and about the effectiveness of his offering. The Egyptian Papyrus Anastase II from the thirteenth century B.C. contains a prayer to the god Amon uttered by a poor man faced with a court trial. Back of the request for vindication is the mythic assumption that Amon could affect the outcome of the case. A memorial *stele* (inscribed stone slab) from the same period thanks Amon for bringing health to an ailing artisan.[11] Again, there is the mythic assumption that Amon was active in the affairs of man and had the power to heal the sick.

Ritualistic acts, such as prayers of petition, utterances of thanksgiving, and in a larger, more inclusive context, the cultic rites performed at festivals, all presuppose the reality of the world of myth. Certain communal rites contain traditions about the acts or revelations of the gods that are pertinent for the present, taking on life and immediacy through cultic dramatization. Personal acts of worship may not be related directly to some past mythic event, but by drawing upon implications in mythic tradition, they respond to a life situation in words and deeds that assume the functional reality of the mythic interpretation. People believed that gods responded to prayers and exercised their powers to benefit certain individuals. Gods, like humans, were assumed to be influenced by pleas and promises and to desire thanks when they have acted on someone's behalf.

MYTH AND HISTORY

When interpretations of events were treated not as happenstance or the results of plots, plans, covenants, and agreements between humans, and when gods were pictured as involved in human affairs, records took on mythological coloration and became mythic in quality. The writers were no longer describing events as events, but were interpreting history as the acts of gods. Thus, when humans began to record the events that affected group destiny, no distinction was made between history and myth. Happenings were recorded and interpreted with mythic terms and implications. For example, Jason of Cyrene or his editor in 2 Maccabees interpreted events in Palestine in the second century B.C. in far stronger mythic terms than the unknown author of 1 Maccabees. A comparison of the two documents readily reveals that the mythic interpretation results in a heightening of the significance of the event. The outcome of conflicts was apprehended as more than the result of human strategy: as an expression of divine will and judgment.

History deals primarily with factual data, with that which occurred. The events are those which relate to and affect groups of people, and the principle characters are usually the leaders or heroes of the group. But historians also engage in interpreting events and judging their significance. A historian who is personally engaged in some action or issue or who is a member of one of the participating groups may be closer to the event by virtue of involvement, but at the same time may tend to write and interpret from the "inside" point of view. His work may reflect partisan judgments.

Another historian, outside the involved groups, will bring a different set of attitudes to his record and interpretation. Events of the past, even if corroborated by the coincidence of data or relevant tangential archeological findings, generally come to us in interpreted form, and suffer further interpretation at the hands of modern scholars.

Mythic history is the interpretation of events as acts of divine beings or as affected by divine beings. Thus, in the ninth century B.C., Mesha, king of Moab, could ascribe Israelite oppression of Moab to the anger of the Moabite god, Chemosh, with his people. Later, when Mesha took Nebo from Israel, it was by the expressed command of Chemosh. Similarly, in the seventh century B.C., Sennacherib of Assyria could relate the success of his Palestinian campaign to the fear-bringing weapons of the god Asshur and to the oracles that provided divine guidance. According to the account in 2 Kings 18:25, the Rabshakeh of the Assyrian forces surrounding Jerusalem mockingly suggested that the Assyrians were there because Yahweh, the god of Israel, had told them to come. When the Assyrians left, the Jewish writers suggested that deliverance came at the will of Yahweh (2 Kings 19:32ff). Cyrus the Great of Persia did not hesitate to give credit for the Persian conquest of Babylon to the Babylonian god Bel-Marduk, and announced that Marduk had looked around for a righteous ruler and had chosen him (Cyrus). About the same time, a Jewish writer in captivity in Babylon wrote that Cyrus came at the behest of Yahweh, whether Cyrus knew it or not (Isa. 45:1,5).

Oracles and omens, dreams and visions were consulted for divine instruction for national and international policy, and the instructions were followed. For example, King Nabonidus of Babylon in the sixth century B.C. explicitly stated that in the exaltation of the moon god, Sin, he was guided by revelatory dreams and omens.[12] Unfortunately, we have no records listing divine instructions as they were given with subsequent notations as to the success or failure of the guidance. We have only later interpretations of events in the light of mythic beliefs. When the Hebrews were defeated in battle by the Philistines, King Saul used sacred dice or lots to obtain an oracle from the Hebrew god, Yahweh (1 Sam 14:36–42). It was assumed that the deity had been offended and had withdrawn divine support for the battle. To remedy the situation, the guilty offender had to be identified and punished. True, no myth is directly involved in the sense of a "story told" about ancient times, yet there are the mythic assumptions that the god was involved in the historical process and in the fighting of battles and that he could be offended if someone broke an agreement. The struggle between the Philistines and the Hebrews, which appears to be historically real, is interpreted by biblical writers as involving the participation of deities. This is most clearly expressed when the Philistines capture the sacred ark, the symbol of the presence of the Hebrew god.

The box-like affair is taken as a trophy of war and placed before the statue of the victorious Philistine god, Dagon. The destruction of the statue, attributed to Yahweh, so dismays the Philistines, according to the biblical story, that they return the ark to the Hebrews. Clearly, the struggle between the two nations has been given a mythic interpretation as well. Unfortunately, we do not have a Philistine account of these events, but certainly such an account would have a different emphasis. If the guidance failed, it could be interpreted as deceptive action on the part of the god who was seeking to punish the nation or the king, or even as guidance or temptation by some anti-deity (1 Chron. 21:1f). Something of the same attitude is represented today in the Muslim "inshallah"—"if Allah wills it"—and in the Christian "as God wills."

MYTH AND ART

To become real to the imagination, the divine must be made concrete. We define our world in terms of objects that have dimension and form, outline and substance, color and texture, smell and sound and taste—all of which impact upon us and call forth a response. The undefinable tends to evaporate in our thinking because it cannot be contained. Immaterial, undefined powers can be frightening as well as overwhelming. As ancient man grappled with self-identity in terms of the human relationship to the cosmos, as he sought to understand experiences believed to manifest divine powers that were beyond human comprehension, as he tried to give meaning to patterns within the topocosm, he concretized his mythological statements, and the artistic expressions became statements in and of themselves.

Gods and goddesses were depicted in forms that could be grasped and held by the mind. Sometimes geographical or geological phenomena were interpreted as manifestations of the divine, and a hill, spring, or stone outcropping became sacred. Artists used both zoomorphic and anthropomorphic imagery to depict the sacred, sometimes combining animal and human forms. The professional way in Babylon from the gate of the goddess Ishtar to the temple of the god Marduk was flanked with walls bearing zoomorphic representations of Marduk. But Marduk was also depicted in human form on a piece of lapis lazuli found in Babylon, and even symbolically in what has often been called a "spade." Ishtar, the fertility goddess, was modeled as a beautiful nude or symbolized as a bundle of reeds with a looped top. A god might be represented by a statue carried in a procession, by an image on a dais in the innermost recesses of a shrine, or by a sacred animal that was believed to express certain divine attributes.

Scenes depicting some aspect of a myth often adorned the walls of sanctuaries, just as today wall paintings and stained glass windows in places of worship both decorate and instruct. Small carved images of divinities—amulets—worn by a worshiper demonstrated allegiance to a particular deity or expressed the individual's need for support and protection by that god, just as today some people wear stars of David or crosses to symbolize allegiance, or mount small Saint Christopher figurines on automobile dashboards in the hope of being protected as they travel. Mesopotamian cylinder and stamp seals, worn on cords hung about the neck and used to sign clay documents, often bore carved representations of divinities, of acts of worship before gods, or of mythological scenes. Such objects brought the gods close.

Like any other creative person, including the mythologer, the artist makes a statement in his work, and that statement, like a mythic statement, is open to varying interpretation by individuals who internalize what they view. The impact of the art can be profound, affecting the way in which individuals view themselves, their society, and the topocosm. A stele in the Louvre, a work from the second millennium B.C., portrays the goddess Ishtar standing on the back of a lion; her sacred animal. The figure conveys not warmth or compassion, but power, authority, aloofness, and stiffness. On the other hand, the third century B.C. alabaster doll figurine of the goddess, also in the Louvre, conveys through the nude body voluptuousness and sensuousness, and the red jewels in the eyes and navel are more than decorative; the glistening stones transmit a sense of mysterious, unearthly, yet desirable beauty, fire to be ignited. The Ishtar myths tell of the goddess's power, of her cold fury when thwarted, of her beauty and her many love affairs. The images concretize the concepts, drawing the worshiper to the goddess but enforcing a respectful distance. The Louvre stele of the Canaanite fertility god, Ba'al, shows him wearing a beard, a pointed helmet, and a kilt. He stands tall with one raised hand holding a thunderbolt, the other a tree—the symbol of fecundity—or perhaps the branched object represents forked lightning. He stands above what may be waves, symbolic of his enemy, Yam, the sea god, or perhaps the hills over which Ba'al holds sway. In diminutive form on the same stone slab is what is usually believed to be the figure of the donor of the carving, small and nonthreatening. The depiction encourages thoughts about the relationships between the god and the worshiper, between fertility and life, and about cosmic patterns—the sea, the earth, the rain.

Temples marked sacred space. They were often located on the site of a manifestation of the divine or where "in the beginning" some divine action had taken place. The sacred area, separated from the profane world, was a place where worshipers might approach and pay homage to the gods and, in some instances, enter into some sort of communion. The temple was the house of the god, modeled on his house in the heavens. Its separate nature was characterized architecturally and artistically. In Egypt, the papyrus columns of temples symbolized the Marsh of Reeds from which the sun god rose each morning. In Mesopotamia, temples were often built on raised platforms. In these high holy places, the human and the divine met; entry into the realm of the divine was made by mortals represented by the priesthood, and simultaneously the gods made direct contact with the world of humans. Enactments by male and female clergy of varying ranks, garbed in special costumes and often wearing symbolic masks, dramatized in ritual and chant the myths and the lofty otherness of the deities. Statuary, symbols, wall paintings, sacred animals and birds, sweet incense, and various kinds of sacrifices and offerings heightened the sense of distance between gods and humans. Yet, through the rituals, humans communicated with the sacred to reenergize the community, to revitalize the individual, and to recommit the people to the revealed ways of the gods.

The total schema of the temple structure and the rites was symbolic, just as today church structure and paraphernalia are symbolic. For example, the vaulted rafters in the roofs of some Christian churches have been interpreted as representing the inverted bottom of Noah's ark, so that the church building and the Church becomes the salvation ship. The domes of Byzantine churches were replicas of the heavens overarching the earth. The octagonal form of some baptismal fonts is related to the New Testament statement, "Eight persons were saved through water" (1 Peter 3:20), again a reference to the biblical flood narrative.

The world of myth was dramatic. It embraced collisions of forces that were either benign or malignant, friendly or hostile, familiar or uncanny, threatening and repellant or alluring and helpful. It is not surprising, therefore, that among the artistic expressions of mythic themes or ritual acts recovered by archeologists, some mythic characters are portrayed in monstrous or frightening forms. For example, the Assyrian *kerubim* (cherubim)[13] are immense bull figures with human faces and gigantic wings. Assyrian palace reliefs depict ritual acts in which priests wore costumes with bird- or animal-head masks. The Mesopotamian wind demon, Pazuzu, and the dreaded female demon appear most fearful on amulets. A Persian relief shows Darius the Great in conflict with a winged monster.

Violent emotion distorts. English conveys these changes in terms of color, size, and physical responses: anger may produce a flushed face with narrowed eyes and tight lips, the body tensed for action; in fear, that same face may be pale with eyes wide, lips trembling, and mouth dry, the body supported by weak knees that seem to have turned to water. These same "feeling qualities," to borrow Cassirer's term,[14] are expressed in myths, where conflicts, tensions, anxieties, and varied emotions abound. Ancient artists accentuated physical distortions and grotesquery, partially to convey the nonhuman aspects of the mythic world, but also to increase the impact of mythic themes. The enemies of the savior god Marduk in the Babylonian creation epic, *Enuma elish,* are described as monster serpents, lion-demons, and dragons with venom for blood, and bore names such as Viper, Dragon, Great-lion, Scorpion-man, and Dragon-fly. Physical representations harmonize with the verbal descriptions, and although we cannot always match archeological finds with myths, the Assyrian wall panels with their fearsome figures provide hints.

CATEGORIES OF MYTHS

For the sake of convenience, we shall divide myths into six basic categories, a division foreign to the ancient mythopoeic societies.

1. *Cosmological myths* suggest cosmic order and meaning. Such myths explain how the world and all that is in it came into being.
2. *Societal myths* or myths of social identification give order and structure to particular societal groups. They define group limits and explain why varying social levels exist within a city or nation. They provide divinely ordained acceptable norms for conduct.
3. *Identity myths* or myths of personal identification enable individuals to understand their role as human beings. Such myths often concern a hero figure who symbolizes man in the search for identity.
4. *Eschatological myths* deal with the end of an age and the end of time. They incorporate such matters as life-death-resurrection, future rewards and punishments, and apocalyptic visions of a golden age.
5. *Death of god myths* discuss the death of one, several, or all gods. They may even become symbols of mythic disassociation, or human alienation from mythic structures.
6. *Discussion of future myths* seek to provide a basis for thinking about mythic patterns that may be emerging now in our society and to project what mythic themes may become dominant in the future.

Obviously, there will be overlap; for example, societal patterns may be implied in cosmological mythology. Actually, all myths are identity myths, because they relate to human efforts at self-understanding and appreciation of the relationship of the self and the topocosm.

NOTES

[1]For a discussion of the Jungian hypothesis, see the essays in C. G. Jung and C. Kerényi, *Essays on a Science of Mythology* (New York: Bollingen Series 22, 1949). For a brief but informative consideration of various psychological approaches to

mythic studies, see the "Introduction" by Robert B. Palmer in his translation of Walter F. Otto, *Dionysus, Myth and Cult* (Bloomington: Indiana University Press, 1965).

[2]Cyrus H. Gordon, *The Ancient Near East* (New York: Norton, 1965).

[3]See Franz Cumont, *Oriental Religions in Roman Paganism* (Chicago: University of Chicago Press, 1911), pp. 73–102; paperback ed. by Dover Publications, New York, 1956.

[4]*Monotheism* is belief in one god and denial of the reality or existence of any other. *Monolatry* is belief in and worship of one god without denial of the reality or existence of other gods. *Polytheism* is belief in more than one god.

[5]Henry A. Murray, ed., *Myth and Mythmaking* (New York: Braziller, 1960), p. 11.

[6]Albert Camus, *The Myth of Sisyphus and Other Essays*, trans. Justin O'Brien (New York: Random House, 1959), p. 91.

[7]"Hymn to Enlil, the All-Benificent," in James B. Pritchard, ed., *Ancient Near Eastern Texts Relating to the Old Testament*, 3rd ed. with Supplement (henceforth *ANET*), (Princeton, N.J.: Princeton University Press, 1969) pp. 573–76, especially lines 131–33.

[8]*Topocosm*, from the Greek *topos* (place) and *cosmos* (world, order), was coined by Theodor H. Gaster in *Thespis: Ritual, Myth, and Drama in the Ancient Near East* (New York: Harper & Row, 1950; rev. ed., 1968), pp. 24f. The term refers to the totality of a place world embracing animate and inanimate elements which constitute the distinctive character of a community. The topocosm extends backward and forward to include the past and the potential future. It is vitally concerned with the reality of the present, but has an ideal, timeless quality extending beyond the present. Gaster suggests analogies in the ideal America which "transcends the present generation" and in symbols such as Alma Mater or La France.

[9]"Oracles Concerning Esarhaddon," *ANET,* pp. 449f.

[10]"Religious Drama in Egypt" *ANET,* pp. 329f.

[11]"A Prayer for Help in the Law Court" and "Gratitude for a God's Mercy," *ANET,* p. 380.

[12]"Nabonidus and His God," *ANET,* pp. 562ff.

[13]The biblical cherubim were probably closer to the Egyptian winged sphinx or lion with a human head than to the bull figure of Mesopotamia. See W. F. Albright, "What Were the Cherubim?" *The Biblical Archaeologist* (henceforth *BA*), Vol. 1 (1938); reprinted in G. E. Wright and D. N. Freedman, eds., *The Biblical Archaeologist Reader* (henceforth *BAR*) (Garden City, N.Y.: Doubleday, 1961), pp. 95f.

[14]Ernst Cassirer, *An Essay on Man* (New Haven, Conn.: Yale University Press, 1944; New York: Bantam Books, 1970), p. 85.

two

Cosmological Myths

In a sense, when we study creation myths, we are dealing with the significance of what man believes about his cosmos. We gain insight into man's understanding of himself and his society. Cosmological or cosmogonic myths are always creation myths. They deal with beginnings—with how the world came into existence—and reveal how man has sought to come to terms with the mystery of his environment and with his experience of power that lay outside human control. Careful observation and thoughtful reflection on cyclic patterns in nature, on malevolent and life-destroying forces and benevolent and life-enhancing factors demonstrated that the world was affected by superhuman powers. All living things died. Plants germinated, blossomed, bore fruit, and died, only to reseed or be renewed to life in the next season. Days varied in length, fading before the lengthening shadows of night, only to expand again and push back the darkness. The sun rose each morning, reached its strength at high noon, then moved west to disappear below the horizon. During the night, the moon shone from the heavens, but it waxed and waned in a measureable cycle. Such cosmic patterns affected man's survival.

Some forces threatened human security. Droughts and floods, destructive winds and rains, plagues and famines upset normal life patterns. Beyond the borders of the organized community was the wasteland, the desert, where plants grew haphazardly, struggled with each other for room to live, or did not grow at all. There wild beasts lurked and strangers wandered. Within the villages, towns, and cities, life was structured and predictable. Fields were planted with crops desired by man. Animals were domesticated. Neighbors were insiders who knew and abided by societal rules. The protective wall about man's place-world separated him from the terrors of the unknown, uncontrolled world and gave him security and identity. He "belonged" to a village, city, or nation. He knew his "limits."

Conjecture? Perhaps, but every Near Eastern cosmological myth, however brief, implies primeval chaos or sterility and begins with a description of the primordial wasteland, the sterile desert, the stagnant pool, or pre-

23

creation chaos. Each myth tells the story of bringing order out of chaos, establishing norms, patterns, limits, and cycles of nature. Creation myths are more than descriptions of the cosmos as seen by man in the ancient Near East; they are his explanations of how and why things came to be as they are. Through the myths, humans expressed their awareness that the cosmos was greater and more enduring than the individual or the society. Mythic language reveals the range of the human response: it is concrete, at times pictorial, and often poetic and emotional. Creation myths do not result from critical analysis of empirical data; they appear to spring from man's awareness of the bigness of his world, from his feeling of helplessness in the face of the chaos "outside," and from his need to understand the chaos and develop some control over it by categorizing, organizing, and labeling what he could apprehend but not comprehend. Of course, categorizing did not change anything, but the very organization of data provided a means for dealing with the world and surviving within it.

The development of cosmological mythic statements may symbolize a deep-rooted human rebellion against or rejection of the concepts of chaos and sterility, and an affirmation of a basic order and fruitfulness of nature. Perhaps there is also reflected human fear of chaos, and the necessity of patterns and understanding for psychic and physical survival. Cyclic patterns demonstrate schemes within nature, and once the patterns are transmuted into broader and more inclusive conjectural designs, confer system and meaning on the whole spectrum of life.

The myths defined cosmic limits. The sky was an overarching hemisphere of solid matter that rested on mountains at the edges of the world. The earth was a disc beneath the heavens, separated from the sky by air or wind, except at its rim. Through louvers or windows (see Gen 9:11), water that was above the sky could be introduced into the hemisphere, falling to the earth as rain. Water that lay beneath the earth's surface gushed forth as springs and the originating points of rivers. The limits were known and observable. The world was subdivided. To know territorial limits and the area within which one belonged was to experience security. Nations, cities, and villages had boundaries, imposed from outside "in the beginning" by divine beings.

The universe of Near Eastern cosmological myths was very personal. Not only had the gods been involved in bringing the cosmos into being, they were in essence the cosmos itself. Wind, rain, earth, sky, moon, sun —all aspects of the known world—had personal natures, emotions, feelings, and attitudes and could react to situations. The universe had a mythological "history," and the gods, like most events in the observable world, also had starting points. A child that grew in the womb and entered the world at birth had a starting point in his parents' act of copulation. So, too, there was a time of beginning for the cosmos and the gods. The limits established "in the beginning" were divinely ordained, and the story of the establishment of boundaries was told over and over in observances that marked the death and rebirth of the seasons and the simultaneous death and rebirth of the topocosm.

The myths that related cosmogonic "history" served as models for the periodic ceremonial ritual reenactment of primeval events. The cult was the interpreter of the divine structure. The sacred history, the cosmological mythic event, was actualized in ritual. What had happened in the distant past happened again in the cultic ritual. Participants and spectators were dramatically and emotionally involved in the clash of forces, helping to overcome chaos and establish order. The ritual of creation, a statement of belief about life and reality, affirmed the goodness and meaning of life, cemented communal bonds, and established cosmic and local order for the coming year.

In an important study of seasonal myths, Theodor Gaster has discussed the characteristics of the accompanying festivals and analyzed the rituals.[1] He notes that the rites are public, that they are social rather than individual, and that they are seasonal or calendaric. Ritual patterns fall into two categories: those associated with *kenosis* or emptying, and those concerned with *plerosis* or filling.

Kenotic rituals dramatize the loss of vitality, the eclipse of life, and the ebbing of the year, and are of two kinds. *Rites of mortification* mark the end of the year, the termination of the lease on life. Observances include the suspension of normal business practices, avoidance of marriages or new contracts, and occasionally the suspension of the king from office. *Purgation rites* emphasize communal ridding by exorcism of evil spirits or demons that threaten the security or health of the group and the continuation of life. Observances include the cleansing of sacred precincts as well as of houses, barns, and so on, and the removal of the accumulated guilt of the community, often through a scapegoat ritual.

Rites of plerosis dramatize the revitalization that occurs as a new lease on life begins with the new year. Again, Gaster subdivides this classification into two categories: invigoration rites and jubilation rites. *Invigoration rituals* may involve mock battles between personifications of life and death, rain and drought, or the like, the antagonists represented by individuals or teams. Sometimes sexual rituals are performed, including mass mating rites to promote fertility for the coming year. In some instances, procedures are designed to produce rain or re-illuminate the sun. *Jubilation rituals* signify both relief and joy as the community begins the new year or the period of a new lease on life, cleansed of the burden of guilt, with the hope and promise of a fruitful and life-sustaining year and the assurance that once again the forces of chaos have been overcome. Commensality rites symbolizing the psychic oneness of the group are marked by feasting and merriment.

EGYPTIAN COSMOGONIES

Egyptian mythology abounds in gods: more than eighty are known by name, and in numerous instances their functions and identities overlap. Each of the forty-two *nomes* or provinces which were to combine to form the united kingdoms of Upper and Lower Egypt had its own official god. Sometimes the same god or goddess was important in more than one district. Battles between the nomes were simultaneously struggles between the representative deities; when one district was absorbed by another, the god of the conquered area was taken into the pantheon of the victor. After Egypt was united, and specific areas emerged from time to time as national cult centers, the chief god or goddess of the particular locale would assume cosmic dimensions and qualities that may have belonged to the god whose status he or she had preempted.

Because local gods had been conceived in a variety of human, animal, and insect forms or combinations of these, the manifestations of divinity during the long period of the united nation were many and varied. A single god might assume many different forms. There developed in Egypt a lack of dogmatism and an open toleration of contradictions. There was no "basic truth," no structured dogma or sacred scripture, no fundamental creed, but rather a variety of unharmonized beliefs that led away from systematized theology. Parallels constituted no problem, but were treated as similar but individual aspects of whatever "reality" might be.

The concept of divinity was fluid. Kings could be gods. At the cult center at Heliopolis, a myth explained that the sun god, Ra, selected the wife of the high priest and, assuming the identity of her husband, copulated with her to produce three sons who were to become the first three pharaohs of the First Dynasty. From that point on, all pharaohs were accepted as sons of Ra. Later, viziers and wise men were believed to be able to become gods after death, a belief which engendered an extensive mortuary religion, originally formulated for the king but extended to queens and nobles.

The fluidity of Egyptian religious thought evoked creative, imaginative mythic patterns. No doubt many Egyptians accepted symbolic animals and human representations of the gods literally, but the sophisticated worshiper, whose beliefs we are slowly coming to understand, recognized in the symbols qualities of the divinity with which certain animals were believed to be endowed. There was a sacred oneness in life. As Henri Frankfort has pointed out, the Egyptian saw the universe "suffused with life" and human life "integrated with the life of nature."[2]

Egyptian mythology centered in two natural phenomena: the Nile river and the sun. Territorially, Egypt was simply the narrow strip of rich black land that bordered the Nile. Here life could be sustained. Soil fertility depended on the rise of the Nile, which began each year when the Dog Star, Sothis (Sirius), appeared on the horizon just before sunrise (July 19). The Nile, fed by rains and melting snow in the headwaters at the Equator, carried down humus and minerals essential for replenishing the soil. Its alluvium-bearing waters were channeled into fields along the Nile and captured by small dams for use later in the season. The earliest literature describes the Nile as flowing from the phallus of Osiris, who as a fertility god was at one time depicted as the fructiferous earth. The sun, which shines on Egypt from an almost always cloudless sky, was recognized as the other life-sustaining force. Manifestations of the sun god ranged from the eye of the falcon to the sun-disc Aton, espoused as the sole acceptable representation by King Akhenaton in the fourteenth century B.C. In the morning, the sun was Khephri, the scarab or dung beetle that rolled the dung ball (the sun) with its hind legs toward the zenith of the heavens. At noon, the sun was Re or Ra, the vigorous young god of Heliopolis. By evening, the sun became an old man, Atum. Or again, in the morning he was born anew as a golden calf from the celestial cow, or as a child of the celestial woman who swallowed him again in the evening. No matter what the manifestation, the sun was the most important factor in Egyptian mythology.

Egyptian mythologies taught that the cosmos, with Egypt and the Nile valley at its center, had emerged from the primeval surfaceless waters, the all-encompassing abyss called Nun. Nun was without form, and void, and complete darkness permeated the deep. The cosmos was a hollowed-out chamber within the waters, protected from their intrusion from below by the earth and from above by the sky. The sky, a hemisphere above the earth, was depicted variously as a cow held up by four legs, as an arched female figure supported by its extended arms and legs, or as a shell supported by mountains or by four posts at the cardinal points. In the beginning, the sun, described sometimes as self-created and sometimes as the child of the sky-goddess, pushed back the abysmal darkness, just as each day the sun's rays push back the darkness of the night. During the night hours, the sun fought its way back through the darkness of the underworld to rise again over Egypt and the world.

Creation itself, attributed to several deities by their respective cult centers, occurred because of some form of sexual activity or through word, which was interpreted as the projection of thought. We will now discuss briefly five cosmogonies associated with cult centers at Memphis, Heliopolis, Hermopolis, Thebes, and Elephantine.[3]

Memphite Cosmology

The city of Memphis was built around 2900 B.C. by Menes (Narmer), who, according to Manethos, the third century B.C. priest-historian, was the first ruler of permanently united Egypt. Memphis was located at the apex of the Nile delta, at the junction of the united kingdoms of Upper and Lower Egypt, and was the center of government and of religion. The Memphite myth augmented the city's claim to exceptional status.

Basic information about the myth has been derived from the Shabaka stone, a product of the reign of the Ethiopian or Kushite Pharaoh Shabaka (Shabako) about 700 B.C. However, that inscription is based on earlier material which may go back to the fourth millennium B.C. The account appears to represent some form of dialogue between gods and was probably designed for dramatic ritual associated with the myth.

Ptah, the high god of Memphis, was designated as creator of the world and master of destiny. His creative activities innovated all that exists, including the cults of other Egyptian gods and the offerings made to them. Creation was by "word," which was the activating power of the thoughts of the god's "heart,"[4] uttered by his "tongue." The heart was, therefore, the symbol of mind or intelligence, the tongue the symbol of command or power.[5] The god spoke, and his utterance took form and became a reality. Ptah incorporated Nun, the primeval waters from which everything came. All other gods were projections of his will and command; all existing things were manifestations of his mind and creative word. The Shabaka account states that the gods entered into their forms in all kinds of wood, minerals, soils, and growing things. Everywhere, within and without, the Egyptian encountered the divine. It is not surprising, therefore, to discover that the Egyptian artisans depicted gods in various animal and human forms and in combinations of these, developing artistic expressions of mythical figures that are most impressive.

The Shabaka account gives no information about the specifics of the cosmological process. There is no reference to the creation of the earth, the sky, the seas, the rivers, and growing things. All was presupposed; Ptah caused the gods to enter into and infuse the world and its contents with the divine. It can be assumed that Ptah created the cosmos just as he caused everything else to be—by his word.

Heliopolitan Cosmology

The ancient city of On, called Heliopolis by the Greeks, was located almost directly across the Nile from Memphis. Here the sun god, sacred to the Egyptians from predynastic times, was worshiped under the name of Atum, later Atum-Ra or Atum-Re, when the two manifestations for the sun god were linked.

Atum was a self-generated god who emerged from the primordial waters of Nun by an act of will. The seventeenth chapter of the Book of the Dead, a compilation of coffin texts that go back to the third millennium B.C., refers to Atum as being "alone in Nun." Self-generation, an idea we will meet again in Hermopolitan and Theban cosmologies, conferred unique authority on Atum. He was his own first cause. His mythic history (mythology) began in and with himself. All other gods had predecessors, Atum alone had none. He was the beginning of the creative process; without him, nothing was made that was made. His power and authority were, therefore, unsurpassed. All other gods and all created things were destined to function and respond to existence in given ways. Atum was above all that he had created, and therefore not under the same controls. He was also embodied in and through his creation, both transcendent and immanent.

In the beginning, because Atum had nowhere to stand, he brought into being the primeval hillock or mound on which the Heliopolitan temple was said to have been built. (The concept of the primeval mound may have originated in the observation of muddy hillocks that emerge as the Nile waters recede after the inundation.) The temple represented sacred space, a holy site, the house of the god. Rituals conducted in its precincts were divine rituals, reenacting cosmic beginnings at the foundation place of the universe.

The Memphite account of creation by Ptah may have been too abstract for worshipers. Heliopolitan mythology described the formation of gods and goddesses in a manner more easily comprehended. Some early texts refer to Atum as the great He-She, a bisexual implication, but it is clear that in the creation mythology, the god is exclusively male. Because Atum's devotees conceived of creation in sexual terms and because Atum was without a mate, he was said to have created by masturbation. The Shabaka inscription notes that the Ennead, the first gods, were created by Atum "by his semen and his fingers." A dedicatory text carved inside Sixth Dynasty pyramids about the middle of the third millennium B.C. provides a variant form of the myth.[6] The name Atum is linked with Khepri, and Atum-Khepri is said to have taken the semen from the masturbatory act

into his mouth and to have spat forth Shu, the air god, and Tefnut, the
moisture goddess, who was both sister and wife to Shu. Clearly, the
concept of life-giving is associated with the male semen, and the woman
might be interpreted as the vessel in which life developed rather than as
a vital contributor to the individual conceived within her.

Atum-Re is also said to have created the "names" of his body parts. In
the very naming, divine beings representing the world came into being:
Geb, the earth god, and his sister-wife Nut, the sky goddess; Osiris, the
fertility god who was to become the chief god of the mortuary cult, and
his sister-wife, Isis; Seth or Set, the rival of Osiris, and his twin sister-wife
Nephthys. Shu and Tefnut were said to have been the parents of Geb and
Nut, who in turn were parents of Osiris, Isis, Set, and Nephthys. In this
variant form of the myth, Atum is the "All," and all gods are extensions
of or parts of Atum.

Mankind was formed by the tears of Atum. Atum, it seems, had but one
eye (*udjat*), which was physically and ideationally independent. Once
when Shu and Tefnut were lost in the murkiness of Nun, Atum sent the
eye to look for them and during its absence replaced it with a substitute.
When the eye returned with the missing gods, it was furious at being
replaced. As appeasement, it was given a place in the forehead of Atum,
where it would be able to rule the world that was shortly to come into
being. Atum shed tears of joy over the return of his children, and the tears
became men. Then, according to this interpretation, Atum left the primeval
abyss and created the world.

Hermopolitan Cosmology

At Hermopolis in Upper Egypt, Thoth, the ancient moon god of the delta,
was accepted as the supreme deity and the embodiment of divine wisdom,
intelligence, and omniscience. His chief manifestation was in the form of
an ibis or an ibis-headed man, although he is sometimes shown as a
dog-faced baboon.

Thoth was self-begotten, emerging in a lotus flower in the primeval
waters of Nun. According to one myth, the ibis god laid the cosmic egg
out of which Re, the sun god, appeared. A variant version depicted Re
emerging as a child when the lotus flower rose from the sea and opened
its petals. In a third version, the lotus flower opened and the sun, in the
form of a scarab beetle, was revealed. The scarab was transformed into a
boy (Re), whose tears became mankind.

Associated with Thoth were the Ogdoad, a group of eight divinities—
four males and their consorts—said to have created the world and ruled
it in a primeval golden age. After their death, they journeyed to the under-

world, from whence they caused the Nile to flow. The names of the male deities personify four aspects of formless precreation chaos, and the consorts' names are simply feminine forms of the male appellations. Nun and Naunet represent the primeval waters, the abyss; Huh and Hauhet, the formless, endless expanse of chaos; Kuk and Kauket, the primeval darkness, the obscure; and Amon and Amonet, the air that moved over the primeval waters.

The holy city was located on the primeval hill that appeared first as an island, called "The Island of Two Flames," in Nun. The sacred lake in the park attached to the temple represented Nun and was called "The Sea of the Two Knives." The temple was believed to be the primeval dwelling place of the Ogdoad.

Many aspects of the ancient myths about Thoth are obscure. In the New Kingdom, which began about the middle of the sixteenth century B.C., a new cult center developed at Thebes, borrowing some aspects of Hermopolitan mythology. According to a fourteenth century text, Thoth, as the moon, was accepted as a substitute for Re and Re's vizier. Ultimately, as the god of wisdom, he was prominent in the Osirian cult of the dead.

Theban Cosmology

When Thebes, in Upper Egypt, became the seat of government in the New Kingdom (ca. 1570–1083), the chief god of the city, Amon, assumed national importance. His early roles as the goose that laid the cosmic egg or as the fertile ram god became less prominent, and Amon was fused with Re as Amon-Re, becoming a solar deity. Facets of Memphite, Heliopolitan, and Hermopolitan mythology were accepted. Like Atum, Amon was self-created. As the god of the air, he was invisible and symbolized the dynamic, creative power of the moving atmosphere or the wind, or even the quality of the breath of life in man and beast. Amon was said to have brought all into being, beginning with the Ogdoad of Hermopolis and then the other gods. As of Ptah, it was said of Amon that all deities were manifestations of different aspects of his nature.

Having created the gods, Amon left the earth. In heaven he was manifested as Re, giving light to the world. At night, because all gods were embodied in him, Amon could be recognized in Thoth, the moon. Amon ruled his creation, sailing in a boat above and below it (through the underworld). A hymn composed in the fourteenth century B.C. and preserved in a thirteenth century document extols Thebes, the holy city of Amon, as the first city ever created. An account recorded on the doorpost of the second pylon at Karnak describes the emergence of the primeval mound out of Nun. Like the mythology of Heliopolis and Hermopolis, this account declares that the sacred domain of the god was located on that mound. Man was created to construct other cities modeled on Thebes.

The topocosm was one. Societal patterns were in harmony with nature, and to disturb one was to disturb the other. Order—*Ma'at*—had to prevail over disorder and disharmony. The pharaoh was the embodiment of the principle of order and power (Amon) and the transmitter of divine stability.

Cosmology of Elephantine and Philae

The two small islands of Elephantine and Philae are located in the Nile at the southernmost boundary of Upper Egypt, just below the First Cataract. Here the ram-headed god Khnum was worshiped from earliest times. According to Elephantine and Philae mythology, Khnum created the heavens, the earth, and the underworld. He brought the Nile up from Nun by way of two caverns, one supplying the waters to the south and the other to the northern part of the river. Thus, Khnum controlled the fertile waters of Egypt. From the Nile mud, Khnum formed man on a potter's wheel. Indeed, every child was said to be fashioned by Khnum.

Khnum was associated with the sun god and recognized under the name of Khnum-Re as the living soul of Re. Thus Khnum became a fertility god linked to the two life-giving resources of Egypt, the Nile and the sun.

SUMERIAN COSMOLOGY

About the middle of the fifth millennium B.C., a people now identified as the Sumerians settled in the lower Tigris-Euphrates river valleys, merging with and supplanting an earlier rural economy. The origin and cultural background of the Sumerians is unknown, but from the melding of the cultures came an explosion of creativity that had effects on the ancient Near Eastern world long after the middle of the eighteenth century B.C., when the Sumerians ceased to exist as a people.

Written mythic materials date from after the third millennium, although they appear to reflect concepts that come from a much earlier date. The literature contains numerous allusions to cosmological themes derived from as yet unknown cosmogonies. The Sumerians believed that before the world was created and subdivided into regions under the control of various gods, there was Nammu, the primeval sea, the mother of all. Heaven (*an*) and earth (*ki*) originated as creations of Nammu. At first they were united (heaven-earth: an-ki), but then the hard metallic shell of the sky was moved away from and vaulted above the earth by Enlil, the god of the air, the wind, and the storm, who occupied the space between heaven and earth. Above the shell of heaven and below the flat disc of the earth were the waters of Nammu. The description projects the image of a three-tiered structure: heaven, earth, and the abyss.

The heavens were placed under the control of the sky god, An, who may once have been the supreme deity. By the middle of the third millennium, his leadership had been usurped by Enlil, who became the chief god of Sumer. Enlil was the creator god. His sacred city, Nippur, was at first inhabited only by divine beings. Enlil brought forth all growing things and the tools necessary for civilization.

The earth was under the control of Enki, son of Enlil and god also of the abyss and the subterranean waters, lord of wisdom, and the organizer of the earth. Enki provided the life-sustaining waters of the Tigris and Euphrates, gave the rain, and taught mankind to farm and build. According to one account, Enki formed mankind from clay in the image of the gods. Man was designed to relieve the gods of the manual labor involved in agriculture. In a competitive spirit, Ninmah, the earth goddess, also formed creatures from clay, but her creations were deformed and defective. The myth of these misshapen figures appears to explain certain groups within Sumerian society. For example, accounts of one creature formed without sexual organs and destined to serve the king seem to refer to the eunuchs employed in the royal palace. A sterile woman served the queen's maids. The other creatures are more difficult to identify. But the contest did not end at this point. Enki created an enfeebled old man and challenged Ninmah to find a purpose for this creature. The details of Ninmah's response are lost, but perhaps this was a Sumerian explanation of the infirmities that beset humans.

The myth of Enki and Ninhursag is known from a six-column clay tablet found at Nippur.[7] Although the tablet dates from the first half of the second millennium B.C., it appears to be based on an earlier version. The poem opens with a description of the land of Dilmum or Tilmun, which some scholars locate at Bahrein in the Persian Gulf and others somewhere east of Sumer. Dilmun is described as a clean, bright location without illness or death. The setting is often interpreted as a paradise, but presumably there was no life and no water, so that Dilmun may be recognized as a clean, sterile, bright desert. The environment was transformed into a life-sustaining realm when Enki, in this myth a definite fertility god, impregnated his wife Ninhursag, the earthgoddess, with his flow of fresh water. After a pregnancy of nine "days," Ninhursag gave birth to Ninmu. Ninmu was impregnated by Enki, and after nine "days" bore Ninkurra, who was also impregnated by Enki and gave birth to Uttu. On advice from her great-grandmother Ninhursag, Uttu refused to have sexual relationships with Enki until he brought her fruits of the field: cucumbers, apples, and grapes. The result of the sexual union between Enki and his great-granddaughter was the sprouting of eight plants, which Enki possessed by eating them. Ninhursag cursed Enki for devouring the plants, and Enki, experiencing excruciating pain in various parts of his body, was apparently dying. A fox, to whom Enki promised the trees and fields of the city of Nippur, brought Ninhursag to the ailing god. Seated "by her vulva," Enki named one by one the parts of his body that were in pain, and for each complaint Ninhursag produced a remedial god. These gods were then given territorial, agricultural, sexual, and time-division jurisdictions.

The myth of Enki and Ninhursag is important because it portrays the place of beginning in terms of the desert. Only when water became available did plant life grow. The people of Mesopotamia, bordered on the west by the desert and dependent on the life-sustaining Tigris and Euphrates rivers, were keenly aware of the relationships between aridity and starvation, water and agricultural productivity. But the myth may have had other implications related to magic and medicine. The plants, associated with aches in different parts of the body and with the healing deities created by Ninhursag, may have been believed to possess healing power. Whether the plants were eaten to cure an illness—when Enki ate them they made him ill—or were bound to the ailing part of the body cannot be known, but the gods associated with them appear to have been invoked by the Sumerians to heal specific ailments.

One myth tells of the birth of the moon god and three underworld deities.[8] Recovered in fragmented form, it describes Enlil's rape and impregnation of Ninlil, the virgin goddess of Nippur. For this act, Enlil was judged by the council of the gods and expelled to the wasteland outside the city. He journeyed to the underworld, followed by Ninlil. At the gate of the underworld, Enlil assumed the role of gatekeeper. In this disguise, unrecognized by Ninlil, Enki copulated with the already pregnant goddess, causing her to become pregnant with another child. Next Enlil assumed the guise of the guardian of the underworld river and impregnated the already doubly pregnant goddess. Finally, as the boatman who would ferry Ninlil across the waters of the underworld, he impregnated the goddess for the fourth time. From the rape, the moon god Sin was born, and from the other three sexual acts came three gods of the underworld, brothers of the moon.

Another myth, known only in part, tells of re-creation after the existing world had been obliterated by a flood. Ziusudra, a priest-king, preserved specimens of life in a ship. When the flood waters subsided, the creatures in the boat were released. About two-thirds of the tablet found at Nippur are missing, but it is clear that the Sumerian myth is a precursor of the biblical flood myth.

Atrahasis

The Atrahasis myth, recovered in part from Sumerian, Babylonian, and Neo-Assyrian sources, included an account of the creation of humans by the mother goddess, Mami or Mama.[9] The section of the myth dealing with the flood will be discussed in Chapter 4.

The creation myth describes a time when the most powerful gods had virtually enslaved the lesser gods, compelling them to labor in heaven and on earth. Rebellion broke out. The lesser gods destroyed their tools and marched in protest before the temple of Enlil. Enlil, roused from slumber, called a council of the high gods and then met with the general assembly, which included the rebel deities. Complaints about excessive labor demands and divine exhaustion were heard. A warning against absentee management is implicit in the complaints, for Enlil was clearly out of touch with the worker-gods. In the arbitration that followed, Ea offered a solution: the goddess Mami (another name for Ninhursag) was asked to create a being that would release the gods from their toil.

Mami formed *lullu,* or savage man, from clay mingled with the blood of the god Illuwe or We-ila, who was sacrificed for this purpose. Apparently divine blood was important for providing life potential in the clay. Fourteen pieces of clay were used to make "mother-wombs" which were animated by incantatory rites. They were placed seven on either side of a brick. Ea assumed the role of surgeon and delivered seven males and seven females. According to this myth, humans were created in pairs, simultaneously, and male had no priority over female. The purpose of humans was to relieve the gods of their labors. Men and women were created to serve the gods.

Despite the lacunae, it is clear that the myth included instructions for the midwife for bringing a pregnant woman to delivery. Every human birth was a reenactment of original creation. Every human was born to enable the gods to enjoy leisure.

THE BABYLONIAN CREATION MYTH

The Babylonian creation myth, *enuma elish,* is named for its opening words, which mean "when on high . . ."[10] It was recited and perhaps mimed during the Akitu festival, which introduced the new year in ancient Babylon, certainly during the seventh century B.C. and perhaps much earlier.

The text has been recovered from tablets found during the excavation of King Ashurbanipal's library at Nineveh and from fragments found at other southern Mesopotamian sites. The earliest fragment from Ashur is dated about 1000 B.C.; other tablets are not so early: Nineveh, seventh century; Kish and Uruk, sixth century or later. On the basis of language and internal evidence, most scholars conclude that the myth in the form now known to us goes back to the Amorite period, the early second millennium B.C., when, during the reign of Hammurabi, the city of Babylon rose to supreme power and Marduk, the city god, became supreme god of the empire. The myth may be based on still earlier Sumerian versions not yet know to us, since the word *akitu* is of Sumerian origin. The present account exalts the position of Marduk and the significance of Babylon as a holy city (Bab-ilim: gate of gods).

The account opens with a description of the basic stuff of creation: water, both salt and fresh, in some form of fluid relationship. There was no heaven, no earth, and no plant or animal life. Apsu (masculine) was the symbol of fresh water, and Tiamat (feminine) of salt water, and these two were to become parents of all gods and consequently of all life forms. There was also one other figure, an advisor to Apsu, called Mummu.

Within the primeval waters, two gods, Lahmu and Lahamu, were called into being by name, for without a name there was no existence. Other gods were formed: Anshar and Kishar and from these two Anu, who would later become the sky god; Ea or Nudimmud, who would be the earth god; and his wife Damkina. At this period, the topocosm was truly one; the new gods appear to exist within the primeval waters.

The new gods were young, vigorous, noisy and disrespectful of their parents. On Mummu's advice, despite Tiamat's reluctance, Apsu planned to kill his children. The plot was foiled by Ea, who cast a spell causing Mummu and Apsu to sleep. Ea seized Apsu's crown, halo, and cloak, bound and killed the father god, and imprisoned Mummu. Ea established himself on the body of Apsu, providing, no doubt, an acceptable explanation for the Babylonians of the fresh waters that seep up through the earth as springs and fountainheads of rivers.

Tiamat sought revenge for the death of Apsu. She created frightening monsters, serpents, and dragons with fearsome names, their veins filled with venom, with the power to frighten to death whoever beheld them. Kingu, her son, was made chief and became the new consort of Tiamat. Around his neck, Tiamat placed the Tablets of Fate or Destiny, the symbol of official control of the future.

When the gods associated with Ea learned of Tiamat's actions, they turned to Ea in terror. This time Ea was not to be the hero; nor was Anu, who was commissioned to confront Tiamat—he turned back, afraid. At last Marduk, the storm god, son of Ea and Damkina, the mightiest, strongest, and most majestic of the pantheon, was persuaded. He had been suckled at the breasts of Damkina.[11] He had been doubly endowed with power and possessed four ears and four eyes (which may have symbolized omniscience).

Marduk was a political strategist. He knew he was needed. Before accepting the responsibility of defending the threatened gods, he demanded that he be made supreme god, that his word, rather than the decision of the assembly, determine the fates, and that his word, once spoken, be unchangeable and effective.[12] The agreement was sealed at a banquet. Seated on his new throne, with the older gods assembled before him, Marduk listened to the pledge of loyalty and the confirmation of his supremacy:

> You are supreme among the great gods
> Your command is without challenge . . .
> Your pronouncements are uncontestable . . .
> All of the gods will have their shrines at your center . . .
> Your weapons shall be supreme . . .
> Spare the life of the god who trusts you . . .
> Destroy the evil god.[13]

As proof of the integrity of the oath, a cloth was set before Marduk and he was told that when he spoke, the cloth would vanish, but his next words would restore the cloth. This happened as predicted, and the cry was raised: "Marduk is king!" Marduk accepted the symbols of office. As the account explained how and why Marduk became supreme god in the Babylonian empire, perhaps it also explained how and why a democratic people came to be ruled by a king. In earliest periods in Mesopotamian cities, decisions were made by assemblies, a practice that gave way to monarchy.[14] As it happened in heaven, so did it happen on earth (or vice versa)—the myth explained the reality.)

Now Marduk mounted the storm chariot. With a net (the gift of Anu), storm winds, bow and arrows, a mace, and lightning, wrapped in a cloak of terror, his fearsome halo on his head, his mouth smeared with red ochre as a protection against evil, and a plant to counteract Tiamat's poison, Marduk went forth to battle. His chariot was drawn by four creatures named Killer, Relentless, Trampler, and Swift. Despite the preparations, Marduk was discomfited when he met Tiamat and his confusion spread to his followers. An exchange of insults brought the combatants to a pitch of uncontrollable frenzy, and Marduk and Tiamat clashed in physical battle. With the net, Marduk enfolded Tiamat. Into her open mouth he drove "Evil Wind" and then shot an arrow down her throat to kill her.

Tiamat's followers fled but were captured and imprisoned by Marduk. Marduk took the Tablets of Destiny from Kingu and fastened them on his own breast. In a final act of violence, he trod on Tiamat's legs, smashed her skull with his mace, and released her blood to the north wind to be carried to an undisclosed place.

While older gods rejoiced in the deliverance, Marduk began the task of creation. Tiamat's body was split in two "like an oyster." One half was arched to form the hemisphere of the heavens, the other half laid flat to become the foundation of the earth. From Tiamat's spittle, Marduk formed the clouds that brought rain, the mists, and the storms which would be under his immediate control. Her head became the mountains, and from her eyes flowed the two rivers, the Tigris and the Euphrates. In the upper regions, Anu, the sky god, was placed in control, while in the lower region, Ea, Marduk's father, the earth god, governed. Enlil, the god of wind and air, had jurisdiction over the space between heaven and earth. Thus were the heavens and the earth created.

Cyclical patterns were instituted. Shamash, the sun god, was given a fixed course. The calendrical waxing and waning of the moon was determined. The stars in the heavens were made in the likenesses of the gods, with three constellations designed for each month. The number of days in the year was designated.

Now the gods complained that there was no one to serve their needs. Kingu, the prime offender among the remaining rebel gods, was killed. From his blood, Marduk created the servant creature of the gods, which he named "man."[15] Clearly, according to Babylonian mythology, the purpose of man was to serve the gods. Kingu's death was redemptive, freeing the gods "so that they might be at ease."[16]

To honor Marduk, the grateful gods proposed that a shrine be built with subsidiary shrines to accommodate them when they were in divine assembly. The divine dwellingplace on earth was a counterpart of the heavenly home. Thus, Babylon came into being. For one year, the celestial gods molded bricks and then constructed Esagila and the ziggurat, which was said to be as high as heaven.[17] Babylon was Marduk's "home," a sanctuary for the gods, and a great religious center. Here the destinies for each year were to be established. In the festivities that followed, the fragmented text seems to indicate that Marduk's bow was set in the heavens as the bow-star.[18]

During the banquet, Marduk's role as king was reaffirmed by curses that would fall on those who violated the oath of allegiance, and by treaties sworn in oil, water, and blood. At the utterance of Marduk's name, the gods were to bow in reverence.[19] His commands were to be preeminent in heaven and on earth.[20] Mankind's responsibilities to the gods were clear: to maintain the sanctuaries, offer up incense, make food offerings,[21] and in every way serve the gods.

The account ends with the recitation of the fifty names of Marduk.[22] At the utterance of each name, some attribute of Marduk was announced. He was praised as the savior of the gods and creation, the bestower of seed and fertility, the sustainer of justice and the punisher of evil, the regulator of life and the creator of permanence. He was supreme, shepherd and lord of all the gods. An epilogue enjoined the leader of the cultic ritual to explain Marduk's attributes, the wise to discuss them, and the father to teach them to his son, that in rejoicing in Marduk the land might be fertile and individuals might prosper.[23] The promise was balanced by the threat of nonsupport from the god, if the worshiper failed to fulfill his responsibilities to Marduk.

Clearly, *enuma elish* embodies more than cosmology. In part it deals with the emergence of Marduk as a savior god who defeats demonic powers and reorganizes the cosmos by bringing order out of chaos. It explains why Marduk should receive the glory given to him in the cult. In establishing Marduk as a single monarch, king of kings, the myth supports the Babylonian political system in which the king of Babylon, like the god of Babylon, is divinely assured of his role as emperor. It is not surprising that the prologue to the Code of Hammurabi should describe the actions of that monarch in much the same way that the listing of the fifty names of Marduk described the god, nor that Hammurabi should win battles against the enemy through Marduk's power.[24] There is little doubt that Hammurabi and other Babylonians actually believed in Marduk and the hierarchy of gods. The cultus and mythology supported the monarchical system, because the structure of Babylonian society paralleled the structure of the heavenly society. Social stratification among humans was similar to that in the divine spheres. The king's authority was like Marduk's authority, the role of the earthly court like the role of the heavenly, the subservience of lesser gods like the subservience of minor kings incorporated in the Babylonian empire. When the gods gathered for the Akitu festival in Babylon, the presence of their sacred images and symbols there, attended by their priests, demonstrated the superiority of Babylon and the god Marduk and formed the basis for similar political councils called by the monarch. When these gods, through their representatives on earth, paid homage to Marduk in cultic ceremonies, they dramatized the homage due to Marduk's chosen king from the royalty of the cities from which the gods originated.

The Akitu festival, in which the *enuma elish* was recited and possibly dramatized, coming at the vernal equinox, gave credence to the life struggle between the forces of chaos and those of order. The festival marked a time of suspension between the termination of the old year and the inauguration of the new, and the recitation and miming of the primordial victory over chaos helped unify the nation and sustain the established norm. When Nabonidus, who claimed that Marduk had chosen him monarch of

Babylon, neglected the Akitu rituals and was suspected of harboring a strong attraction for another god—possibly the moon god, Sin—he lost the support of his clergy and his people.[25]

The Akitu Festival

The Akitu festival, the most important annual festival in Babylon, was celebrated each year at the vernal equinox, from the first to the twelfth days of the month Nisanu (Hebrew *Nisan* = March-April).[26] Activities centered in the temple of Marduk, called Esagila (house of the uplifted head), which stood near the great ziggurat called Etemenanki (house of the platform of heaven and earth).

Our information about the Akitu festival is derived from texts belonging to the third and second centuries B.C., which point back to much earlier materials, parts of which may come from Sumerian times. The writings of the unknown Jewish prophet who lived in Babylon just before the conquest by Cyrus the Great in the sixth century reflect patterns of the festival.[27] Because the Akitu festival is one of the few rites about which we have detailed information, and because it has mythic implications for modern times, we shall outline its activities in detail.[28]

The Akitu Festival was more than a simple interpretation or dramatization of *enuma elish.* At its center stood the ancient myth of creation, but the celebration of creation and of Marduk's victory over chaos had accumulated a vast accompaniment of mythic interpretations, many of which simply cannot be understood at this time.

Through mythic interpretation, the organized cult had generated a strong sense of uncertainty and insecurity among the people by appealing to guilt feelings. Cosmological myth described the polarity of chaos and order, evil and good, and the implications of that tension were transferred to the realm of human behavior. Like Christians and Jews, the Mesopotamians were a guilt-burdened people constantly reminded of their faults and violations of divine rules. They existed in danger of judgment and punishment. To break the divine commands that gave order and structure to the cosmos and to society was, in a sense, to enhance the power of the forces of chaos, against which Marduk and presumably the Mesopotamian people were pitted. And as we shall see, purification from sin and guilt was an essential part of the Akitu ritual.

What we of the twentieth century lack most is the emotional response of the Mesopotamian worshiper. The pageantry, extended over many days and marked by the arrival and departure of gods with their retinues from surrounding cities, generated high excitement. The Lenten restrictions and the emphasis in the festival on the termination of a time-lease on life probably produced solemnity and some insecurity about the coming year. The requirements of animal and human sacrifice—for only by giving life could life be preserved—would, we imagine, generate a deep inner response in the participants. Nor have we records that enable us to grasp the sense of release from the burden of guilt, the joy in becoming clean and new, that would result from the purgation rites. Perhaps the closest we can come is statements of contemporaries who have experienced "salvation," "forgiveness," or "newness of life" in religious experiences.[29]

Preparatory rituals began on the first day of the festival, two hours before dawn. The *urigallu* priest washed himself with water from the Euphrates, donned a linen vestment, and entered Marduk's shrine. Before the statue of the god, he recited a prayer in which the deity was acknowledged as "lord of kings, light of mankind," and was asked to "grant mercy to your city, Babylon" to establish the "liberty" of the people. Following the opening prayer, the doors of the temple were opened and other categories of priests entered to perform rites before the god and his consort Zarpanit.[30] Apparently, instrumentalists and singers were involved, and some rituals were associated with the attire of the deities.

The second and third days were also set apart for preparation for the central rites. Woodworkers carved two statues from tamarisk and cedar, and metalworkers overlaid the images with precious metals and jewels from the treasury of Marduk. One figure held a snake in its left hand and raised its right hand in salute to Nabu or Nebo, son of Marduk and chief god of the neighboring city of Borsippa. The other also raised its right hand to Nabu, but held a scorpion in its left hand. The statues were clothed in red. Until the sixth day, they remained in the house of the god Madan, the judge. The mockery of the manufacture of idols by the Jewish prophet (Isa. 40:18–20, 41:7) ignored that the images were symbols, not gods, and that the artisans who made them were persons chosen for the specific tasks associated with manufacture of such items.[31]

On the morning of the fourth day, the *urigallu* priest ritually washed and clothed himself. In the presence of the statues of Marduk and Zarpanit, he called on Marduk as lord of Babylon, whose hands held the fates of all the other gods, to grant release and to have mercy on Babylon. He addressed Zarpanit as one who caused the poor to become rich and the wealthy to become impoverished, who released the prisoner and raised the fallen. For himself, the petitioner sought life, health, and joy. Then the priest went to the courtyard and three times blessed the temple Esagila. In the late afternoon, after other rituals, the *urigallu* priest recited *enuma elish* to the god Marduk. During the recitation, the tiara of the sky god, Anu, and the dais of the wind god, Enlil, were covered.

On the fifth day, purification rituals were performed. The temple was sprinkled with water and fumigated with incense, and the kettle drum was beaten. Incantations exorcised the building. During the *kuppuru* ceremony, a ram was decapitated and its body rubbed against the walls of the temple of Nabu, called Ezida, to purify the temple. The body of the sacrificed animal was believed to absorb all the pollution accumulated during the year and to render the structure and its precincts clean and pure. The head and torso were then thrown into the river, and the men involved with the animal—the slaughterer and the priest—compelled to remain in a remote place outside the city until the festival ended.[32]

Within the temple of Marduk, the king abdicated his office. He was stripped of royal regalia, and the scepter, ring, and sword were set apart in Marduk's temple. Priests slapped the king's face and dragged him by the ears before Marduk's image, where he made a negative confession, stating that he had not sinned or neglected the responsibilities of his office, and that he had protected Babylon and had neither plotted its overthrow nor neglected temple ritual. He further confessed that he had not humilated his subordinates. Following the confession, the *urigallu* priest uttered words of absolution, comfort, and reassurance and promised the blessing of Marduk. Now the symbols of office were returned and the king's cheek struck. If tears flowed, it was a sign that Marduk was pleased and friendly; if they did not flow, then Marduk was angry and there was threat of disaster.[33] The day concluded with an evening ritual involving a white bull, called the "Divine Bull," perhaps symbolic of the constellation Taurus.[34]

It is possible that the death of Marduk was observed on the fifth day. The texts, though unclear, appear to record lamentations for the dead god. There are references to a cultic act where Marduk seems to be wounded and lying in his own blood and is presumed dead. A ritual search was conducted for the missing god. Then the records explicitly state that the *enuma elish* was recited over the dead god, presumably in some sort of ritual attempt to release him from death. There were also rituals in which Zarpanit appears to have washed Marduk's wounds, and there is a reference to the killing of a pig on the eighth day, which may have symbolized the destruction of Marduk's killer. Because of gaps in the text, we can only assume that Marduk was dead or missing for part of the festival.

On the sixth day, Nebo and his consort, Tasmet, arrived from Borsippa. The small statues fashioned during the preparatory period were presented to the god, decapitated, and thrown into the fire. Also on this day, a scapegoat rite of purification took place. Just as the temple environs had been purified and made ready for the inauguration of the new year, so the community was required to achieve a state of pristine purity. A human victim was required to remove the weight of communal sin and guilt. The sin-bearer, a felon or deformed person, was driven through the streets of the city and scourged to rid the community of guilt, sin, and evil that could not be definitely related to individuals or to specific acts or events.[35] The scapegoat was believed to absorb into himself the sin, guilt, and accumulated social impurities of the community. Perhaps the burden of sin was transferred by a ritual act wherein the priest confessed the evils of the community and by the laying on the hands transmitted the guilt to the scapegoat, just as the high priest in ancient Israel conveyed Israelite sin to a live goat (Lev. 16:20ff), or just as in the modern-day ordination ceremony, a bishop by certain utterances and by laying on of hands confers apostolic authority to a priest. Perhaps the sin-bearer was believed to draw social pollution to himself simply by being driven through the city as a magnet draws fragments of metal. As a soiled cleaning cloth is discarded, so the individual bearing society's uncleanness could be eliminated. If the scapegoat was killed, it was assumed that the evil, guilt, and sin died with him.[36] It is not clear that the Babylonian scapegoat was put to death.

The seventh day of the Akitu festival was marked by a solemn procession from the temple Esagila to a place called the *akitu* house, concerning which little is known. On the eighth day, a pig was sacrificed. We know nothing of the ninth day, but on the tenth it appears that Marduk was resurrected, an event marked by the sacrifice of oxen and sheep and the pouring of libations of wine and milk. The image of the god was removed from one station to another, symbolizing the change in Marduk's status or condition.

On the eleventh day, the gods met in solemn assembly in the chamber of destiny to determine the destiny of the new year. S. A. Pallis believes that the ritual implied something positive. Rather than involving an attempt to predict individual events or to catalog specific dangers or evils of the coming year, the assembly sought to create positive influences toward prosperity, peace, and happiness.[37] The forces were set in motion through the use of magic. During the year, divination rites would determine good or evil days and the pleasure or displeasure of the gods, related to specific events.

A sacred marriage was enacted, a fertility rite symbolizing the coming together of Marduk and Zarpanit. The limited textual data describe the goddess, full of love, reclining beside Marduk. Probably, the king and the high priestess dramatized the text in a copulation rite performed before the populace. The virility of the king was of paramount importance in the Near East, for the king embodied the topocosm, and an impotent king symbolized an impotent people and world.[38]

A processional along Marduk's way in which Zarpanit accompanied her lord and Nebo and Tasmet also participated, culminated in a celebration called "Marduk's Feast." During the processional, the king is said to take the god's right hand. It has been suggested that this action is symbolic of the king leading the god to the shrine. On the other hand, it could equally well signify to the watching populace that the god Marduk had chosen the king to rule for the coming year. Divine approval of the king was vital to retaining the throne.[39]

The twelfth and final day of the festival was marked by the sacrifice of great numbers of sacred cattle and by a banquet in which gods, priests, king, and people participated. The rite symbolized the sealing of relationships for the coming year, the bonding of the gods, the cult, the people, and the ruler in a giant commensality ritual.

The Akitu festival was a threshold ritual marking the passing from one time boundary to the next, the separation of old time from new time. To move across boundaries in the physical world was to encounter opposition from those whose territory was being invaded. Tiamat symbolized the forces of opposition; the festival achieved group cohesiveness against that opposition. The totality of the past had died, and the whole topocosm had been born into the new. The disruption of normal function for the twelve-day period symbolized transition. The rite also held agricultural significance, for it ensured the feritility of the coming year. Politically, it marked a new beginning with new energy and vitality. Most of all, through the myth, it restified to a belief in cosmic order that was always threatened by potential disruption.

THE CANAANITE MYTH OF BA'AL

The Canaanite myth of Ba'al is not strictly cosmogonic, but it contains motifs that link it to creation accounts: in the beginning, the world was controlled by the god of primeval waters, conflicts between gods introduced order, the earth was subdivided, and different areas were assigned to different gods. Six cuneiform tablets under the heading "Concerning Ba'al" were among the documents recovered by Professor Claude Schaeffer of Paris during the excavation of the ancient city of Ugarit in northern Syria. Unfortunately, some of the tablets were found in a damaged state, so there are significant gaps in the mythic account.

The myth records a series of battles for control of the world. Yam or Judge Nahar,[40] god of the primordial waters, (also called Lotan (Leviathan), "a slippery serpent," "a dragon, "a tyrant with seven heads,") battled Ba'al or Hadad, the "rider of the clouds," god of fertility and rain. Mot, god of sterility and death, dweller in the nether regions, fought Ba'al and Ba'al's consort-sister Anat, who is called "the virgin" despite her sexual relationships with Ba'al. All were part of a pantheon, children of the father god, El, whose epithets included "the bull" and "creator of creatures," and his wife, the Lady Asherah of the sea, the creator of the gods.

The fragmented opening of the myth calls to mind the primordial waters of Egyptian and Mesopotamian mythologies, for the Canaanite account indicates that El had given Yam control of the world. Soon Yam's messengers appeared before the divine assembly gathered at Mount Saphon in the recesses of the north and demanded that the gods pay Yam tribute and that Ba'al and his holdings be turned over to the water god. Infuriated by Yam's arrogance, Ba'al overreacted, abandoned his divine dignity, and would have killed the envoys with a knife had he not been restrained by Anat and Ashtoreth, the Canaanite counterpart of Astarte or Ishtar. Thus the stage was set for a dramatic encounter between Yam, god of waters and symbol of chaos, and Ba'al, god of rain and symbol of the fecundity that made possible the civilized, ordered world. Ba'al assumes the role of the divine warrior, the life-giving savior-king.

Like Marduk, Ba'al acquired two weapons, manufactured by the artisan god Kothar-and-Khasis (Skillful-and-Clever), whose territory was Egypt and perhaps also Crete. The weapons were some sort of missiles, spears, or perhaps thunderbolts, magically empowered by incantation. The first was dispatched with the following chant:

> Your name is Yagrush ("Chaser").
> Yagrush, chase *(grsh)* Yam!
> Chase *(grsh)* Yam from his throne,
> Nahar from his throne!
> Swoop like a falcon from Ba'al's hand
> And strike Prince Yam's shoulders
> Between Judge Nahar's two hands!

The bolt felled Yam, but it was not enough to overcome the powerful god. So the second weapon was launched:

> Your name is Aymurr ("Driver").
> Aymurr, drive *(mr)* Yam!
> Drive *(mr)* Yam from his throne,
> Nahar from his throne!
> Swoop like a falcon from Ba'al's hand
> And crush Prince Yam's head,
> Judge Nahar's forehead!
> Let Yam collapse and fall to the earth.

The second missile dethroned Yam, and Ba'al was disuaded from dispatching the defeated god. We can probably assume that the defeated Yam was confined to his proper sphere—the oceanbed and the river basins—thus marking the emergence of the land, which was to be under Ba'al's sovereignty, that is, the lands made fertile by rain.

Now the cry was raised, "Ba'al is to be king!" At a victory banquet, Ba'al and his daughters Padriya (mist) and Taliya (showers) were honored with food, wine, and song. Anat arrived after having indulged in a gory slaughter of people in cities to the east and west. She is described as plunging her knees in warriors' blood and wearing heads at her waist and palms on her sash. The significance of her act is not understood; perhaps she was overcoming areas still loyal to Yam. Ba'al called for peace, and Anat raised the challenge:

> What foes will rise against Ba'al?
> What enemy against the Rider of the Clouds?

In response, a pledge of allegiance was given:

> No foe will rise against Ba'al,
> No enemy against the Rider of the Clouds.
> The message of the triumphant Ba'al
> The word of the brave victor is:
> "War on earth is against my will . . ."

Ba'al was now established as the supreme god, and like Marduk, he required a palace. Permission to build was given by El and the artisan god, Kothar-and-Khasis, was brought from Egypt. During the discussion, while the divine architect was royally entertained, he argued that a window must be included in the mansion. Ba'al's protest revealed his fear that Padriya and Taliya might escape. Despite his objections, the window was built. When Ba'al opened the window like "a rift in the clouds," his "holy voice" rang out, causing the earth to tremble and quake. Some ritual of sympathetic magic may be involved here, so that when a priest opened a window in the temple on earth which was, presumably, a replica of the heavenly abode, the window in the heavenly temple was simultaneously opened to permit the rain to fall (see Gen. 7:11) and Ba'al's voice to be heard as thunder.[41] Ba'al's utterance was a challenge:

> Enemies of Hadad, why are you dismayed?
> Why are you dismayed at the weapons of our defense?
> Ba'al's eyes guide his hands
> When the cedar (spear) is waved in his right hand.
> When Ba'al returns to his mansion
> Will anyone—king or no king—
> Make the earth his dominion?

Ba'al next challenged Mot:

> Truly I will send an envoy to Mot
> A herald to the hero, the beloved son of El
> To summon Mot to his grave,
> To conceal the loved one in his tomb.
> I alone will be king of gods
> That gods may grow fat
> And that mankind, the multitudes of the earth, be satisfied.

The statement was delivered by Ba'al's two messengers, Gupan and Ugar. Mot returned a message which reaffirmed Ba'al's victory over Yam:

> You smote Lotan (Leviathan) the slippery serpent,
> You defeated the writhing serpent,
> The tyrant with seven heads . . .
> Truly you will come down into Mot's throat,
> Into the miry gullet of El's beloved hero.

Mot's message may have been an invitation to Ba'al to visit and feast in the underworld, for Ba'al does disappear into the realm of Mot. Before descending into the underworld, however, Ba'al copulated with a heifer, mounting the animal innumerable times (seven and seventy times . . . eight and eighty times), and a son was born. What the gods did in the myth, the gods' representatives enacted in ritual. It is probable that a sexual rite involving a heifer was publicly performed at Canaanite shrines, with a priest assuming the role of Ba'al; such a rite may have been designed to increase the fertility of flocks and herds.[42] (The biblical prohibition of bestiality in Leviticus 18:23–24 refers to the Canaanite practice. The legislation in Exodus 22:19 invokes the death penalty for bestiality, and the ritual in Deuteronomy 27:24 pronounces a curse. The Hebrew attitude seems to be directed against participation in rites associated with the god Ba'al, rather than at any inherent evil or immorality in the act. What was sacred to one god was often taboo to another.)

The text is broken at this point; we are told simply that Mot overcame and killed Ba'al.[43] In grief, El descended from his throne and sat on the ground, wearing sackcloth and pouring ashes over his head. Then he wandered through the hills, gashed his face, forearms, chest, and back, and wailed, "Ba'al is dead!" Anat also roamed the forest and hills, gashing herself, weeping, and searching for the missing god. When she found his body, the sun goddess helped her load it on her shoulders, and Anat carried it to Mount Saphon for burial. The funeral rite included the sacrifice of large numbers of wild and domestic beasts.

During Ba'al's absence, Athtar, "the terrible," ascended the empty throne, but found himself too small for the task. Some scholars have suggested Athtar may represent artificial irrigation, which would be inadequate for the Levant, (the countries bordering the eastern Mediterranean),[44] or perhaps water stored in cisterns.[45] Size, strength, and virility were important attributes in a ruler.[46]

The next battle of the gods involved Anat and Mot. As sister and consort of Ba'al, Anat was, in a sense, the female counterpart of the life-sustaining god. The description of the battle employs symbols of the harvest:

> She seizes Mot, son of El,
> She cuts him with a [sickle] sword
> She winnows him in a sieve
> She roasts him in a fire
> She grinds him with millstones
> She scatters him in a field
> The birds eat his remains.

The image is of reaping, winnowing, drying or roasting grain, and grinding it into flour. Some of the winnowed grain falls outside the threshing pit, to be devoured by birds and beasts.

Ba'al returned, but the texts do not indicate how his resurrection was accomplished. His coming was anticipated by El in a dream of heavens raining oil and ravines flowing with honey. Anat cried:

> Where is the victorious Ba'al?
> Where is the prince, lord of the earth?

The final battle between Mot and Ba'al is more vividly portrayed than any of the others. The two gods are described as bulls goring and kicking, biting one another like serpents, first one and then the other falling and rising. The battle ends with the proclamation of Ba'al as victor and king.

The entire myth may have been recited and enacted at the autumnal equinoctial festival before the beginning of the rainy season and the commencement of the agricultural year. The cries and ritual gashing by the prophets of Ba'al, described in 1 Kings 18:28f, echo the grieving words and actions of El and Anat in the Ugaritic account. That the rains came after the contest between Elijah and the Ba'al worshipers (1 Kings 18:45) suggests that a new year ritual was enacted, probably in late October or during the month of Tishri (September-October), when the winter rains begin in Palestine.[47] However, the myth anticipates other aspects of the agricultural cycle and in a sense projects the seasonal pattern. The defeat of Yam and the inauguration of Ba'al as king, the establishment of the fecundity of the soil implying ordered cultivation by civilized people, and the dedication of the Ba'al shrine all belong to the new year ritual. The temple window was opened and the rain came. The cultic rite of bestiality fits best into the spring breeding period, in April. Ba'al's descent into the underworld marks the beginning of the summer period and the time of greatest aridity. The Anat–Mot conflict, with the emphasis on the harvesting of grain, coincides with our month of July, the time of ripened grain in Palestine.

BIBLICAL CREATION MYTHS

A number of differing cosmological themes seem to have been accepted in ancient Israel. Scattered throughout the Old Testament are references to cosmogonic patterns that reveal the influence of Canaanite thought. One creation account, labeled "J"[48] and believed to have been recorded during the reign of King Solomon in the tenth century B.C., extends from Genesis 2:4b to 3:24. Another, different and contradictory, was appended, probably during the last years of the fifth century B.C. It is known as "P" (priest) and includes Genesis 1:1–2:4a.

It is not surprising to discover Canaanite mythic themes in Hebraic thought. Yahwism and Ba'alism coexisted for centuries, at times peacefully but often in violent conflict. The traditions associated with Elijah and Elisha (1 Kings 18 to 2 Kings 10) reveal the intensity of the struggle. Hosea's oracles (Hos. 2:2–13, 4:12–13, 4:14–16, 8:5–6) and the description of the temple reform by Josiah in the seventh century B.C. (2 Kings 23) clearly demonstrate the influence of Ba'alism and other religions at Yahwist centers. In addition, biblical legislation which seems to have been directed against Canaanite practices suggests that Canaanite mythic concepts become so pervasive that cultic laws were necessary to keep the Hebrews from being drawn into Ba'alism.

Although the evidence has been disputed, some scholars have suggested that Yahweh may have been included as a member of the Canaanite pantheon.[49] In the opening of the Ugaritic myth of Ba'al, El (Lutpan), the father god, states:

> The name of my son is Yw-el (or Yo-el)
> And he proclaimed the name YW (or Yo).

Yw or Yo is one form of the name Yahweh and, as Cyrus Gordon has pointed out, it is found in the name of Moses' mother, Jochebed, which is Yw-kbd or Yo-kbd (see Num. 26:59) and in the name Jo-el.[50] In Deut. 32:8, a passage which refers to the allocation of territories to the various sons of the father god, Yahweh appears as one of the sons of Elyon:

> When Elyon portioned out the nations
> When he separated mankind
> He set the boundaries for the people
> According to the number of the sons of god.
> Yahweh's portion was his people,
> Jacob his allotted inheritance.

In Genesis 14:18, the term *El Elyon* (god most high) refers to the pre-Hebrew Canaanite god of Jerusalem. The title "Elyon" was given to Yahweh, and Yahweh assumed the role of the most high god (Pss. 21:7, 46:4, 47:2, 91:1, and so on).

In some mythic settings, Yahweh displaced Ba'al. For example, there are numerous references to Yahweh's battle with Yam, the sea. In Isaiah 51:9, Yahweh is called to battle:

> Awake, awake, put on strength, O arm of Yahweh!
> Awake, as in ancient times, in generations of long ago!
> Did you not cut Rahab, wound the dragon?
> Did you not dry up Yam, the waters of the great deep (Tehom)?

Isaiah 27:1 makes specific reference to the conquest of Leviathan, the sea monster, in terms that echo the Ba'al myth:

> In that day Yahweh with his hard and great and strong sword will punish Leviathan, the fleeing serpent, Leviathan, the twisting serpent, he will slay the dragon that is in the sea.

Job 38:8 refers to the harnessing of Yam:

> And (who) shut up the sea (Yam) with doors when he burst forth, issuing from the womb, and I made clouds his garment and thick darkness his swaddling band, and decreed limits for him and set bars and doors and said: Up to here you may come, but not farther, and here your proud waves will stop.

There are numerous other references to the battle with Yam (Isa. 30:7; Ezek. 29:3–5 and 32:2–6; Hab. 3:8ff; Pss. 29, 74:13–14, 89:9–10, 93; Job 26:12–13),[51] and in Psalm 68:4, Yahweh has been given Ba'al's title, "Rider of the Clouds."

Gen. 2:4b–3:24 [J]

The J creation account opens a longer mythic epic which traces the relationship of the Hebrew god Yahweh to his people Israel from creation to the Solomonic era, when the account was recorded. It sketches the story from the first humans, through a series of failures of Yahweh and mankind to come together, through the ideal hero, Abraham, and Moses the lawgiver, through the struggles to achieve identity as a people, to nationhood.

The creation myth opens in the middle of the plot. Yahweh-Elohim had created the heavens and the earth, but no growth had begun because there was no rain. A mist moistened the soil enough to make it malleable. Like Khnum of Egypt, Enki of Sumer, and Marduk of Babylon, Yahweh molded man out of the plastic earth and animated the clay model by breathing life into its nostrils, just as Arab midwives still initiate breathing for newborn children. Man was designed to be Yahweh's servant or slave, a gardener in the divine estate which Yahweh next brought into being. Man, a vegetarian, was permitted to eat the fruit of any tree but one—the tree of knowledge of good and evil—on pain of immediate death.

Yahweh modeled and animated other life forms—birds and beasts—as companions for man. Man gave each of them a name or label, by which they were separated from him and from each other. None proved to be an acceptable companion. Yahweh's last creation was an extension of man himself[52] composed from a rib extracted from the man while he was asleep. On awakening, the delighted man accepted this last creation, perhaps recognizing that she was part of him and that he was incomplete without her. The god, the two humans, and all the animals seemed to live harmoniously within the garden of Eden.

The second part of the myth explains the change in relationships between man and the god, man and Eden, and man and the animals. The serpent, symbol of chaos in other cosmological myths, is depicted in J as the most astute of Yahweh's created beings. It recognized the deception in Yahweh's threat of immediate death as punishment for eating of the tree of moral awareness. When the woman and then the man ate, they did not die, as Yahweh had threatened, but, as the serpent had promised, they suddenly acquired the knowledge which had, until that moment, been reserved for divine beings—knowledge of good and evil, right and wrong. This act marked the transition of the two humans from what they had been —members of the animal kingdom—to a status but one step removed from the gods (see Psalm 8:5). They lacked only immortality to achieve divinity. However, the angry god prevented them from eating of the tree of life (immortality) and expelled them from the garden. Nor could they reenter, for the gate was guarded by ferocious monsters (cherubim) and a magic, fiery sword.

Before their expulsion, Yahweh, like a stern parent, not only terrified them into admitting their act, but pronounced punishment. The woman, Eve (whose name means "life-giver"), would bear children in pain, and though she might desire not to do so, still her sexual drives would bring her to her husband, who would cause her to bear ("rule over her"). The relationship between man and the land was to be one of struggle for survival. Man was compelled to face the chaos of the disordered world outside the protection of Yahweh. He knew the divine patterns of order from his life in Eden, and now he attempted to create his world based on the paradise he had experienced. Cultivated fields were constantly under siege from the wilderness, and weeds and thistles competed for soil energy with life-sustaining plants. Yahweh would not plant for him. Man had to plant for himself: it was his own garden, his own plot that he attended, and his survival depended on it. The harmonious relationship between man and animals also ended. Animosity would henceforth exist between man and the snake. Later, Yahweh made animal skin garments for man, presumably from some of the beasts originally created as his companions.

The motifs are familiar. The primeval paradise is like that of the Egyptian myth of Ra, when men and gods lived together. When man plotted to exceed his god-given status, the relationship was broken and Yahweh became a transcendent god. As in the Babylonian myth, man was created to serve. Animals were created from clay, just as man was, and man and beast lived in harmony until one of the creatures led man to oppose the divine will.

If the J creation myth was mimed or recited at the new year festival in the Hebrew temple in Jerusalem, then its emphasis, unlike the Canaanite myth, was not primarily on rain. It explains man's attachment to the soil —his destiny is to be a cultivator of the ground. The myth does not originate in an early Hebrew nomadic setting; it relates to a settled culture. Man, a farmer, has intimate knowledge about the soil, perhaps revealed "in the beginning" by Yahweh. The myth is associated with hoeing, weeding, preparing, and planting the soil, all of which must be done before the coming of the fall rains. The myth explained a reality: man's struggle to exist. Gardening was no longer a sacred task performed in the precincts of Yahweh's garden; it was a profane struggle for survival. The myth also explained why man was free to decide and act according to his own reasons, even when that act violated some command of the god.

Much later, Jewish and Christian mythologists realigned the mythic figures and developed new patterns of relationship. The wise serpent became a rebellious member of the divine family and was identified with Satan, the anti-god. The thrust of the myth was changed. Instead of explaining how man ascended from an animal state to moral maturity, responsible for his decisions, the myth was transformed into a symbol of decent, a fall from a divine state. Eve, who liberated man from subservience in the garden, became a symbol of weakness, through whom "original sin" was transmitted. The J creation myth may also have served another purpose, perhaps more closely related to societal patterns. It reminded worshipers that man and god had lived together in harmonious fellowship until man violated a divine ruling. The new year festival, a celebration of the successful termination of one time period and the inauguration of the next, may have been in part the Hebrew society's attempt to reconcile itself with Yahweh, to cleanse itself of accumulated guilt, to rediscover the primal relationship between the sacred and the profane, and through mythic tradition to renew awareness of the divine will.

Genesis 1:1–2:4a [P]

Like J, the P story is part of a larger writing which also traces Jewish identity from the creation of the world through a long line of ancestors beginning with Shem, one of the survivors of the flood. The writing is ascribed to an author with cultic interests because of its heavy emphasis on priestly paraphernalia, orders of priests, ritual, and so on.

The introductory statement depicts the primeval chaos:

> When Elohim began to create the heavens and the earth, the earth was formless and empty and darkness was on the face of the deep (*Tehom*) and Elohim's wind (spirit) moved (hovered) over the face of the waters.

There are reminiscences of *enuma elish* here. The Hebrew word meaning "create" is *bara'*, which implies giving shape by cutting, just as Marduk formed the boundaries of the cosmos by cutting Tiamat in two. The word *tehom*, the "deep," corresponds to Tiamat.

The bringing of the cosmos into being is accomplished by an act of will expressed through verbal utterance, just as Ptah of Egypt also created by his word. The P order of creation differs from that of the J account:

1. Darkness and light were created and named "day" and "night."
2. Heaven, or the firmament, is designated by the Hebrew term *rakia,* which implies that the arched sky was composed of something firm or beaten out, like metal, and this structure was suspended within the primeval sea.
3. Earth appeared when the waters beneath the dome of heaven were restricted to specific areas to form the sea.
4. Plant life was created.
5. Sun, moon, and stars were made to give light and establish time sequences.

6. Sea life and flying creatures appeared.

7. Earth's animal life was created.

8. Mankind was formed in the divine image, with orders to control or subjugate the earth.

9. The seventh day was a day of rest.

The entire creative process was accomplished within six days, each extending from sunset to sunset, as does the Jewish day. The seventh day, which closed the week, was a rest day corresponding to the Jewish sabbath and thus giving divine sanction for the observance of the sabbath. The priestly writer restricted diet for all living creatures to plant life until after the flood, possibly to make possible survival of species within the microcosm of the ark (Gen. 9:1–7).

The priestly source includes a second creation myth in its account of the flood.[53] Elohim had decided to return the earth to its primeval watery state, thereby eliminating the evil that had developed in human society. The windows of heaven were opened, the fountains of the deep unplugged, and the space between the earth and the inverted shell of heaven began to fill with water. Bobbing on the rising surface of the waters and withstanding the rain was the ark, the container built by Noah, which contained representations of all life forms. When the earth had been submerged, the creative process began again. As in the first priestly myth, the wind of Elohim again blew across the face of the water (Gen. 8:1), the tops of the mountains emerged (8:5), and the land finally dried enough to support life (8:13). The multitude of life forms left the ark to fulfill their natural functions of survival and reproduction (8:18). Man received permission to eat the flesh of any living creature, providing it had been ritually killed (9:1–7).

TWENTIETH CENTURY THEORY

No single hypothesis about the evolution of the universe is accepted by all twentieth century scientists. Continuing research into the history of the cosmos, our solar system, our world, and man tends to make every theory tentative and subject to change in the light of new evidence. Like the ancient Egyptians, we accept certain basic concepts, with variations endorsed by different intellectual-cult centers.

A general thesis concerning our solar system might be that eons and eons ago ("In the beginning . . ."?) there was space—endless space—and there was time—eternity—in some sort of fluid relationship. Within space was a great cloud of stellar gas and dust; where or how it originated is not known. The gas mass began to contract, the very contraction and coagulation of particles imparting a rotational spin and forming the sun at its center. When the sun had contracted to about the size of the orbit of Neptune, great masses of gases and solids were discharged from its equatorial region, where the centrifugal forces were greatest—a process of contraction and discharge that continued until the sun reached its present size. Some larger lumps of discharged matter became planets. (According to a different theory, some lumps collided and fused to form planets and other large masses, such as the moon, which are held as planetary satellites by various gravitational forces.) Smaller lumps of matter became asteroids, meteors, and meteorites.

One of the planets was the earth, at first lifeless and waterless because of fierce internal heat. In time the surface cooled, moisture formed, seas took shape, and rain began to fall. Or perhaps the gaseous earth forms condensed into moisture and in further cooling became a solid mass with land and seas and atmosphere. In the sea—the womb of life, according to some theorists—organic compounds were catalyzed and rearranged, perhaps by lightning or through solar radiation; complex organic molecules, including amino acids, were formed; and life began. After several billion years of evolution, there emerged the particular double helix form of DNA which is man.

Our general statement is, of course, an oversimplification, vulnerable to attack. For example, we noted earlier that man is more than DNA. Some scientists suspect that life may have begun not in the sea, but on land. The exact process by which the earth and the seas were formed is also debatable. The hypothesis of a whirling mass of gas in space does not account for the retrograde revolution of certain planets, such as Venus, or for the orbits of some of their satellites. Finally, the thesis deals only with our solar system, ignoring the totality of space and other heavenly systems. Nevertheless, as a general statement, it embodies the essence of what is now being taught in one form or another in life-science classes.

ANCIENT COSMOLOGY AND MODERN MAN

We are free individuals, living in the second half of the twentieth century, but we have not broken the hold of the past. Intellectually we have changed. The old cosmologies are meaningless. The Copernican revolution has run its course. Man has journeyed into space, where he has photographed and relayed for earthly television viewing the image of the earth as a small blue planet spinning in orbit about a relatively small sun in the vastness of seemingly endless space. We are no longer at the center of the universe.

The Darwinian revolution has also run its course. We are a species of life form, not radically different in physiological makeup from other life forms. Our *homo* lineage goes back only some two million or so years, a very brief interval in the four to five billion years estimated as the age of the earth.

The astronauts who looked at the earth from space could ask half-jokingly, "Is it inhabited?" Alone in the void, we must shout "Yes!" into the emptiness, in chorus—a response from a human life form that is, so far as we know, utterly unique in the cosmos. Despite the mathematical probabilities, it is possible that we are aliens in space, flukes in cosmic history. We live a brief moment and then merge into the elements of our planet. In terms of cosmic time and history, we really do not matter, either individually or as a life form. We matter only to ourselves and to one another, and only in our "nowness."

The demythologizing of our thinking has not run its course; in fact, mythically we have not really changed. Even though nearly two thousand years ago the Greeks of Alexandria moved away from the three-story world concept, despite Copernicus's teachings in the fifteenth century, despite telescopes and other astronomical gear, space travel and space photography, despite classroom teaching of the new cosmologies, millions of Westerners continue to respond to the cosmos in terms of ancient mythic patterns. They live as though the earth is the center of the universe.[54] Where the individual is, is the center of the world.

Discussions with groups of older adults reveal the deep insecurities that accompany acceptance of modern cosmological concepts. Some people refuse to give any extended thought to the implications of modern cosmology because those implications are frightening and distressing. Many refuse to abandon their earlier training in ancient mythic thought. Billy Graham and thousands like him still speak comfortingly of "heaven," while pointing to the skies, as though there were some actual place to be recognized. The so-called "Jesus movement," the revived stress among conservative Christians on "Biblicism," and the publicizing of apocalyptic thought by certain youth groups, involve the acceptance of ancient mythic cosmologies including heaven and hell. Nor are these fundamentalist or conservative positions very far removed from the teachings of many churches and synagogues, including some of the so-called "liberal" groups. The old exists within the new; the new has not overcome it.

From biblical and other Near Eastern mythology, we have inherited the concept of creation and a creator. Some person or power beyond our human selves and our cosmos planned and brought into being all that is. Some people argue that this creator must be one who was not created, but who exists and has existed throughout eternity, above and beyond all that is, yet within all that is. This creator planned what happened and initiated the process that brought everything to its present status. At this moment, the hypothesis of a creator god or power cannot be rejected out of hand as irrational; nor can it be proven or disproven. We can only recognize it as one hypothesis for the theory of a creator is as "logical" as the theory of no creator.

Some have sought to reconcile biblical mythology and modern scientific hypothesis. For example, the P creation myth states that Elohim created fish and fowl on the fifth day and land creatures and man on the sixth, an order which fits roughly into the generally accepted evolutionary hypothesis. The six "days" of creation become six periods of undefined time. However, attempts to explain the presolar day and night patterns in P are something less than convincing.

Others point out that human concerns have not changed over the past few thousand years; only our awareness of topocosmic boundaries has changed. The protecting arch of the heavens has been pushed back, now that we are conscious of space. The gods have become more distant, but perhaps more intimate, too. Like the Egyptian followers of Ptah, we can understand that the divine has infused everything and everyone and is manifested in a multitude of forms. Man still experiences the "power" of that which is other; put another way, that which is other continues to be manifested. Nothing has changed except the dimensions of time and space. Man's insecurities and need for identity remain. Some answer to those insecurities and needs can be given through the recognition of the validity of ancient cosmological intuitions which, in myth, ritual, drama, and art, expressed man's intuitive and intellectual response to his world and his place in it. Such a hypothesis, which comes close to a humanistic appreciation of myth and of man, is excellent theory, but the reality may be somewhat different.

We do not know how the process began, but it clearly has not ended. We have a sketchy history (evolution) of the development. We are vitally conscious of the present, and abstractly aware of the continuation of the process. Like the rest of the cosmos, we are part of the process, and we are in process. Awareness of our individual relationship to the whole links us to our ancient Near-Eastern forbears and their I–thou response to the topocosm, and simultaneously joins us to the future of mankind and the universe, in that how we think and what we do may affect the continuing process on earth and possibly elsewhere.

It is confrontation with the terrible littleness and aloneness of man in the cosmos that is so overwhelming. We have left behind old cosmologies with their comforting stress on purpose and meaning. By crossing the frontier of space, we have been able to see ourselves as we are—momentary creatures that fade into the dust of our planet. Even the modification of the ancient myths is not enough; eventually, present myths and modern cosmologies will be studied together with the myths of Egypt, Sumer, Babylon, and Israel as man's interesting but outmoded efforts to establish his identity in the cosmos. The transition may not happen until man has moved to other astral bodies and established colonies with controlled atmospheres, hydroponic gardens, and new attitudes toward what it means to be human. Perhaps only when other planets become "home" will we develop language to convey how the concepts of the cosmos, the earth, and man will have been altered.

Meanwhile, theologians will still discuss the implications of the "fall" and "original sin" as found in the J creation myth, continuing to explain man's mortality, suffering, and evil behavior mythologically. Man will still stand in need of forgiveness from the cosmological god who created him. The cosmological concepts that stemmed from ancient Sumer and Egypt will continue to affect twentieth century man's thinking, for the acceptance of ancient cosmology is reinforced through modern-day social and cultic observances.

We recognize reminiscences of seasonal myths in current festivals. For example, Hanukkah and Christmas are celebrated at the time of the winter solstice, which the ancients associated with the birth of the sun, the triumph of light over darkness and chaos, an event which they marked or enabled by lighting fires. In Hanukkah, the fire symbolism has been transmuted; Hanukkah lights are associated with temple lamps, and the festival is based in the history of the Maccabean period. The date of Jesus' birth is unknown, but a non-Christian festival has been adapted and given new meaning as Christmas through association with a historical figure. An echo of ancient observances of solar rebirth which appear in Malachi 4:2 can be heard in the third verse of the popular festal hymn, "Hark, the Herald Angels Sing," composed by Charles Wesley in the late eighteenth century:

> Hail, the heaven-born Prince of Peace!
> Hail, the Sun of Righteousness!
> Light and life to all He brings,
> Risen with healing in his wings.

The firing of yule logs is borrowed from ancient rites designed to rekindle the sun. The twelve days of Christmas and Twelfth-night, which terminates Twelfth-tide, the season leading to epiphany (January 6), when the Magi were supposed to have visited the infant Jesus, all hearken back to a twelve-day solstice festival.

Passover and Easter are also anchored in cultic interpretations of history. These seasonal celebrations occur at the time of the vernal equinox and coincide with the period of the Akitu festival in Babylon, which took place during the first twelve days of Nisanu (Hebrew: Nisan = March–April). Earlier we noted the double reading of *enuma elish* in the Babylonian rite. In Judaism, the triennial cycle of reading the Torah began on the first Sabbath in Nisan; of course, this reading included Hebrew creation mythology.[55] Now, Passover commemorates a new creation: the beginning or coming-into-being of the Israelite people, in addition to their freedom from enslavement. Purgation symbolism might be read into the passage of the Israelites through the waters of the Sea of Reeds, which marked the abandonment of life in Egypt and the initiation of new life as the people of Yahweh. Easter celebrates the triumph of life over death and the emergence of a new people. We recognize purgation symbolism in the human sacrifice of Jesus, which, through the mysterious cleansing power attributed to shed blood, freed the believer from accumulated sin and, according to some interpretations, from the hold of the power of darkness or the devil. Jesus' resurrection marked the birth of the new life.

Rosh Hashanah, the Jewish new year festival, is observed at the time of the autumnal equinox, which precedes the coming of the winter rains in Palestine. In Canaan during this period, worshipers celebrated the resurrection of the fertility and rain god, Ba'al.[56] Ancient Hebrew scapegoat rituals purged the community of sin on Yom Kippur. Present-day observances mark the cleansing of the individual by acts of introspection, confession, and atonement, as preparations for entering the new year regenerated. Ancient Canaanites celebrated the coming of the autumnal rains as evidence of the defeat of Mot, the death god, the rebirth of Ba'al, and the commencement of a new year with a new hold on life. Today, Jewish believers celebrate the sovereignty of God, the creation of the world, the covenant marking the beginning of peoplehood, and the experience of personal renewal.

Ancient mythic symbolism exists in the secular world, also. In patterns reminiscent of ancient Mesopotamian thinking, two primeval powers contend with each other: good and evil, order and chaos. Only the identities of the antagonists differ from ancient mythology. Seasonal changes and natural forces are no longer interpreted as acts of gods. Floods, earthquakes, tornadoes, and hurricanes still wreak havoc, but apart from giving female names to hurricanes, man does not personify these natural environmental phenomena. The I–it attitude of twentieth century man toward nature assures him that he can find means to cope with such forces. Massive dams, strategically placed and operated by modern technological devices, harness flood waters. Better construction reduces the destructive effects of earthquakes and violent winds. Weather prediction enables man to prepare for approaching storms.

The conflict of good and evil, light and darkness, order and chaos has been transferred to societies, peoples, and nations. Threats to the way of life of any group come from those who espouse different political systems, different beliefs and customs, and different societal groupings. The threat of chaos is from other people. Communism, socialism, atheism, and the like represent the forces of chaos. It is not surprising that religious organizations align with secular groups in making similar identifications. Preachers proclaim that unbelievers live in darkness, that "atheistic communism" represents a threat to good. Ample support for religious claims exists in the New Testament, for example, Romans 2:19 or Ephesians 6:12. However, we have now brought the discussion to sociological factors and societal myth, which we shall discuss in Chapter 3.

NOTES

[1]Theodor H. Gaster, *Thespis: Ritual, Myth, and Drama in the Ancient Near East* (New York: Harper & Row, 1950; rev. ed., 1968).

[2]Henri Frankfort, *Ancient Egyptian Religion: An Interpretation* (New York: Harper & Row, 1948; rev. ed. 1961), pp. 28f.

[3]For succinct statements, see E. O. James, *The Ancient Gods* (London: Weidenfeld and Nicolson, 1960), pp. 200–208, and Veronica Ions, *Egyptian Mythology* (Middlesex: Hamlyn Publishing Group, 1965, 1968), pp. 24–38. For the Edfu myths not discussed here, see E. A. E. Reymond, *The Mythical Origin of the Egyptian Temple* (New York: Barnes & Noble, 1969).

[4]In Egypt, as in other parts of the Near East, the heart, not the head, was recognized as the source of thought. See Prov. 6:18, 16:9, and so on.

[5]Creation by "word" foreshadows the creation by utterance in the priestly creation myth, Gen. 1:1–2:4a, and in the gnostic mythology of John 1:1ff.

[6]E. A. Wallis Budge, *The Gods of the Egyptians* (Chicago: Open Court, 1904; New York: Dover, 1969), pp. 308ff.

[7]"Enki and Ninhursag," *ANET*, pp. 37–41.

[8]S. N. Kramer, *The Sumerians* (Chicago: University of Chicago Press, 1963; rev. paperback ed., 1971), pp. 146f.

[9]W. G. Lambert and A. R. Millard, *Atra-hasis: The Babylonian Story of the Flood* (Oxford: Clarendon, 1969); *ANET*, pp. 99f; W. F. Albright, "From the Patriarchs to Moses," *BA*, Vol. 36, No. 1 (1973), pp. 5–33, particularly pp. 22–26.

[10]This method of naming writings was common in earlier times. For example, the book of Genesis in the Hebrew Bible is titled *Bereshith* after the opening Hebrew word; Exodus is called *We'elleh shemoth;* and so on.

[11]In Egypt, the king's divinity was symbolized by the myth of the monarch nursing at the breast of a goddess. Here it may signify that Marduk was a king among gods.

[12]See Isa. 55:11, where the unknown Jewish prophet in Babylon applies this concept to Yahweh's word, saying that it "shall not return . . . empty," and "it will accomplish . . . and prosper in the thing for which . . ." it is sent.

[13]This paraphrase captures the essence of the commitment. For the full text, see *ANET*, p. 66.

[14]See Thorkild Jacobsen, "Primitive Democracy in Mesopotamia," *Journal of Near Eastern Studies,* II (1943), pp. 159ff.

[15]In the Assyrian version, Ninhursag, who replaces Marduk as the chief god, creates primitive man from clay, using the blood of a slain god to animate man. See also Gen. 9:4; Lev. 17:11, 14; Deut. 12:23. In Hebrew thought, blood was equivalent to life.

[16]The redemptive death has a counterpart in the Akitu festival (see below), and is one interpretation of the death of Jesus who, in Christian mythology, redeemed men from the burden of sin.

[17]See the tower of Babel mythology in 11:1–9, where the proposed structure was to have "its top in heaven."

[18]See Gen. 9:12–17, where in biblical mythology the rainbow is a reminder to God of the agreement he has made never to destroy life again by flood, a decision not to return the cosmos to the primitive watery chaos from which it came. See also Gen. 1:1–2; 7:17–8:5.

[19]See the reference in 1 Kings 19:18 to the seven thousand who had not bowed their knees to Ba'al, which seems to suggest some cultic act. See also Phil. 2:10: "That at the name of Jesus every knee should bow, in heaven and on earth and under the earth, and every tongue confess that Jesus Christ is Lord, to the glory of God the Father."

[20]The fragmented text on which this paragraph is based has been given some meaning in the translation by J. V. Kinnear Wilson in *Documents from Old Testament Times,* D. Winton Thomas, ed. (New York: Harper & Row, 1961), p. 13.

[21]Some reminiscence of the gods' mythological hunger for food is apparent in the flood myth contained in the Gilgamesh epic. When Utnapishtim, the survivor of the deluge, offered a sacrifice, poured out libations, and burned incense wood, the gods, on smelling the sweet odor, "gathered like flies" around the sacrificer. In the biblical myth, Noah's animal offering was also smelled by Yahweh (Gen. 8:20–21).

[22]Compare to the numerous designations of the sun god in Egypt, and the ninety-nine names for God in Islamic mythology.

[23]In Deut. 6, a similar admonition is made concerning the teachings about Yahweh, with a similar promise of blessing.

[24]See "The Code of Hammurabi: Prologue," *ANET,* pp. 164ff; "Texts from Hammurabi to the Downfall of the Assyrian Empire," *ANET,* pp. 269f.

[25]See the texts in *ANET,* pp. 309–15.

[26]For a detailed discussion of the festival, see S. A. Pallis, *The Babylonian Akitu Festival* (Copenhagen: Andr. Fred. Host, 1926).

[27]These writings, appended to writings of the eighth century prophet Isaiah of Jerusalem, constitute chapters 40–55 and parts of 56–66 of the book of Isaiah. See G. A. Larue, *Old Testament Life and Literature* (Boston: Allyn & Bacon, 1968), pp. 301–13, 323–27; and *Babylon and the Bible* (Grand Rapids, Mich.: Baker Book House, 1969), p. 70.

[28]For a translation of the text of the festival by A. Sachs, see *ANET,* pp. 331–34.

[29]Numerous Roman Catholics have commented on the joy and sense of renewal they experience after confession and absolution. Testimonials of Christians who have been "saved" often contain references to release from the burden of sin. The Samaritans I observed participating in the Paschal rites on Mount Gerizim were

overjoyed when the sheep were slain and blood from the sacrificed animals was smeared on the foreheads and cheeks of believers. They were, as one Christian hymn puts it, "washed in the blood of the lamb." See 1 Cor. 5:7: "Christ, our paschal lamb, has been sacrificed."

[30]Later Marduk is fused with Ba'al and becomes Bel Marduk, and Zarpanit is called Beltiya.

[31]In much the same way, accoutrèments of worship including vestments, communal wafers, and the like, are manufactured by religious personnel in the Roman Catholic communion.

[32]The men involved in the Jewish atonement rite (Hebrew: *kippur*) were considered to be ritually unclean and had to perform ablution rites. See Lev. 16:26.

[33]The precise meaning of this act is not known. It has been suggested that it was associated with the bringing of the spring rains.

[34]See Sidney Smith, "The Practice of Kingship in Early Semitic Kingdoms," in S. H. Hooke, ed., *Myth, Ritual, and Kingship* (London: Oxford University Press, 1958), p. 39.

[35]See note 456, p. 555, in J. G. Frazer, *The New Golden Bough*, T. H. Gaster, ed. (New York: Criterion Books, 1959); and "Scapegoats," in Frazer, *The New Golden Bough*, p. 554.

[36]See also Lev. 16:21–22, where a goat is the sin-bearer, and John 1:29, Heb. 10, where the scapegoat motif is apparent in the interpretation of Jesus' death as a sacrifice for sin.

[37]Pallis, *The Babylonian Akitu Festival*, p. 196.

[38]When King David of Israel became impotent, his son Adonijah sought to replace him as king (1 Kings 1:1–5). The plan failed, and Solomon became king by virtue of a palace plot. Solomon made plain his virility (1 Kings 11:1–3).

[39]Cyrus claimed divine support from Marduk for his rule in Babylon, and indicated that Nabonidus failed because he did not worship Marduk. The unknown Jewish prophet of the exile wrote that Yahweh had taken Cyrus's "right hand" (Isa. 45:1), reminiscent of an acceptance or investiture rite.

[40]The word *Yam* means "sea," and *Nahar* means "river," so that it is possible that Canaanites envisioned the primieval waters in much the same way as their Mesopotamian neighbors. The term *judge* is reminiscent of the ancient custom of tossing an accused person into a river so that the waters might determine guilt or innocence. See the Code of Hammurabi, law 2, where sorcery is judged in this manner, and law 132, where it is suggested that a woman accused of adultery might establish her innocence in this manner (*ANET*, pp. 166, 171).

[41]Gaster, *Thespis*, p. 195.

[42]See Cyrus Gordon, *Ugaritic Literature* (Rome: Pontificum Institutum Biblicum, 1949), p. 8; Gordon, *Ugarit and Minoan Crete* (New York: Norton, 1967), p. 24.

[43]There are differing views on the interpretation of this section of the text. Gordon (*Ugarit and Minoan Crete*, pp. 80–81), says that a seven-year drought cycle is involved; Gaster (*Thespis*, pp. 124f), relates Ba'al's disappearance to the dry summer season.

[44]Gaster, *Thespis*, p. 219.

[45]Compare with the search for water during the drought in the time of King Ahab (1 Kings 18:5).

[46]Note the emphasis on such features in Saul (1 Sam 9:2), David (1 Sam 16:12), and Absalom (2 Sam 14:25). When a king became ill, as Uzziah did when he contracted leprosy (2 Kings 15:5), or impotent, like David (1 Kings 1:1–4), he was deposed or had to share his throne with a more healthy, virile ruler.

[47]Martin Noth, *The Old Testament World* (London: Adam & Charles Black, 1966), p. 29.

[48]The label *J* reflects the German translation of the divine name, the Tetragrammaton, as *Jahveh* (pronounced "Yahweh" in English). Hebrew scriptures omit the vowels so that the name reads *YHWH.* The P account prefers the term *Elohim* for the designation of the god.

[49]W. F. Albright, *From Stone Age to Christianity,* 2nd ed. (Baltimore: Johns Hopkins, 1946); reprinted by Doubleday, 1957). Cyrus Gordon supports the thesis (*Ugarit and Minoan Crete,* p. 244).

[50]Gordon, *Ugarit and Minoan Crete,* p. 244.

[51]See Gaster, *Thespis,* pp. 142ff, 442ff, for a discussion.

[52]The biblical writer punned on the Hebrew words for man and woman, implying that *ish-shah* was a female form of *ish.* Despite the similarity in sound, no etymological relationship has been established between the two words.

[53]Genesis 6:5–9:17 is actually a fusion of J and P flood myths. The recreation motif is most clearly demonstrated in the P portions, particularly in the repetition of the language of Genesis 1.

[54]The continuing controversy between religion and science is succinctly demonstrated in the essays in the "Problems in American Civilization" series, Gail Kennedy, ed., *Evolution and Religion: The Conflict Between Science and Theology in Modern America* (Boston: Heath, 1957). See also C. C. Gillispie, *Genesis and Geology* (New York: Harper & Row, 1951; reprint ed., 1959).

[55]J. B. Segal, *The Hebrew Passover* (London: Oxford University Press, 1933), p. 149.

[56]Gaster, *Thespis,* pp. 135ff.

three

Societal Myth

Society is constantly faced with choices: between individual freedom and communal security; between highly structured order at one extreme, and anarchic disorder at the other; between regulations that protect personal liberty and rules that infringe or ignore the rights of individuals or minority groups. Somehow, patterns of relationship emerge, laws are made, systems are formulated, and an accepted code of behavioral standards is developed. The more societal control, the less is the amount of individual freedom. The more laws restricting individual behavior and the stricter their enforcement, the greater are the insecurity and persecution of those who chafe under strict rules of conduct. The greater the societal insecurity, the greater is society's tendency to restrict individual freedom of expression.

Societal myths give form to communal living. They provide foundations for human interaction by projecting a *Gestalt* intrinsically defining the group ethos. They establish the basis for peoplehood; for identity; for acts and attitudes; for the artifacts, experiences, and interpretation of experiences that characterize a given group. The individuals are made aware by way of societal myths of their otherness, the group-separateness which distinguishes them and holds them apart from other humans. So powerful are societal myths that even among those people who intellectually affirm a basic human oneness, the societal myth operates emotionally to create a paradoxical isolation of groups of persons.

Societal myths project generalities about human classifications, justifying mistreatment of certain groups. For example, women have traditionally been considered the weaker sex, more emotional than intellectual in responding to situations and less stable and pragmatic than men. However, many modern women, liberated from the prescriptions that confined so many in the past, are demonstrating the fallacious (and stupid) nature of such broad stereotypes. These male-made assertions, often lent mythic support by traditions that women were created weaker by God, have sustained the male role in male-dominated society. They separated male and female roles and occupations, dividing societal and social responsibilities on the basis of presuppositions which were not challenged until recent times, although the lives of some women have historically demonstrated the fallacies of these assumptions.

We have no way of knowing how the earliest human societies were organized. Animals live in both large and small colonies, some as couples mated for life, some mated for a season, some with several mates in a pride. In some animal species, parents cooperate in raising the offspring; in others, one parent is responsible; in still others, the young are left to fend for themselves. The earliest human patterns we know of indicate that the family was the core unit, with parents assuming long-term responsibilities for raising the young. Cooperation was the key to survival. We do not know what constituted "marriage," or even the nature of the family and the principle governing intermarriage between groups.

Literary evidence from the ancient Near East describes varied social structures and many value differences. Each nation sustained its social system with societal myths that gave an ordered pattern to prevailing life-styles. Myths provided rules and acceptable norms for living. They explicated mores and supplied divine sanction for existing social patterns. Societal myths enabled the individual to know that his society was superior to others, and to understand why the laws of his land were the correct laws and why his ways of behaving were more acceptable than those of the other peoples. Societal myths established barriers between groups by defining the lines of separation.

Separation barriers are usually inwardly defined. On the surface, they may appear shadowy or unclear, but to the individuals and groups that embrace them, the invisible inner lines become sharp and hard in specific social settings. Societal myths that empower acts of separation are rooted in ancient times, when the will of the god who gave identity to the group was expressed. The pattern becomes inbred, part of the societal structure into which persons are born. Violation of the concept of separation from outsiders can produce hurt and pain. For example, separation myths can be used to justify cruelty to and even killing of humans who are not members of the in-group. The enslavement of nongroup persons, it may be argued, is divinely sanctioned. Such mythic arguments have been used to justify the mistreatment of blacks in America.

Even when outsiders are permitted to become part of the community, they are not completely accepted—they remain foreigners, resident aliens, foreign-born, other. Acceptance of outsiders is generally on an individual basis. Individuals or families are admitted to the in-group perhaps because the group respects their power or wealth. Wholesale acceptance of other people can occur in time of social upheaval or war, when societal barriers crumble or are violated. Peoples commingle, not because they want to, but because they must. Rape blends genetic patterns, commingling is accepted, and a new societal pattern emerges. Then the old myths are reinterpretated, but even with continuing reinterpretation, they tend to remain separatist in emphasis.

Despite the universalism implicit in cosmological mythology, gods of the ancient Near East belonged primarily to the specific groups that recognized and worshiped them. Thus, cosmic gods were actually national gods whose real concerns were territorially determined. Some societal myths imply and others state explicitly that certain peoples were chosen by a deity or deities. The Egyptians believed themselves singularly blessed— the gods who had provided them with the Nile established a second Nile in the sky to provide rain for less fortunate countries. The Egyptians' gods were Egyptian and only Egyptians and residents of the territories administered by them paid homage to Egyptian gods. Babylonians worshipped Shamash, not Ra, as sun god, and hailed Marduk as chief god of the empire. Assyrians revered Ashur, when they conquered foreign lands such as Israel or Egypt, they required the subject nations to acknowledge the supremacy of Ashur, no matter what rites were performed for local deities.

National gods were believed to provide guidance in the art of living. Each nation was convinced that it was, in most ways, superior to other peoples, that its way of life was the best and was in accord with the wishes of the deities. To live as the gods wished was to win blessings; disobedience brought punishment and disaster. But how could one know what the gods wanted? Through revelation. Revelatory myths recorded encounters with the divine, the holy, the god by seers, diviners, priests, prophets, wise men, and heroes. In these encounters the god's will was revealed concerning proper action for a specific situation or correct conduct for communal living. These precepts were transmitted either explicitly or implicitly through the cult, law courts, "wisdom schools" and teachings, hero stories, and the weight of established tradition and custom. In ritual, the cult dramatized the revelatory basis of societal myth, and cultic verbiage conferred profound meaning on societal patterns: "We are this way because we are the followers of a particular god, who has revealed his will to us."

Justice was the maintenance of divinely revealed societal order, establishing harmony, balance, and peace within the nation. The protection of individual rights was often an issue, but there was little attempt to rectify patterns that might have done injustice to specific individuals.

Ancient legal codes that have been discovered disclose some of the precepts undergirding the laws of the land. Slavery was accepted. Some persons were worth more than others. Males were more valuable than females. A virgin bride was preferable to a nonvirgin. The legal structures sustained the system.

Young men aspiring to public office were instructed by the wise, whose observations about life were set forth as aphorisms and in manuals of behavior. Proverbial lore guided students in everything from establishing a home and raising children to impressing higher officials.

Tales about heroes whose feats were beyond the ability of ordinary men because of their peculiar or particular relationship to the gods dramatized what was possible and acceptable in society. Heroes were models of what should and should not, could and could not be attempted.[1] They gave the ordinary man insight into the meaning of existence and the potential and limits of mortality.

Because societal patterns became fixed and because those who ruled preferred neatly organized systems and smoothly running societal machines, there was resistance to change and strong reaction against the rebel who insisted on following his own pattern. Law courts, schools, hero tales, strong ruling authorities, and inertia, all enhanced by societal myth, tended to perpetuate existing patterns. The individual raised within such a cultural framework was programmed to think and respond according to traditional modes. The goal was harmony and balanced relationships within the topocosm. To violate divine edict was to rebel against the god and the state and to endanger societal balance. Crimes that ignored the revealed law and were not punished provoked the gods' anger, resulting in divine retribution on the nation by natural disaster or conquest. Thus, King Mesha of Moab recorded that because the national god Chemosh was angry with the Moabites, the Moabites came under the control of Israel.[2] Similarly, because Marduk and the gods of Babylon were angry, the Assyrian Sennacherib was able to impose humiliating punishments on the people of Babylon.[3] In the moving "Lamentation over the Destruction of Sumer," the poet stated that disaster came when the sky-god An frowned and other usually friendly gods became estranged.[4] The author of the Hebrew lament over the destruction of Jerusalem in the early sixth century described Yahweh as the enemy, bending his bow against his own people.[5] Hebrew prophets warned of destruction by the hand of Yahweh if the Israelites failed to follow rules established by their god for their well-being (Amos 2:6–6:14, Isa. 3, 5,). When the gods were pleased, there was prosperity, security, and peace. Clearly then, disaster could be attributed to punishment because of some violation of the divine will.

SOCIETAL MYTH IN EGYPT

So far as we know, the Egyptians never developed a legal code. To be sure, the governance of the kingdom must have required ordinances, and the ancient literature refers to arrests and trials. Most of our limited information dates after the sixteenth century B.C. We know, for example, that great importance was placed on oath-taking, and that perjury was punished by death. Traitors who revealed state secrets had their tongues pulled out. People convicted of falsifying weights or forging documents lost their right hands. Women convicted of adultery were disfigured by having their noses cut off, although their male partners were only beaten.

An eighteenth dynasty document relates that Thoth, the chief god of Hermopolis and the inventor of writing, composed forty-two volumes containing the wisdom of the world, and that these volumes were introduced into courts of law for reference. The composition by the "Master of the words of the gods" supposedly contained the divine wisdom which established the laws of the kingdom. We do not know exactly what was in the books but it may have constituted the basic law of Egypt.

From time to time, royal edicts met specific problems. During the reign of Har-em-heb, the general who became king in the late fourteenth century, B.C., edicts were issued to correct malpractices that characterized the disorder of the Amarna age. Military and state officials misused power for personal enrichment while many ordinary citizens were impoverished. Har-em-heb sought men of character to run the courts and judge the cases. The courts, not supported by local taxation, were free from the obligations that such financing might bring, and could therefore function more impartially and objectively.[6] Each man had the right to accuse and prosecute, but there was a social hierarchy in the legal procedure. The vizier was the administrative head and the pharaoh, the final court of appeal. Beneath these two were various levels of magistrates.[7]

It has been suggested that Egypt had no written legal code transmitted as a once-for-all-time revelation of the gods, because the pharaoh was recognized as god dwelling among men, and the mythic concept of an incarnate deity moved Egyptian thought away from a prescribed legal system, lest it reflect negatively on the living pharaoh. We have observed that there was in Egypt the idea of immanence, the infusion of all parts of the topocosm by the divine. How the essence of the sacred came to be manifested or concentrated in one individual to the exclusion of others is unknown. One Egyptian myth looked back to a time when gods and men dwelled together in accord with a divine plan. However, the system failed, because of the rebellious intent of men, and the gods removed themselves from the human environment. The pharaoh alone represented the divine consortium, still present among men. He was, in a sense, the successor to the golden age and as such the symbol of an idealistic mythic projection that the conditions of the golden age might once again prevail. The very concept that the pharaoh was god incarnate meant that the dream for the future was in process. To avoid the unpleasantness of the earlier experience, justice—the will of the pharaoh-god—had to be maintained.

The myth of the miraculous birth of the king which developed at Heliopolis during the fifth dynasty might also have given credence to the divinity of the ruler. What had happened in ancient times, occurred over and over with the birth of each king. The enthronement of each new monarch symbolized the entry anew of the divine into the realm of the human and was accompanied with hope that new divine–human relationships might be established. The accession hymn dedicated to Merneptah expresses the joy of newness because "good times have come" and "the gods are happy . . . and life is spent in laughter and wonder."[8] The concept of the holy family may also have had its start here, for the reigning queen was the mother of god; the reigning pharaoh was Ra or Horus, the sun god immanent, in the flesh, among men; and the heir apparent was both son of god and god to be, for just as the reigning pharaoh would become Osiris at death, the prince would become Horus when he assumed the crown. The king was, therefore, divine by birth, not by appointment or by rites that added divinity to his human status.[9] The divine-royalty myths partly removed the king from the world of humans and provided a pharaonic mystique for kingship.

The importance of the notion of divinity in the fifteenth century B.C. is indicated by Hatshepsut's announcement that her mother had been visited by the god Amon and that she (Hatshepsut) was the child of the god. The myth was reenforced by another inscription which depicted Hatshepsut fashioned on a potter's wheel by Khnum. Much later, in the fourth century, Alexander of Greece conquered Egypt. He found it expedient to travel to the shrine of Amon at the oasis of Siwa in the western desert, where he was recognized as the physical son of the Egyptian sun god.

In any event, the pharaoh was, in a formal way, the epitome of divinity. Because he was divine and simultaneously the ruler, there was no separation of church and state. The divine oneness permeated all patterns of society. Pharaoh was the embodiment of *ma'at,* a term which signified security, stability, justice, the norm. The word of pharaoh was the law of the land, which was *ma'at.* Because *ma'at* was, in a sense, born anew in each pharaoh, and because there was no codified legal statement, the law tended to be flexibly interpreted. Judgments were made in accordance with *ma'at* in a practical way; disputes were worked out in terms of a general understanding of *ma'at,* rather than according to a single fixed code. The proper approach to *ma'at* was unquestioning acceptance. The quiet, non-challenging man was the ideal. The impatient, unrestrained questioner of the status quo was abhorred. *Ma'at* ordered society, maintained proper behavior in the land, and gave peace and inner order to the individual. *Ma'at* constituted the right thing to do, that which was proper, the acceptable norm—in John Wilson's words, "the cosmic force of harmony."[10]

The will of the pharaoh was transmitted politically through the nobility, who were the chief officers of state, to provincial governors, local magistrates, and thence through law courts to craftsmen, merchants, and peasants. The divine power was enhanced through the cult, with its hierarchy of priests. A variety of myths, dramatized in liturgies and festivals, imparted divine sanction to the social structure. Heliopolitan myth stated that the existing social order was the creation of Shu, the air god, and his consort Tefnut. Memphite mythology taught that Ptah, the god who created by his word, established the moral order and pharaonic power. Ptah determined the ranking of the gods. He decreed the functions of government and the acceptable social standards. The actions of a good and peaceful man conformed to the divine pattern; those of a disobedient man violated Ptah's will.

The Book of the Dead, texts associated with mortuary rituals, is best known from the Papyrus of Ani, an eighteenth dynasty papyrus roll which contains the texts previously written inside coffins and in royal pyramids. Chapter 125, which the deceased was to recite before forty-two deities sitting in judgment, contains a repudiation of forty-two sins. The list of sins gives us insight into Egyptian social values—at least into behavior that was not approved. Among the evils not committed by Ani were acts of violence, murder, disturbing the peace, theft, deceit, slander, blasphemy, and cursing. Nor did Ani cause another to suffer or weep. He did not engage in masturbation, homosexual acts (which were considered a perversion), or adultery.

In an additional statement made in the Hall of Ma'at, the deceased declared that he had done the will of god and had given bread to the hungry, water to the thirsty, clothing to the naked, and river transportation to the man without a boat.[11] Clearly, one of the most powerful forces motivating adherence to accepted social values was fear of judgment in the afterlife. This belief, first associated with the pharaoh's continued existence after death, came to include nobles and then common people.

The Words of the Wise

Accepted norms were taught in scribal schools by the wise men. Some of these precepts have been recovered, often from texts copied by student scribes. The wisdom sayings were supposedly written variously by a pharaoh, who recorded advice for his son, by a vizier or other court official, and in at least one instance by a man of somewhat lower sociopolitical standing. Maxims not associated with the pharaoh often contain statements that they are in harmony with the royal will and attitude; in other words, wisdom sayings sustained the norm and were in harmony with *ma'at,* and the pharaonic concept of justice.

Many teachings concerned the art of governing or obtaining success in political offices and were composed primarily for those seeking state and administrative positions. The ethical principles supported accepted norms, and the reasons given for unquestioning acceptance of these norms were generally practical: to ignore the precepts was to court failure; to violate the ethics was to invite punishment and social disaster.

Pupils for the temple schools were drawn from the upper echelons of Egyptian society. Although a variety of administrative posts was open to candidates, sons often succeeded their fathers in office. Reading and writing were taught and, from the limited evidence, it appears that considerable care was exercised in selecting material to be copied. Schools were establishment-oriented and students were encouraged to hear, to obey, and to accept without argument the prevailing norms.

Hor-dedef's Advice.   Among the earliest collections of wise sayings are those attributed to Prince Hor-dedef, son of the fourth dynasty pharaoh Khufu (Cheops). Hor-dedef seems to have succeeded his father as ruler,[12] but his fame is associated with his counsel. Unfortunately, only a few maxims have survived on ostraca (fragments of pottery containing written inscriptions) from the thirteenth or twelfth centuries B.C. Hor-dedef advised his son to take a wife, beget a son, and prepare a place for the son and a burial site for himself.

The basic social unit in Egypt was the family, including the father, one or more wives, and their children. Incestuous marriages were accepted as normal. Because property was inherited through females, the father stood to lose when his wife died, for the daughter inherited the estate and the daughter's husband assumed control. Therefore, it was not uncommon for a father to marry his daughter, or for a brother to marry his sister. Brother-sister marriages were common among the gods, the pharaohs, the courtiers, and those of lower social status. The god Min, sometimes called the "bull of his mother," was hailed in the harvest festival: "Hail Min, who impregnates his mother! How mysterious is that which you have done to her in the darkness."[13] Pharaohs often safeguarded their interests by marrying all possible heiresses, so that if one wife died, the pharaonic properties were protected.[14]

Ptah-hotep's Instructions.   Ptah-hotep's instructions are supposedly the reflections of the famous vizier of the court of King Izezi of the fifth dynasty (twenty-fifth century B.C.). The aged administrator looked back over his years of leadership and offered advice on living, most of which involved the art of leadership and getting ahead politically and socially. Ptah-hotep gave instruction on how to play the social games necessary for approval and for winning favors. For example, one should bend one's back and bow before a superior, look down in humility when he spoke, and laugh after he laughed, so that he might feel good.

According to Ptah-hotep, a responsible man should have a family. His wife should be carefully chosen and provided with food, clothing, and ointments so that she might be happy, for she was the source of children and, in particular of sons. The husband was warned to avoid legal disputes with his wife and to keep away from other men's wives.

Filial obedience and the desire to succeed in business were stressed. Sons should heed their fathers' instructions. A son who rebelled against parental authority and talked authoritatively on the basis of his limited experience, or who developed other poor manners, should be disowned as one whom the god had condemned within the womb.

Humility was counseled. One should not be puffed up because one was wise, or be too proud to take counsel with the ignorant, for no single individual could know everything. Justice was to be sought and all taint of fraud or dishonesty eschewed.

The Instructions for Meri-ka-Re.   "The Instructions for King Meri-ka-Re" may be the teachings of Meri-ka-Re's father whose name is not known but who was one of several rulers seeking power during the disordered First Intermediate Period (after the twenty-second century B.C.).[15] Presumably, the divinity of the ruler was not challenged at this time; thus, royal wisdom designed to prepare the prince for the responsibilities of the role of god living among men had sacred implications.

The instructions taught that men were the "cattle" of the sun god, who provided plants, animals, fish, and fowl for human nourishment. The god was both transcendent and immanent, for although far removed from men as he sailed above, it was said "he knows every name" and was aware of petitions made and tears shed before his shrine. The pharaoh was the appointed ruler of men, and Meri-ka-Re was given advice about administering the kingdom. He was warned against disturbers of the peace and those who caused factions: such persons were traitors and should be denounced and removed. Arrests and beatings were preferable to the death sentence. The pharaoh was to comfort the mourner, be impartial in judgment and uninfluenced by the wealth of plaintiffs. He was not to oppress the widow or to seize a man's patrimony.

The Instructions of Amen-em-opet.   "The Instructions of Amen-em-opet," a lengthy document from the fourteenth century or shortly thereafter, repeats many precepts found in earlier documents and expands others. The teachings were designed to supply the basic principles for happiness and prosperity. Amen-em-opet directed his readers away from greed for wealth and power by theft, fraud, dishonesty in business, and taking advantage of others. He warned against association with quarrelsome persons and urged that one think before speaking. His ideal was the temperate man who performed good deeds and kindly acts and lived one day at a time. The wise man did not mock the deformed and the unfortunate. He extended his arm to assist the elderly drunk, rather than to strike him down, and when reproached by an older person, he accepted the abuse and kept his peace. The wise man shared his good fortune with the poor.

The Advice of Ani. The advice of Ani, which appears to have been given during the thirteenth or twelfth centuries B.C., includes the familiar emphasis on beginning a family and begetting a son. Ani urged that the wife be left to handle her household without supervision from her husband, presuming, of course, that she was efficient. Students were cautioned against the wiles of a woman from another community who might be traveling without her husband, particularly against becoming involved sexually with such a person. In fact, Ani recommended suspicion of all strangers until one was sure of the relationship, for an incautious word could bring trouble. Respect for elders and the importance of maintaining right relationships with the god were stressed.

Societal Attitudes

The words of the wise reflect the attitudes of those who would preserve the existing state of affairs. They give almost no credence to the point of view of the young, emphasizing instead the traditional wisdom of the past. Family life was important, and other sources reveal that warm bonds held families together. The husband's recreation and sport were at times shared by his family. The status of women was especially high in Egypt, probably because of inheritance customs, and women appear to have had exceptional freedom to travel and participate in social activities. Many tomb paintings portrayed the wife accompanying her husband at his daily duties. Scenes of social gatherings depict the wife enjoying herself with both male and female guests. The goddess Isis is usually considered the model for the Egyptian wife. According to the Osirian myth, when Osiris was abroad spreading culture, Isis managed his kingdom and protected his interests. When he was murdered, she gathered his dismembered body and reconstituted and embalmed it.

The words of the wise and other documents disclose the stratification of society. The recurring plea for equity in dispensing justice and the warnings about the influence exercised by rank or wealth in lawsuits suggest that there were inequalities in the administration of *ma'at*. The story of Khun-Anup, the eloquent peasant who was robbed of his goods by a vassal of the chief steward, is set in the First Intermediary Period (twenty-first century B.C.). So fixed were the class stereotypes that it was automatically assumed that the peasant must be in the wrong. The magistrates pointed out that vassals had the right to beat peasants and seize property when the peasant sought to leave his patron—which Khun-Anup was not trying to do. They imposed a minimal fine on the vassal. Khun-Anup's eloquent appeals won him a rehearing. When the pharaoh, Neb-kau-Re, heard of the case, he permitted the appeals to be postponed time after time. After nine appeals and several beatings, Khun-Anep received justice and the dishonest vassal was punished. Khun-Anup's statements are liberally sprinkled with appeals to tradition, implying that the basic teachings of the wise and the myths about divine concern over justice were known throughout the various social levels in Egypt. However, only through persistence did Khun-Anup obtain justice. Whether the pharaoh was actually aware of his appeals and was waiting with sadistic pleasure to see how Khun-Anup would respond cannot be known for sure; the story states that he became aware of the case early and permitted its continuance. Possibly the account was meant to assure those who heard the tale of the god-king's knowledge of what took place in his kingdom, thereby explaining his failure to exercise divine power to ensure justice. The peasant could not be sure that the divine pharaoh would act in his behalf. He had to persevere and by his importunity get a hearing.[16]

The Egyptians carried on extensive trade, business, and political relationship with the outside world, including Nubia, which lay above the first cataract of the Nile and which was incorporated into the empire; Cush or Kush on the Indian Ocean; Palestine and Lebanon; Anatolia, which was occupied by the Hittites; and the various peoples settled along the Euphrates and in Mesopotamia. Despite intermarriages, much correspondence, and the borrowing of words to label new products, the Egyptians distinguished sharply between themselves and outsiders. The Egyptians were men as distinct from gods, humans as distinct from animals. Outsiders or foreigners were something else, for it was foreign influence, according to Egyptian thinking, that caused social breakdown. Hence, the term for foreigners suggested a category not quite up to the Egyptian concept "human," and in certain literature, outsiders were grouped with animals. Perhaps, as Wilson has suggested, isolation accounted in part for this attitude; however, once outsiders settled in Egypt and adopted Egyptian ways, they might be accepted as "people," except that the very language programmed the Egyptian attitudes toward others.[17]

MESOPOTAMIAN SOCIETAL MYTH

The most ancient Sumerian society may have been a democracy which was both urban and agricultural. Some acreage was owned by the temple, administered by the priests, and worked by tenants who paid a portion of the harvest as rental. The remaining land was held as private property by freemen, some controlling large estates and others small plots. Some people raised livestock, some were hunters or fishermen, some were artisans and merchants, some were traders importing and exporting by land and water routes, and some were professionals—scribes and doctors. The business of the city was conducted by an *ensi,* an appointed city manager who was considered of equal status with the freemen—not above them. Crucial decisions concerning civic welfare and security were made by a council of elders and freemen.

However, this system changed. Social, economic, and political pressures, largely from the outside, threatened the survival of the people and led to the development of military leadership which was subsequently transformed into a hereditary monarchy. A new class structure emerged: king, nobles, commoners who were freemen, laborers who were freemen, and slaves, either reduced through poverty to selling themselves and their families or prisoners of war from neighboring areas.[18] The king, although not treated as a god, was recognized as the agent of the god, subservient to the divine will. The god was the real king; there appears to have been no way in Mesopotamian thought for the ruler to claim divinity for himself.[19] The structure of earthly society was modeled on the heavenly system, where councils decided on proper action. Thus, the Mesopotamian ruler was responsible to the gods and to the councils.[20]

The basic social unit was the family, and both monogamy and polygamy were accepted. Marriages usually developed not out of courtship, but from contractual arrangements between the fathers of the two families. In Sumer, property was passed through the males, but the woman controlled the dowry given by her father at the time of her marriage. In case of divorce, the woman retained her inheritance. A man could divorce his wife for failing in what seems to have been vaguely termed "wifely duties," which included bearing children, so that a woman who did not bear could be divorced and another taken in her place. Women could own property and conduct businesses. Children were under the absolute control of their parents.

Some of the best insights into Sumerian societal patterns come from the surviving remnants of legal codes. Such codes sought to establish a balance between truth and justice. "Truth" was god-given; the just administration of this "truth" in the affairs of men was a primary obligation of the monarch. "Truth" was not fixed and immutable; there is ample evidence that law codes were updated from time to time when the king issued new prescriptions.[21] In fact, certain of the presently known Mesopotamian codes are composite and incorporate revisions.[22] However, law was not subject to change at the royal whim; its execution was strictly governed by existing codes.[23] One of the earliest codes was promulgated in the name of King Ur Nammu, founder of the third dynasty of Ur during the twenty-first century B.C. No doubt there were earlier legal formulations which also provided a mythic interpretation for the societal structure, but so far they have not been recovered.

The Ur Nammu Code. According to the prologue of the Ur Nammu Code, the city of Ur had been assigned to Nanna, the moon god, by An, the sky god, and Enlil, the wind god. Nanna, in turn, chose as king Ur Nammu, described as a child of the goddess Ninsun. Ur Nammu developed laws in accordance with the will of Utu, the sun god, child of Nanna and patron of justice. Thus we know that by the twenty-first century, and probably much earlier, there was acceptance of the myth that a particular city had been assigned to a particular god, that the king had a divine birth, and that he had become ruler by virtue of having been selected by the city god. Furthermore, the laws that sustained the society had the approval of the god of justice. Violation of the revealed law and opposition to the rule of the monarch were tantamount to blasphemy and endangered the security and well-being of the community. The community sought to achieve what the gods approved. Violators had to be punished, mostly by fines, to protect the city.

From the parts of the code that have survived, we learn that Ur Nammu standardized weights and protected the rights of widows, orphans, and the poor. Some of the laws concerned sexual relationships. Adultery was condemned. A married woman accused of adultery was subjected to the river ordeal. If proven innocent, she received a compensatory payment in silver from her accuser. If she had actually used her charms to seduce a man other than her husband, she was killed, and her lover freed. The rape of a virgin slave was punishable by fine. A man who divorced his first wife made a separation payment to her, but if she had been a widow before marrying him, the payment was decreased by half. However, a man who had been cohabiting with a widow without a marriage contract made no payment upon separation.

Many other charges were tested by the river ordeal. A man falsely accused of a misdemeanor and proven innocent by the ordeal received payment from his accuser in an amount nine times that paid to a woman accused of adultery. The ratio of payments reflects the social status of woman. Physical injuries and mutilations were punishable by fines. A slave woman who insulted her mistress had her mouth scoured with a quart of salt.

Another Sumerian code known as YBC 2177 and dated about 1800 B.C.[24] discriminates between deliberate and accidental injury causing abortion to a woman of the free citizenry rank. Deliberate injury called for a double fine. A son who rejected his parents forfeited his inheritance and could be sold into slavery. If the parents rejected him, they forfeited their estate. A virgin daughter of a freeman, if she was raped in the street, could be compelled to marry the rapist if she had been walking about without parental consent. If she had had her parents' consent, and if the rapist swore that he was unaware of her status as a free citizen, he was freed without penalty.

Other laws in the fragmentary list have to do with business responsibilities. For example, a boat captain who changed his itinerary, causing a loss to the ship, was held responsible to the owner for the value of the vessel. A herdsman was held responsible for an animal carelessly allowed to stray and killed by a predator.

The Lipit Ishtar Code. Little by little, Semitic influence infiltrated Sumerian cultural patterns. During the first half of the nineteenth century B.C., Lipit Ishtar, the fifth Semitic king of the Isin dynasty, included both Sumer and Akkad in his official title. Only half of his law code remains. Like Ur-Nammu, Lipit Ishtar announced that he had been summoned by gods (Anu and Enlil). Although he made no claim of divine birth, in the epilogue he called himself "the son of Enlil"; in this instance, sonship seems to indicate faithful fulfillment of the divine will, since he said that his actions were in accord with "the word of Enlil." Both prologue and epilogue listed benefits brought by Lipit Ishtar to his people, including freedom, family stability (fathers had to support and stand by their children and children were required to support and sustain their fathers), the abolition of rebellion and enmity, and the establishment of peace. Some of Lipit Ishtar's laws were concerned with matters of taxation and with disputes over property, including slaves. The treatment of certain humans as property with monetary value, characteristic of Sumerian and Babylonian law, was current practice throughout the ancient world, appearing again and again in societal patterns. The value placed on slaves is shown by international treaties that dealt with slaves who had fled from their masters and crossed national boundaries in much the same way that they dealt with stolen goods transported across national borders.[25] Family matters covered by the codes included inheritance problems, status, and responsibilities. For example, if a man's second wife bore him children, her offspring shared her dowry and divided the man's property equally with the children of the first wife. The master's children by a slave had no claim on the property. If a harlot bore him children and he had no offspring by his wife, the harlot's children became his heirs and had to be supported, although the harlot could not live in his house so long as his wife was alive. In cases of marital disaffection that did not terminate in divorce, the man could take a second wife but was compelled to support the first.

The Eshnunna Code. The laws of the city of Eshnunna bear the name of King Bilalama and come from about the same period as the Lipit Ishtar code. There are laws dealing with business and responsible labor, with theft, and with legislation pertaining to the treatment of slaves, who are clearly considered to be property. A man who seized and held another's slave girl and caused her death had to repay the real owner with two slaves. The child of a female slave belonged to her master, and should she give the child away, it could be reclaimed by her owner. When a palace official adopted the child of a palace slave, payment was made to the royal coffers, not to the slave woman.

Some laws dealt with marriage. If a man had paid the marriage fee and his intended bride was raped by another man, the rapist was killed. There was no marriage if a man and a woman lived together without a marriage contract and without the permission of the woman's parents. A wife caught in the act of adultery was killed. A citizen who became a prisoner of war could claim his wife on his return, even if the woman had remarried and borne a son to her second husband. Those who voluntarily abandoned their city had no such familial claims. A man who divorced a woman who had borne him children so that he could marry another was free to pursue his new love, but forfeited all his property.

The Hammurabi Code. The most famous Mesopotamian law code is that of King Hammurabi of Babylon (ca. 1728–1686 B.C.). The black stela (inscribed stone slab) which was found at Susa, the Elamite capital, where it had been taken as a trophy of war, is now on display in the Louvre, and its contents have been published and studied throughout the modern world. Hammurabi borrowed the format of his predecessors, claiming that he had been chosen for kingship by the gods Anu and Enlil and commissioned by Marduk to promote human welfare and justice and to destroy the wicked. He described himself as the shepherd and savior of his people, a great ruler and warrior and a devout man who established law in the language of the people under the authority of Shamash, the sun god and patron of justice. He did not neglect his religious obligations, but supported and beautified temples sacred to the various deities and faithfully performed rites of worship.

Justice under Hammurabi was harsh. The death penalty and *lex talionis* (law of retribution) were frequently invoked. The code opens with laws designed to protect the individual against false accusation. For falsely accusing another of murder, the accuser was killed. A charge of sorcery was tested by the river ordeal; if the charge proved false, the accuser was put to death and his estates went to the accused. On the other hand, if the accused drowned—indicating guilt—his estates went to the accuser. False testimony in cases involving the life of the accused was punishable by death, but in cases involving money or grain, the perjurer paid a fine. A man who made unproven accusations against a married woman or a woman engaged in religious work had half his hair removed.[26]

Crimes of theft were severely punished.[27] Stealing or receiving property taken from the church or state was punishable by death, although if boats or animals were involved, thirty-fold restitution was required. Theft of a boat or animal from a private citizen called for a ten-fold repayment, and failure to pay was punishable by death. Humans were bought and sold as property, and stealing a slave or aiding a slave to escape were punishable by death.

In Babylonian thought, wars were holy and the gods were involved in victory and failure. The date formulary of Hammurabi referred to oracles from Anu and Enlil and noted that those two gods marched before the army.[28] By virtue of the power granted by Anu and Enlil, Hammurabi defeated his foes. Marduk was also praised for providing conquering strength.[29] Therefore, to neglect duties was a serious crime. Military service was voluntary or by conscription. Failure to go on a campaign when ordered, or hiring a substitute to serve, earned the death penalty and the substitute soldier took possession of the citizen's estate. The difficulty of maintaining an estate during military service was recognized; laws protected the absentee soldier's interests. A captured soldier who could not afford to buy freedom without giving up his estate could be ransomed by a merchant who, in turn, was reimbursed by the local temple or the state. An officer who misused his rank to acquire the property of an enlisted man was killed.

The bulk of the code of Hammurabi was concerned with business matters: renting and exchanging property, liability suits, and lending and borrowing money. Women could own property and operate wine shops, but were thrown in the river for overcharging, and could be put to death, should the shop become a congregating place for outlaws. Women in temple service were burned for entering a wine shop.

Numerous laws dealt with marriage and the family. A family consisted of the father, one or more wives, and the children by the wives or servant women. Without a contract, cohabitation did not constitute marriage, but once a marriage was legally consummated, the woman was subject to severe punishments for any violations of the contract. Adultery had to be proven; a woman accused by her husband was believed to be guiltless if she took an oath to that effect. If the accusation came from a man other than her husband, she took the river test. If they were caught in the act, both she and her lover were drowned. However, if her husband wished to spare her, then the state might spare her lover. The wife of a captive soldier might live with another man with impunity only if she were impoverished. On the return of her husband, she returned to him, leaving any children by her interim mate with their father.

The dissolution of marriage was initiated by either the man or the woman. Marriage was for the purpose of establishing a family;[30] thus, a woman who failed to bear a child could be divorced and dismissed with her dowry and her marriage price or a cash settlement. It was much easier for a man to obtain a divorce than for a woman. An Old Babylonian marriage contract states that if the wife should ever announce to her spouse, "You are not my husband," she would be bound and thrown into the water. On the other hand, if the husband should say, "You are not my wife," he paid only a separation fee.[31] According to the code, a woman of good repute could seek divorce and leave her husband taking her dowry; a woman of bad reputation was thrown into the water for desiring divorce. If a woman wanted a divorce so that she might go into business, and if she had humiliated her husband, the divorce could be granted only with his approval, and there was no financial settlement. If the husband contested the divorce, it was denied, he was thereafter free to take a second wife and to reduce the first to the status of a servant. A fever-ridden wife could leave, taking her dowry with her, but if she wished, she could remain married, leaving her husband free to take a second wife.

Slaves occasionally bore children to their masters. If on any occasion the master acknowledged the children, they shared his inheritance with his other children; should he not recognize them, they could not share the inheritance. A man married to a temple woman might be given a slave to bear children, and in such cases, divorce was impossible unless the slave-substitute bore no children. The slave, having borne children to her master, might claim equality with her mistress, and although the temple woman was not at liberty to sell her, she might mark her. If the temple woman did not provide a slave, the man was free to marry a lay-priestess, who would rank lower in the household than the first wife.

A woman found guilty of bringing about her husband's death so that she might marry another was impaled. A certain Nin-dada, who failed to identify her husband's murderers, was indicted as an accessory on the assumption that she must have had a lover.[32]

Incest was forbidden. Although in Egypt, where incest was practiced by the gods, it was also acceptable in the human realm, that Mesopotamian deities engaged in incest did not make the act acceptable for men. For example, in the Enki and Ninhursag creation myth, Enki copulated with his daughter and granddaughter without condemnation. According to another myth from the ancient city of Dunnu, the gods were born in pairs.[33] The first couple were Hain (male) and Earth (female). Earth invited her son

Amakandu to engage in sexual relations. After the sexual encounter, Amakandu murdered Hain and buried him in Dunnu. Amakandu then copulated with his sister, Sea. Amakandu was later murdered by his son Lahar, who assumed sovereignty. The incest-murder pattern continues in the account, but unfortunately the text is broken and the conclusion is missing, so we cannot determine whether some sort of tabu concerning incest may have concluded the myth. So far as we now know, incest was acceptable in divine behavior but was prohibited among men. A man was exiled for having intercourse with his daughter. Sexual relationships with a future daughter-in-law before the marriage was consummated required return of the dowry and a financial settlement; if the marriage had been completed, the guilty father-in-law was bound and thrown into the river. For incest involving a mother and son, both were burned, but a man engaging in sexual relationships with his step-mother who had borne children to his father was merely disinherited.

Hammurabi set forth numerous laws to protect the individual against violation of his person. Rape in which the man had bound the woman was punishable by death. Most injury cases were settled by inflicting an equal injury on the violator, or by fine. Because of the stratification of society, there were different penalties for different individuals. A man of rank who caused physical harm to someone of equal status was repaid in kind—blow for blow, injury for injury, eye for eye, tooth for tooth. Injury to someone of lower social standing was settled by reparations geared to the individual's status. If one in a lower social echelon injured a man who ranked above him socially, the punishment was severe. For striking the cheek of a superior, a man could receive publicly sixty lashes with an oxtail whip. A slave's ear was cut off if he struck a member of the aristocracy. Where injury to a woman caused miscarriage, financial settlements were made, but the amounts decreased markedly for women of lower status. If the woman died, further payments were required, except when the woman was the daughter of an aristocrat, in which case the penalty was death.

The code concluded with a long roster of laws to protect persons and property from broken contracts and from acts performed by irresponsible persons. In the epilogue, Hammurabi enjoined his successors to heed his legal prescriptions, and pronounced curses on anyone who altered or abolished his laws or dared to inscribe another's name in the place of that of Hammurabi.

Mesopotamian Wisdom Writings

In Mesopotamia, as in Egypt, the proverbial lore that was copied and recopied as part of the training in scribal schools supported prevailing notions about law and order, status, and rights, as set forth in legal codes.

The importance of ritual responsibilities to the gods was emphasized, for there were no clear distinctions between moral-ethical and ritual violations. When the nation was in trouble, it was because the gods had been offended; when the individual suffered, he knew he had violated the will of the gods. In both instances, certain procedures had to be followed to determine the act or sin that had triggered divine hostility and to know what actions would placate the angry gods. Some individuals invoked personal gods to intercede with the higher gods on their behalf, for just as in human society, so among the gods there were hierarchical orders. Woe betide the nation or individual unable to determine by introspection, oracles, or divination the nature of the offense or the identity of the offended god. Certain writings express the frustration of individuals caught in such dilemmas.

One Babylonian wisdom text from about 700 B.C., perhaps based on a much earlier writing, suggests that some teachers emphasized the virtue of prudence, modesty, economy of speech, and avoidance of hostility and impertinence.[34] When disputes and quarrels arose, the wise man followed a course of noninvolvement, lest he be compelled to testify. Gifts to the poor pleased Shamash, the sun god, who would reward the giver. Slander, evil talk, and even hasty speech brought divine retribution. To obtain the blessings of a long life, prosperity, and happiness, one should worship daily, make sacrifices, offer prayer, and prostrate oneself. Sin, a violation of the divine will, could be atoned for through prayer. Young men were warned to avoid certain kinds of women when selecting a wife and establishing a family: the harlot and the sacred prostitute were unreliable and unfaithful.

Ahikar's Words. The words of the wise Ahikar, supposedly a vizier in the courts of King Sennacherib and King Esarhaddon of Assyria (seventh century B.C.), circulated throughout the Near East in several languages for centuries. The earliest version is a fragmented copy in Aramaic from the fifth century, found at Elephantine, Egypt. Ahikar, entrapped by an unfaithful nephew who coveted his position, had barely escaped death. This experience may be reflected in some of his sayings.[35] Ahikar warned against sharing secrets with friends (which he had done with his nephew) and against self-aggrandizement (which was characteristic of the ambitious nephew). He counseled humility, mistrust of others, avoidance of evil, and careful fulfillment of responsibilities. A father, he stated, should not spare the rod, for only by punishment was a son saved from wickedness.

The mark of a good man was obedience to the accepted norms. Signs of divine approval of such behavior were wealth, power, and status. Personal tragedy, including physical illness, was interpreted as punishment. Once the offending action and the offended deity were known, the individual could make amends. But what happened when an individual faithfully kept the rules and still suffered misfortune?

A Man and His God.   According to one Sumerian poet, the proper response to individual misfortune was to approach in humility one's personal god, flatter that deity with words of praise, and then with lamentations bewail one's miserable state.[36] If pleased, the personal god would plead the suppliant's case. In this instance, the worshiper was a man of honor whose words had been turned against him, a friendly person whose friends had betrayed him. In his misery he approached his god. He did not deny guilt. In fact, he expressed the mythic conviction of his time that no child had ever been born sinless. The Sumerians believed that deceit, evil, and discord were ordained by the gods as normal, inborn human behavior.

The account had a happy ending: the unfortunate man's god heeded his cry and alleviated his misfortune, whereupon the relieved worshiper praised his god in thanksgiving.

A Prayer to Every God.   A miserable Babylonian worshiper, unable to determine which god or goddess he had offended, composed an appeal "to whom it may concern" that has been titled "Prayer to Every God."[37] The author made no claim of being sinless, but said that the act that had brought about his misfortune had been done in ignorance. That he received no response to his outcries made him wonder whether the offended deity was even listening. The poem concluded with an appeal to the offended god or goddess that his/her heart be quieted, and with the promise that if the sin was forgiven, he would sing the praises of the deity.

"I Will Praise the Lord of Wisdom."   The worshiper who composed "I Will Praise the Lord of Wisdom" faced a similar situation, but experienced a happy outcome.[38] His plight made no sense: suffering and social misfortune had befallen him, although he had been righteous. Faithfully and joyfully he had kept the laws of the land, fulfilled social responsibilities, and worshiped the gods. In his bewilderment, he cried:

> O if I only knew that these things were pleasing to a god!
> What seems to be proper for oneself may be an offense to one's god.
> What seems despicable in one's mind may be proper for his god.
> Who can understand the will of the heavenly gods?
> Who can comprehend the desires of the underworld gods?
> Where have confused mortals learned the god's way?

The standard answer to his questions was that the gods had revealed their desires in codes and cultic rites, but he had gone that route, and even consultation with omen-interpreters, diviners, and magicians provided no insight or guidance. He believed he was dying, and those who wished him ill thought so, too, and were rejoicing. Finally, release came through Marduk, lord of wisdom, who healed him of his illness, revived his strength, and made him whole. The jubilant man was convinced that Marduk could reach into the grave and raise up a dead man. He called on all breathing, living creatures to glorify Marduk. (There is no indication that the worshiper ever discovered what he had done to offend, or what deity he had offended. What mattered was that Marduk as cultic king had taken action on his behalf.)

A Satirical Dialogue. Myths about structuring life and society according to the ordinances of the gods, pronouncing that men were the creatures of the gods and destined to serve them, and revealing rules by which life was to be lived, did not face the question of "meaning" in life. What was the purpose of life? Speculation about such matters led one unknown Mesopotamian author to compose a satirical dialogue between a slave and his master, a man of wealth and status.[39] Following the social teachings of the wise men, the slave automatically agreed with everything his master uttered. Only when he was directly asked for his opinion did he venture a comment, usually seen to be the writer's message.

The master decided to drive to the palace, and the slave agreed that it would be a good thing to do. When the master decided not to drive, the servant observed that that, too, was good. The master wanted to drive into the country and then did not want to drive, to dine and then not to dine. With each shift in desire, the slave found the action wise. To love a woman or not to love was one question. In support of love, the slave commented that "one who loves a woman forgets sorrow and fear"; in support of not loving he stated that "woman is a pitfall" and "a sharp iron dagger that cuts a man's throat." The ambivalence extended to religious duties, to sacrificing to the master's personal god. The servant observed that sacrifice made a man happy and provided benefits. The refusal to sacrifice, on the other hand, made the god subject to the man, for when the god demanded, "Perform my ritual," the man declared his independence by refusing to comply. Nor did the question of duty to one's country receive a simple answer. The servant noted that acts on behalf of one's country lay eventually in the hands of Marduk, presumably for reward and blessing by the national god. The master's decision not to do something for his country prompted the suggestion that the master climb among ancient ruins and look at the exposed human skulls and skeletons, trying to determine which had been "an evil doer and which a benefactor." Finally the master asked, "What is good?" The slave responded, "To have my neck and your neck broken and be thrown into the river." When the master said, "No, I will just kill you and let you go first," the slave replied, "Would my lord want to live three days after me?" The slave indicated the futility of any sort of striving by quoting from an ancient source:

Who is tall enough to reach the heavens?
Who is big enough to encompass the earth?

The discussion was a rejection of the normative value structure that ranked one kind of action over another. Ultimately, it did not matter whether the master rode to the palace, went hunting, ate, performed rituals, engaged in love, or did anything else. He should do what pleased him, and should he require a rationale, that too could be provided. Another generation, looking at his skeletal remains, could not know whether he had been great or small, rich or poor, good or evil. Death was the final solution, for there was no ultimate meaning in anything and no ultimate value structure.

Gilgamesh. One of the most remarkable documents reinforcing Mesopotamian societal patterns is the story of Gilgamesh. So important was this tale that it was repeated and in some instances remodeled for centuries throughout the ancient Near East. Some aspects of the story enter the realm of problems associated with human identity and with identity myths, but basically the account contributed to conformity to the existing societal patterns.

The epic tells of a hero-king's legendary quest for personal meaning or identity and for life beyond death. In the Sumerian King List, Gilgamesh is the fifth king of the first dynasty of ancient Uruk (biblical Erech), which would suggest that he lived about the middle of the third millennium B.C. It is recorded that he reigned for 120 years, a figure that is obviously exaggerated but very modest in a roster which lists twelve monarchs as having ruled for a total of 2,310 years.[40]

Present translations of the Gilgamesh epic are based primarily on twelve fragmented tablets found in the ruins of the library of King Ashurbanipal at Nineveh. During the seventh century B.C., Ashurbanipal, an ardent antiquarian, dispatched scribes throughout his empire to copy and translate historical and religious literature, including the Gilgamesh epic. The source is supplemented by partial texts found at Boghazkoy, a Hittite site in Asia Minor, and at Megiddo in Israel. From these records, we can reconstruct the main features of the epic, despite the remaining lacunae.[41]

The epic opens with a description of Uruk, the holy city of the sky-god Anu, head of the divine assembly. Within the strong city walls was the temple Eanna, sacred to Anu and to Ishtar, goddess of love. The projected image is one of security, wealth, and beauty—but there were grave injustice and unhappiness, too. King Gilgamesh, who appears to have been very young at this point, rejected the traditional concept of the king as a shepherd concerned for his people. Instead, he ruled as an arrogant despot. He ignored socially acceptable patterns of relationship and established personal behavioral codes. He flaunted recognized societal regulations and sought self-fulfillment at the expense of his people, whom he seems to have treated as objects rather than as humans. Nor was there any way to stop him, for not only was he invested with the authority of the throne, but from his mother, the goddess Aruru, he had received a nature two-thirds divine, only one-third of his nature coming from his human father. Moreover, he was bigger and stronger than all others. Finally, his unbridled energy, his disdain for the rights and feelings of others, and his ruthless indulgence in his pleasures, which drove him into restless action both day and night, led the people to complain to the gods. Aruru was summoned by Anu. To curb Gilgamesh's misuse of power, to redirect his energies and interests, she created from clay a wild, hairy, beastlike man named Enkidu.

Enkidu was, in a sense, the alter ego of Gilgamesh. Like Gilgamesh, he was powerful, but where Gilgamesh was a man of the sophisticated city, Enkidu was of the untamed wilds. Gilgamesh lived among men, Enkidu associated with wild beasts. Whereas Gilgamesh was estranged from the populace by his misuse of power, Enkidu appeared happy and at one with the animals he befriended.

The first steps toward humanizing and urbanizing Enkidu were accomplished by a temple harlot. Enkidu had thwarted the hunters by freeing animals and destroying traps, so the hunters consulted Gilgamesh, who explained that sexual involvement with a woman would rob Enkidu of his primal innocence and alienate him from his animal friends. The harlot enticed Enkidu, and after spending six days and seven nights with her, he discovered that he was no longer acceptable to the animals, which now ran from him. The enemy of settled life, the hero of nature in the raw, the one who had struggled to protect the ways of the wild, had succumbed to the temptations of urban ways. Enkidu, estranged, was compelled to seek identity among humans. To prepare him for his new life, the courtesan taught him to eat like a human being and tore off part of her clothing to provide a garment for the still naked man.

The encounter between Enkidu and Gilgamesh was a violent test of strength and endurance, a turning point in both their lives. Gilgamesh had been forewarned by dreams of the coming of Enkidu; the omens made him both expectant and uneasy. The meeting took place within Uruk, where Gilgamesh appears to have been about to exercise his authority and sexually possess a bride before her husband. The text is broken, but the ensuing battle seems to have been a draw, although some scholars would have Gilgamesh the victor and still others, Enkidu. In any event, the result was the same: the two men became fast friends—brothers even, for Aruru adopted Enkidu. Tyranny in Uruk had been curtailed by Enkidu, and the two heroes now directed their energies to adventures that promised to bring meaning to life and immortality through fame.

Gilgamesh and Enkidu decided to attack Huwawa, monster guardian of the Sacred Cedar Forest, which belonged to the god of air, Enlil. By this time, Gilgamesh and Enkidu had become the beloved of the people of Uruk. Out of fear for the safety of their heroes, the citizens and elders sought to dissuade them from this enterprise. But Gilgamesh was firm, perhaps because of his "restless heart," which his mother Aruru said was given to him by the sun god Shamash, perhaps because of immature enthusiasm which prompted him to embark on a venture he could only dimly comprehend. Perhaps he was being transformed from the physical man who found identity through the use of brute force to the romantic man of action who envisioned himself a hero. In any case, the restless drive within led him to seize on Huwawa as the object to be overcome to achieve inner satisfaction, despite the protestations of the people and the reluctance of Enkidu.

The Sacred Forest is believed to have been on the slopes of Mount Amanus in northern Syria. The two heroes traversed the distance in record time. Before the battle, omens were consulted. With help from Shamash, who buffeted and confused Huwawa with tempestuous winds, the brothers slew the monster.

Now Gilgamesh and Enkidu bathed and changed from battle attire. Ishtar, drawn by the physical beauty of Gilgamesh, invited him to be her lover and promised him untold power, treasure, and honor. Proudly, scornfully, he disdained her offer. Mocking the depth and reliability of her love, he recounted her past failures as a lover as evidence of her fickle nature. Defiance of a goddess prompted reprisal: the bull of heaven was sent against Gilgamesh. At the crucial moment, Enkidu seized the bull's tail, enabling Gilgamesh to kill it. As a crowning insult, Enkidu hurled the bull's thigh at Ishtar—an act that brought the gods into divine council. Meanwhile, the two victorious warriors were welcomed by the cheering populace and with chants by the young women:

> Gilgamesh is the most glorious of heroes.
> Gilgamesh is the mightiest among men.

Whether there is some cultic significance in the rejection of Ishtar cannot be known. Possibly, Gilgamesh was refusing to participate in a temple ritual that called for the king to become the consort of the goddess, represented by a priestess or a temple courtesan. It is also possible that the bull of heaven symbolized the coming of a plague or some other disaster as punishment for Gilgamesh's refusal to comply with Ishtar's desires. The danger was averted by the defeat of the bull.

In the heavenly council, charges were preferred against Gilgamesh and Enkidu by Enlil: the divine forest had been violated and Huwawa killed, Ishtar had been insulted and the celestial bull slain. Enlil called for Enkidu's death. Shamash defended Enkidu, arguing that the bull and Huwawa had been killed at Shamash's decree. Shamash failed to win his case, and Enkidu learned in a dream that he was to die.

Enkidu's end was not pleasant. He died not as a hero, but as a pathetic victim of the gods, bemoaning his fate and cursing the events that removed him from his secure world among the animals, until Shamash reminded him of the joys he had experienced in the friendship of Gilgamesh. The description of the place of the dead, where Enkidu would go, is gloomy: the dead ate mud and resembled bedraggled birds dwelling in darkness. Enkidu's illness lasted thirteen days, during which time he grew weaker and weaker until he died in the arms of his friend.

At first, Gilgamesh rejected the reality of death. For six days and seven nights, he refused to bury the body of his friend, in the vain hope that life would somehow return. But when a maggot fell from the dead man, he was compelled to acknowledge the truth: Enkidu was dead and would not be revived. Gilgamesh's mourning and the mourning rites of the people of Uruk did not assuage him. In mad frenzy he fled through the land, trying to escape his fears: "When I die, will I not be like Enkidu?"

Gilgamesh had not yet ended his romantic quest for meaning. The determination that had led him to attack Huwawa now drove him into battle against death itself. He began a search for immortality. According to Sumerian mythology, only two humans had gained immortality— Utnapishtim, a distant relative of Gilgamesh, and Utnapishtim's wife. To reach Utnapishtim, Gilgamesh had to undertake a dangerous journey to the mountains at the edge of the world, where terrifying scorpion-men guarded the entrance to a subterranean passageway, the road traversed by the sun through the underworld. Because he was two-thirds divine, Gilgamesh was allowed to pass through the darkness of the tunnel to the glorious sea which lay beyond, where trees bore precious stones. Here he met Siduri, a barmaid, who attempted to dissuade him:

> Gilgamesh, where are you running?
> You will not find the immortal life you seek.
> When the gods created man
> They ordained death for man
> And kept immortality for themselves.
> Make merry day and night.

Make every day a day of joy.
Dance, play, day and night.
Wear dazzling clothes,
Bathe your head. Refresh yourself with water.
Cherish the child who grasps your hand.
Let your wife rejoice in your bosom
For this is the fate of man.

Gilgamesh paid no heed to this advice, but obtained directions to Utnapishtim's boatman, Sursanabi, who conveyed him over the waters of death to Utnapishtim. Gilgamesh's conversation with Utnapishtim was not particularly satisfying. Utnapishtim pointed out that nothing lasts forever, that life has an ever-changing, ever-developing pattern. Death comes by divine decree; no man has any choice but to accept it. Gilgamesh could not accept this fact, because Utnapishtim himself had escaped death. Utnapishtim then related the story of the flood, in which he had preserved life in his huge boat. For this act, the gods had rewarded him and his wife with immortality. What had happened in his case could not be repeated for Gilgamesh.

Gilgamesh still refused to yield, and Utnapishtim challenged him to a test—to overcome sleep for six nights and seven days. (Sleep is an image of death, and the word is often used as a synonym for death.) Of course, Gilgamesh failed. In consolation, Utnapishtim told Gilgamesh of a plant called "the old man becomes young" that had the magical power of rejuvenation. Gilgamesh acquired the plant from the bottom of the sea, but decided not to use it until he became old. He came to a well and decided to bathe. He set the plant aside while he swam, and a snake, attracted by its fragrance, devoured it and fled into the sea. This story, of course, provides an etiological explanation of why the snake sheds its old skin and seems to renew its youth. The plant was lost to Gilgamesh.

The epic ends as it began, with a comment on the walls of Uruk. It leaves unanswered the question of what Gilgamesh did next, but perhaps the epic itself is the answer. Reciting the story of Gilgamesh gave the hero a symbolic relationship with the listeners. He became the bearer of wisdom, of profound spiritual truth about human mortality, life, and how to live it. He was the aged hero, the wise man whose experiences conveyed insights. We assume that he did not revert to his former wayward patterns, that he became a wise shepherd to his people, that he conformed to the image of what a king should be, that he became the wise teacher whose life story was in itself instruction.

The epic is more than an entertaining hero tale. Gilgamesh is the representative man of Uruk in search of identity, but unlike ordinary men, he can do as he pleases, for he is a semidivine king. His portrayal both emphasizes the limitations of ordinary man and details ordinary man's inner dream of absolute freedom from responsibility. Gilgamesh discovers that the abuse of power for self-gratification is not satisfying, and he moves from physical gratification to romantic adventures. However, romantic adventures cannot forever ignore the harsh reality of death, and when Enkidu died, not in glorious battle but of a lingering illness, Gilgamesh embarked on a desperate, frantic search for immortality. His search failed when he lost the plant that could have rejuvenated him. What was left but to return to Uruk and fulfill himself in the accepted role of king?

The point is clear: if the superhero failed to acquire immortality, could not be rejuvenated, and found no real satisfaction in power and romantic adventure, then what could the citizens of Uruk (or other centers where the legend was told) do but acknowledge the reality of death as the end for all men and fulfill themselves in their appointed (god-determined) roles? As for how to live within such a context, the answer was given by Utnapishtim and the barmaid. Utnapishtim observed that nothing remains forever, that life and death are allocated by the gods, with the time of death kept secret from man. The barmaid gave the answer to the question of how to live within the human life span.

BIBLICAL SOCIETAL MYTH

Societal myth in the Old Testament moves rapidly from universalism to particularism, from divine interest in the world to Yahweh's concern for one people: Israel. The mythic structure of the opening of Genesis exposes the god's repeated failures to come to terms with man's aspirations and to establish meaningful relationships with mankind in general. The garden of Eden experiment failed—man did not slavishly obey, but refused to do the expressed will of Yahweh and thereby rose above animal status to a position a little lower than divinity (Ps. 8:5). Yahweh expelled man from the garden and from proximity to the tree of life.

In the next myth (Gen. 6:1–4), divine beings copulated with human females to produce offspring who became heroes, but whose life span was limited by Yahweh to 120 years, despite the divine infusion.[42] Apparently, this particular divine–human relationship was such an abject failure that Yahweh decided to destroy all life by a flood. Noah was chosen as the new Adam, and he and his immediate family and selected pairs of living creatures were spared to become the new creation (Gen. 6:5–10:32). All seemed to succeed until men attempted to invade the realm of the gods by building a tower that would provide a ladder to heaven (Gen. 11:1–9). The Tower of Babel myth developed from Hebrew evaluation of the ziggurats, the multistaged temple-towers that were important in Mesopotamian religion.

Yahweh frustrated this human effort by confusing the language of the workers. Thus, the Hebrew myth explained how mankind, descended from one family, acquired a multitude of languages.

In Genesis 12 the myth of chosenness, the election myth, introduces Yahweh's next attempt to relate to his creatures and records the narrowing of Yahweh's interests to one people. Yahweh chose Abraham, promising him divine protection, land, descendants, and a nation in return for faith and obedience (Gen. 12:1–3, 15:5–6). Subsequent chapters recording his life (Gen. 12–25:8) present Abraham as a model of blind obedience, responding without question to such severe, traumatic testing as Yahweh's command that Isaac be sacrificed (Gen. 22:1–4). Even in bargaining for the lives of the people of Sodom and Gomorrah, Abraham did not challenge Yahweh's determination to destroy the cities. Through covenant mythology the Abraham (Jewish)–Yahweh relationship assumed a contractual nature, signed and sealed with the symbolic mark of circumcision (Gen. 17). Accounts of subsequent patriarchal heroes restate the election and covenant myths and exhibit these heroes as additional models of faith and obedience in their responses to the continuing revelations of Yahweh (Gen. 26:24, 35:10–12, and so on).

The specifics of the covenant are found in another myth, which stipulates that Yahweh's laws were revealed to Moses on Mount Sinai-Horeb (Exod. 20). Critical analysis of the Torah demonstrates that several different law codes were combined and harmonized during a period of some five hundred years. Some laws may have come from non-Hebrew sources, but whatever was borrowed was hebraized and became the basis for the legalistic structure of Judaism.

Like other Near Eastern codes, the Torah claimed a divine origin. Its contents delineate the particular likes and dislikes of Yahweh, what kind of behavior was acceptable to him and what was offensive. Unlike other codes, Hebrew law was said to be authored by the deity and guaranteed by him; the king was neither involved nor mentioned. The aim of the law was *ṣedeq,* usually interpreted as "justice" or "righteousness" or perhaps a combination of these. But *sedeq* also embodies the concept of the norm. *Ṣedeq* meant that which was normal—accepted communal patterns. The Deuteronomist called on the people to observe the principle:

Ṣedeq, ṣedeq you shall pursue that you may live and inherit the land which Yahweh your god gives you. (Deut. 16:20)

Despite the statement in Exodus 12:49, "You shall have but one law for the home-born and for the outsider who lives among you," distinctions were made among the citizens. The classifications are not spelled out so

clearly as in the Hammurabi code. There were citizens and slaves, sojourners who passed through the land, resident aliens, and there were men and
women. Social responsibilities and penalties for violation of sacred laws
varied among these classes. One unique Deuteronomic law reads as follows:

> You shall not give up a slave who has escaped from his master to you. He shall dwell
> among you in the locale he shall choose in one of your towns, where it pleases him most.
> You shall not oppress him. (Deut. 23:15–16)

It is doubtful that the ruling applies to a Hebrew slave fleeing from a
Hebrew master, or even to a Hebrew slave fleeing from a foreign master.
In both cases, the slave would probably flee to his family or clan; therefore,
the regulation seems to deal with a foreign slave who fled into Hebrew
territory and who was to be given sanctuary without fear of extradition.

Nowhere was any demand raised for equal treatment for all men. The
social and political inequities were accepted throughout the ancient Near
East as economic realities or as the natural results of warfare, and as
approved by the deity. Perhaps in an effort to bring kindness into master-
slave relationships, Deuteronomic law enjoined humane treatment and
reminded the Hebrews that they had been slaves in Egypt.

Justice was publicly administered by local gatherings of elders, heads of
families or clan leaders, and apparently the sentences they imposed were
carried out immediately by townspeople (Deut. 21:2ff., 19; 22:15, and so
on). Judges were also appointed (Deut. 16:18f, 19:16ff). Certain cases were
sent to Jerusalem for trial by priests and an appointed magistrate (Deut.
17:8–13). Some cases could be referred to the king; for this purpose, the
Solomonic palace included a judgment court.

Basically, the social unit comprised those bound by blood ties and those
who lived together. The unit could be a family, household, clan, or tribe,
and included the father, mother, children, slaves, widows, orphans, resident aliens, and temporary sojourners who had been given shelter. So tight
was the bond that the unit could be understood as having one corporate
personality, one life, one blood (Lev. 17:11: "For the life of the flesh is in
the blood"). Misfortune or good fortune to one was misfortune or good
fortune to all. Injury to one was injury to all and required vengeance by
the next-of-kin, the redeemer in blood. On this basis, Joab justified the
murder of Abner, for Abner had killed Joab's brother (2 Sam. 3:26–30). In
the event of an unsolved murder, guilt settled on the community nearest
where the dead body was found, and expiation rituals were required because of the mythic assumption that spilled blood, unless redeemed, contaminated the ground and reduced its fertility (Deut. 21:1–9).

The social concept of the corporate group was not restricted by ordinary time-space limitations, but extended backward to the dead and forward to the unborn. According to this manner of thinking, a living group could be said to enjoy blessings engendered by an ancestor who had pleased the deity. Similarly, the unborn might have to bear punishment for sins of their dead ancestors. The Deuteronomic enunciation of this principle was related to the jealousy of Yahweh and the demand for complete loyalty:

> . . . I, Yahweh your god, am a jealous god, visiting the iniquity of the fathers on the children to the third and fourth generation . . . (Deut. 5:9).

The principle opened the door to political expediency. David was able to blame a famine on his predecessor, Saul, and to claim that he was expiating guilt by murdering seven of Saul's sons who were potential political rivals (2 Sam. 21:1–9). Rejection of this principle is also found in the Old Testament; each individual was said to be responsible for his sins (compare Deut. 24:16; Jer. 31:29–30; Ezek. 18). Both concepts were apparently alive during the first century A.D. Jesus' disciples supposedly asked him whether a man was born blind for his own sins or for those of his parents (John 9:2).

The tight bond associated with blood contributed to the concept of the holy war. One man violating the taboos associated with the war could endanger the entire army, as Achan did during the battle of Jericho (Josh. 7). When Hebrew tribes fought, the deity fought with and for them (Josh. 5:13, 10:10–14; Judg. 5, and so on). The Hebrews vowed to sacrifice to the god all or part of the defeated enemy and enemy property in a holocaust (Josh. 6:17–21). This act, known as the *herem,* carried overtones of a covenant agreement. Violation of the agreement resulted in the withdrawal of divine help and disaster for the Hebrews (Josh 7–8). Warfare thus assumed a beyond-the-secular dimension. Battles were entered into after consultation with and reception of oracles from the god. The *herem* was not exclusively Hebrew, for the ninth century B.C. Moabite stone shows that the *herem* was practiced by the Moabites.[43] Documents from other nations record that national gods were consulted before engaging in war or battles. In war, as in peace, the concept of psychic unity prevailed.

Family structure was primarily monogamous. Those who could support more than one wife were free to enter into multiple marriages. King Solomon appears to have established an all-time record, with seven hundred wives. Wealthy men could also have concubines, and again Solomon led the rest with three hundred. Slave women might bear their master's children, and a barren wife might provide her husband with a slave girl to bear a child, just as Sarah gave Hagar to Abraham (Gen. 16:3–4). However, the child of a harlot could not inherit property from its father (Judg. 11:1–2).

Couples could fall in love and marry, but most marriages were arranged by fathers. The groom paid his father-in-law a marriage price (*mohar*), and the bride left her home to join the household, clan, or tribe of her husband. The exception to this rule was in *Sadiqa* marriage, when the woman remained within her father's household and was visited by her mate. The marriage of Samson to the Philistine woman of Timnah was such a marriage (see Judg. 14–15, especially Judg. 15:1) The *mohar* was partial recompense for the loss of a daughter; its amount varied according to the social standing of the woman's family. However, there may have been other dimensions involved. The purpose of marriage was to produce offspring, and because the Hebrews believed that immortality consisted in the continuation of an individual's name, it was important to legitimize the children as members of the father's group rather than of the mother's.[44] There is also a feeling that the psychic strength of the bride's family was diminished by her departure, and the *mohar* may have served as partial compensation.

Some marriages were between first cousins, some between members of the same clan or tribe, some across tribal lines, and some with foreigners. Apparently in David's time, a man could marry his half-sister, as Tamar informed Amnon before he raped her (2 Sam 13:13). One account says that Sarah was Abraham's half-sister (Gen. 20:12). Before her marriage, a woman captured in war underwent a rite symbolizing the termination of her relationship with her country of origin (Deut. 21:10ff). During the late fifth century B.C., marriages to foreign women were condemned by Ezra and Nehemiah.

Children were important; childlessness, a disaster (Gen. 11:30, 20:17f, 30:1, 2 Sam. 6:23). A Psalmist wrote:

> Behold, sons are a heritage from Yahweh.
> The fruit of the womb is a reward. (Ps. 127:3)

Male children were preferred, as a male had more commercial value than a female. A scale of worth is set forth in Leviticus 27:1–8. Persons dedicated for service in a sanctuary could be released from that responsibility by payment of money. The service of all persons, and presumably the value of all individuals, was not equal. The money-worth of females was half that established for males, and the value of the very young and of the old was also less.

Daughters, but not sons, could be sold into slavery (Exod. 21:7), although whole families might enter into bondage because of debts (Lev. 25:39ff). Children had few rights. They were commanded to honor their parents (Exod 20:12). Should a son curse or strike his parents, he was killed (Exod. 21:15–17). At certain periods, children were sacrificed to Yahweh or to other deities. For example, Jephthah's daughter was sacrificed to Yahweh (Judg. 11:30–40), and children were burned to the god Molech in the valley of Hinnom outside Jerusalem in the seventh century B.C. (see 2 Kings 23:10; Jer. 32:35). Exodus 13:1 and 22:29 call for the sacrifice of the first-born son, and Exodus 13:13 and Numbers 18:15 provide for a substitutional sacrifice by which the child was redeemed. Numbers 3:12 and 8:17–18 state that the Levitical priesthood was a substitution for child sacrifice. The mythic legend that involved Abraham in the near-sacrifice of his son Isaac may have been a sermonic device giving additional divine sanction to the substitution of a sacrificed animal for a human (Gen. 22).

Sexual taboos abounded, and the penalties for violations were harsh. Incest was forbidden (Lev. 18:6–18); those who transgressed the law were cursed (Deut. 27:20, 22, 23) and both parties were killed (Lev. 20:11–12, 14). The incestuous relationship of Reuben with Bilhah, his father's concubine (Gen. 35:22), is reported without reference to punishment, but the act was mentioned by Jacob in his deathbed blessings (Gen. 49:3–4). According to Ezekiel, during the Exile in the sixth century B.C., incest was common in Jerusalem (Ezek. 22:10–11), and although the prophet condemned such relationships, the death penalty does not seem to have been enforced.

There was a mythic taboo against viewing the naked body (Lev. 20:17–18). Priests were required to wear garments covering their sexual organs ("bare flesh") when ministering in the temple. One Hebraic legend told of a curse on the Canaanites, pronounced because Ham, son of Noah and father of Canaan, looked at the naked body of his drunken father. Perhaps some condemnation of Canaanite homosexual practices was implied,[45] for at least two biblical accounts suggest that homosexuality was accepted within Canaan. Judges 19 relates that a sojourning Levite protected himself against the men of Gibeah by giving them his concubine for their sexual pleasure.[46] Sodom and Gomorrah were destroyed for their "sinfulness," which included homosexuality (Gen. 19). Under Hebrew law, homosexuality was punishable by death (Lev. 20:13).

The story of Onan (Gen. 38:1–11) is usually interpreted as a condemnation of masturbation and/or coitus interruptus. Onan refused to fulfill the social requirements of the Levirate or brother-in-law regulation of Deuteronomy 25:5–10, according to which he should have copulated with the widow of his dead brother and provided a son to continue the dead man's name and lineage. Onan was killed by Yahweh for letting his semen fall to the ground, either by withdrawal before ejaculation or as a result of self-manipulation.

Bestiality, a sexual relationship between a human and an animal, was punishable by death (Exod. 22:19; Lev. 18:23). In Deuteronomy 27:21, the individual who committed bestiality was cursed, but Leviticus 20:15–16 called for the death of both the human and the animal. No reason for the taboo is given: the act was simply abhorrent to Yahweh. Perhaps some rejection of Canaanite ritual was involved, for in Canaanite myth the god Ba'al, represented by a priest in the ritual, copulated with a heifer. Hosea may have referred to the cultic act in his derisive comment on men kissing calves (Hos. 13:2). If the animal involved was a sheep, the condemnation might have had a basis in concern for health, since syphilis can be contracted through copulation with sheep.

Children born to an incestuous or otherwise disapproved marriage were labeled bastards and prohibited from participating in religious assemblies (Deut. 23:2). The prohibition did not extend to their parents, but the descendants of illegitimate children were forever barred from religious groups.

One law declared a woman unclean during her menstrual period, capable of contaminating anyone who touched her and anything she sat or lay on (Lev. 15:19–24). Sexual intercourse during the menstrual period was forbidden, for it rendered a man unclean (Lev. 15:24, 18:19), and it was punishable by expulsion from the community (Lev. 20:18). The emission of semen was considered unclean, even when it occurred during the sexual act. The persons involved were considered unclean, and any garment touched by the semen was impure (Lev. 15:16–18).

Adultery was condemned, for it rendered both participants ceremonially unclean. It was considered a crime against one's male neighbor and was punishable by death for both the man and the woman, regardless of whether the woman was married or engaged (Lev. 20:10; Deut 22:22ff). The male was forbidden to desire his neighbor's wife or other property (Exod. 20:17; Deut. 5:21). Adultery was a violation of property rights.

A woman was expected to be a virgin when she married. Should her husband accuse her of not being a virgin, if she was unable to produce the blood-stained bridal sheets to prove the hymen had been broken by her husband, she was stoned to death. If the charge was false, the husband was whipped and compelled to recompense his father-in-law for bringing dishonor on the family (Deut. 22:13–21). A betrothed virgin raped in the city was stoned together with the rapist, on the assumption that she could have cried out for help. If the rape occurred in the country, only the man was killed. If the virgin was not betrothed, the rapist paid the girl's father fifty shekels of silver and married the girl, with no possibility of future divorce (Deut. 22:23–29).

A man could divorce his wife simply by finding in her something of which he disapproved, according to the rather vague statement in

Deuteronomy 24:1. He was required to provide her with a writ of divorce, and she was then free to remarry. Should her second husband die, the first husband could not remarry her (Deut. 24:1–4). Ordinarily, women could not divorce their husbands, but a fifth century B.C. marriage contract from Elephantine, Egypt, which appears to be the product of a Jewish community, states that Yehoyishma' could divorce her husband by stating "I divorce you, I will not be wife to you."[47]

Like others in the ancient Near East, the Hebrews found ways to exalt themselves at the expense of their neighbors. Canaanite religion, its myths and rituals so concerned with fertility, was condemned by prophets such as Amos, Hosea, Isaiah, and Jeremiah. As we have noted, the conquest of the Canaanites by the Hebrews was traced to Ham, who had viewed his naked father. The Amonites and Moabites were described as children of incest (Gen. 19:30–38). Israel's enemies were cursed by the prophets, who explained any disaster caused by enemies according to the blessing-curse mythology enunciated in cultic laws (Deut. 28). Even the proclamation of monotheism in the sixth century did not change anything, and as we have noted, by the fifth century B.C. intermarriage with foreigners was treated as pollution of the holy people (see Neh. 13:23–31; Ezra 9–10).

Any protest against the concept of exclusiveness was not really heeded. The books of Ruth and Jonah, for example, seek to demonstrate the validity of a more open societal point of view. Ruth traces the lineage of King David to the Moabitess Ruth. Certainly one thrust of the book is its emphasis on Ruth's foreignness. Her marriage to a leading citizen of Bethlehem was acceptable to the total community. The child of the union was formally adopted by Naomi, and the great-grandchild of the union was David. Obviously, if David, the model king, was descended from a mixed marriage, then there was good reason to accept foreigners into the assembly of Israel. In comparison with the harsh edicts of Ezra and Nehemiah, the book of Ruth exhibits an attitude of magnanimity toward those whose origins lay outside Israel.

The highly dramatized mythic tale of Jonah discloses Yahweh's concern for other people—in this case, the Assyrians, hated enemies of the Jews—and points to Jewish responsibility for making Yahweh's ways known. Because the people of Nineveh repented, they were open to divine salvation. Yahweh's concern and salvation were not limited to Israel, despite the particularistic views of Ezra, Nehemiah, and their followers. The mythology of a universal god meant that he was concerned for *all* humanity, not solely his chosen people. The stories of Ruth and Jonah, however lacked the mythic weight of the law and the covenant. It was easy to point to King Solomon's many marriages with non-Jews and argue that the division of the kingdom had come about because of Yahweh's anger at the mixed marriages and the accompanying apostasy.

Separation of the Jews from others was reinforced by food taboos. Certain meats, fish, and fowl were not to be eaten, nor were certain mixtures of food, such as milk and meat. Even though the pork taboo might have been an effort to avoid trichinosis, modern efforts to demonstrate that the other prohibitions rested in health concerns are not convincing. The food traditions are based on cultic myths. The milk-and-meat restrictions may have stemmed from a reaction against some Canaanite cultic rite in which a young goat was boiled in milk; one fragmented Canaanite text mentions this food. On the other hand, before the Sinai revelation, Abraham was supposed to have served just such a meal to Yahweh— perhaps in a Canaanite cultic rite or as a typical bedouin feast (Gen. 18).

Hebrew Wisdom Literature

The Hebrew wisdom literature collected in the book of Proverbs is, like the wisdom of Egypt, largely attributed to royalty—to King Solomon (1:1, 10:1, 25:1), and to an otherwise unidentified King Lemuel, who recorded his mother's precepts. One collection is supposedly from a man known only as Agur, son of Jakeh. Chapters 22:17–24:22 contain ten parallels to the sayings of Amen-em-opet of Egypt; indeed, the Hebrew collection may have been deliberately modeled after the Egyptian wisdom. Scholars have recognized several small collections within the book of Proverbs. Although some of the sayings may go back to Solomon's time, the majority appear to come from later periods.

Regardless of authorship, wisdom was said to have been revealed by Yahweh (2:6). Those who accepted its guidance were promised blessings of plenty, security, and ease (1:33, 8:1–21, 10:3ff); protection against evil ways (1:10ff., 2:12ff); and knowledge about proper action and justice (2:6). Two classes of men were recognized: the wise, who were good men, and the foolish, who were evil. The wise man adhered to wisdom teachings; the stupid man ignored or abandoned them. The wise man was a good citizen, discreet, prudent, reliable, honest, of gentle speech, humble, conforming, industrious, impartial in judgment, and observant of cultic responsibilities. The foolish was the opposite.

There were also two classes of women, good and evil. The good woman is described as an ideal wife (Prov. 31:10–31). Her major concern was the welfare of her husband and her household. She worked long and diligently to succeed as a home manager, an astute businesswoman, a manufacturer and seller of garments. Her reward was the approval of her family and the knowledge that her husband boasted of her among the men. The evil woman was an adventuress, against whom wise men cautioned their students. A wanton, she openly sought lovers and boasted that her husband was away and her bed was ready. She represented the way of folly and the road to disaster (Prov. 7:6–27, 9:13–18).

Wise men realized that marriages could be marred by personality conflicts and quarrels, and expressed concern for the man who had a garrulous or nagging wife (Prov. 15:17f, 17:1, 19:13, 21:9, 19). There was no solution, except to warn young men to choose a wife carefully and to treat her well.

Children were to be disciplined, raised according to accepted standards. Little respect was accorded to youthful insights (22:15).

Table manners were taught, with emphasis on proper social conduct in the home of the wealthy and powerful (23:1–8). Young men were warned against associating with those considered troublemakers, social misfits, drunkards, or gluttons.

The wisdom of Agur, son of Jakeh of Massa, demonstrates that not everyone accepted the validity of revelatory myths without question (Prov. 30:1–6). Agur was a skeptic. He began in mock humility:

> Surely I am more brutish than human and am without human understanding.
> I am not schooled in wisdom nor in the knowledge of the sacred.

He then taunted the wise men about their claims to know revealed wisdom:

> Who has gone up to heaven and come down again?
> Who has gathered the wind in his fists?
> Who has bound the waters in a garment?
> Who has determined the ends of the earth?
> What is his name? And what is his son's name? Surely you know!

The response of the wise men to his challenge was to recite the tradition:

> Every word of God is certain. He is a shield to those who trust him.
> Do not add to his words lest he reprove you and you are found to be a liar.

The skeptic asked only two things: honesty or integrity and his daily bread. He sought no extremes of wealth or poverty.[48]

Job.   During the late sixth century B.C., an unknown Jewish wise man living in exile in Babylon struggled with the issue of theodicy, the balance between sin and suffering. He reworked the old dramatic story of Job to convey his thoughts. The setting is introduced in the prose prologue, which alternates between scenes in heaven and situations on earth. Job is presented as a righteous wise man who accepted without question the accepted traditional mythic lore and who never deviated from, but piously fulfilled, all social and cultic responsibilities. Indeed, in his caution he often went beyond legal requirements. Job had been rewarded by Yahweh with wealth, fame, power, position, respect, and a healthy, happy family. However, Job was unaware of the conversations in heaven between Yahweh and one of his sons, The Satan. The Satan had wagered that once Job was deprived of wealth and family, he would curse his god. Job lost his children and possessions, but did not curse the god.

Then the Satan wagered that if Job himself were personally afflicted with bodily suffering, he would utter curses. The main body of the writing deals with Job's struggle with the problem of theodicy, in the depth of his losses and his physical misery. He knew that he was innocent of wrongdoing and could not understand what had happened to him. Although he cried out to know from his god what he had done to deserve such treatment, Job still did not curse Yahweh.

Three counsellors or wise men were introduced by the Jewish author as foils for Job's argument. These men were persuaded that the revealed tradition was unchallengeable, that sin produced punishment and suffering, and that Job therefore must have sinned. Eliphaz observed, "I have seen that those who plow sin and sow trouble reap the same" (Job 4:8). Bildad suggested that because God could not pervert justice, Job's children must have sinned, and thus they were justly eliminated (8:3–4). Zophar argued that Job was being punished less than he deserved (11:6). When Job, who knew that he was innocent and who felt no guilt, responded with hostility to these innuendos, Eliphaz replied with the platitude that no man could be clean before God (15:14f).

After three cycles of speeches, the deity interceded. At no point did he answer Job's query, What lies behind the misery? Instead, the deity flaunted his power, his majesty, his unfathomable wisdom, his control of the mysteries of the universe. Before such a magnificent verbal display, Job was silenced. Because he could not fathom the complexities of the topocosm, he was made to feel that he could not presume to question divine action that affected him personally. The epilogue provides what students have labeled a "Hollywood ending": everyone lives happily ever after. Job's fortunes are restored, he produces a new family of seven males and three females, and the wise men are reprimanded.

Although Job never learned of the factors that brought on his suffering, the reader knows, for he has been privy to the heavenly conversations. He knows that Job had done nothing to invite disaster, nothing to offend the god, unless being a model of pious obedience could be said to constitute a challenge. What was the author of this dramatic narrative trying to convey? We believe that he was saying that the convenient formula— disobedience to the revealed will of Yahweh brought punishment and obedience resulted in reward—did not always work, that the pious tradition did not account for every situation, that in reality men could not always know why certain things occurred as they did (although the author did not question that all things occurred because of divine will). Just as the complexities of any topocosm defy simplistic answers, so the problems of human suffering are more complex than a mythic formula.

In the face of inability to comprehend his life situation, what could a man do? The answer is clear: do as Job did—keep the faith! In good times and bad, in health and sickness, man must not waver in faith and loyalty to Yahweh. Men may not understand why the righteous suffer and the wicked prosper; those issues belong to the deity. They can only remain steadfast in the knowledge that Yahweh is just and that, optimally, periods of tribulation pass and blessings follow.

Ecclesiastes (Qoheleth). Shortly after the writing of the Job story, another document, Ecclesiastes, suggested a different approach to life. Like the epic of Gilgamesh, the book of Ecclesiastes relates the life of a famous king, in this instance Solomon, king of Israel. Ecclesiastes reflects the same fruitless search for meaning and identity as that found in the Gilgamesh epic, and the same basic philosophy about how to live life.

Solomon was a tenth century B.C. monarch of the United Kingdom of Israel and Judah. His reputation for wisdom, for buildings, for trade and commerce, and for multiple marriages is preserved in 1 Kings 1–11. Various legends grew up around him, and during the last decades of the fourth century or the early years of the third century B.C., while Alexander the Great and his successors were in control of the Near Eastern world, Ecclesiastes was written. The writer posed as Solomon in his old age, reflecting on the past and evaluating the accomplishments of his life. He has become the culture hero, the wisdom giver, stressing the emptiness of great achievements and the importance of small personal pleasures.

The writer assumed the name Qoheleth, which seems to refer to one who calls together or administers or lectures to an assembly, a school, a congregation, a council, or perhaps a nation. His thesis, that there is no ultimate meaning in anything that exists or in anything that man does, is clear from his opening cry of *hebel. Hebel* is popularly translated as "vanity," but its real meaning is "vapor" or "breath"; what Qoheleth is saying is that everything is like vapor, unsubstantial and void of meaning. The seasonal cycles, life and death, work and play, are ultimately meaningless. Nevertheless, like Gilgamesh, Qoheleth found himself involved in a quest for meaning and identity, able to indulge in experiences not always available to most people.

First, Qoheleth sought wisdom and understanding by the amassing knowledge, a path never explored by Gilgamesh. He found only frustration. Indeed, when he realized that the wise man and the fool have the same end—death—there seemed to be little sense or value in struggling for wisdom.[49]

Having achieved wisdom, Qoheleth next embarked on a mad search for identity through pleasure by creating buildings, gardens, and pools, acquiring possessions, and indulging in wine and women. Soon he realized that his creations would be inherited by others who might not appreciate or respect what he had accomplished. The way of possessions and the desperate search for physical satisfaction were therefore also void of meaning.

His search brought despondency, as he contemplated foolish pursuits and competition among men. What, then, is man to do? How is he to live? Like the barmaid in the Gilgamesh epic, Qoheleth observes:

> There is nothing better for a man
> Than he should eat and drink
> And find enjoyment in his work.

Qoheleth evaluated the accepted standards for living. He dismissed progress through rivalry and hard work: "One handful gained quietly is better than two handfuls acquired by toil and racing after the wind." He judged worthwhile friendship and family ties. Obviously, it was better to be wise than to be a fool, although ultimately it does not matter. He warned against the folly of offending God, suggesting that instead of zeal, piety, or indifference in religious obligations, one should simply do what was necessary. Qoheleth would never have indulged in the reckless insults which Enkidu and Gilgamesh hurled against Ishtar.

Qoheleth observed that certain attributes more than others are apt to produce contentment and joy. For example, a good name and wisdom with an inheritance are desirable. But some negative factors also have value. Sorrow in the house of mourning is a reminder that death comes to all. Reproof from a wise man (which is ultimately meaningless) is certainly better than praise from a fool (which is obviously meaningless). To be alive is better than to be dead. In the grave, all men are equal—both good and evil, wise and foolish. Qoheleth advised his hearers to live life joyously in youth, to seize each day and to drain each moment, for with old age come physical infirmities, and the potential for enjoyment fades.

There is a quiet fatalism in Qoheleth's thinking, a resigned acceptance of what cannot be changed (such as the natural order). He did not indulge in arguments about justice, about the differences of wealth and poverty, but simply acknowledged that God ordained things as they are. He deplored misuse of power. Ultimately, he questioned whether life is worth the struggle for prestige, possessions, wealth, and wisdom: "What has man to show for all his trouble and work during his brief lifetime under the sun?" The answer is, clearly, nothing. Things, position, and power are futile. An attitude of calm acceptance and an openness to the sweet pleasures of food, drink, associations, and opportunities for enjoyment are commendable. Ultimately, death ends all human endeavors and efforts. The value of life is the joy of living, not the futile search for meaning, for there is no meaning. " 'Emptiness, emptiness, all is empty of meaning,' says Qoheleth."

ZOROASTRIAN MYTH

Between the sixth and fourth centuries B.C., Persia dominated the Near Eastern world. From Persia, Zoroastrian mythology flowed to other parts of the world. Certain Zoroastrian mythic themes entered Judaism and were given a Jewish interpretation.

Zoroastrians developed a myth of cosmic dualism. Ahura Mazda was the supreme god (according to Zoroaster, the founder, the only god), from whom came all the good and positive factors: wisdom, light, and truth. Evil principles emerged from Ahriman, the opposing spirit, the symbol of darkness and the lie. These two counter-forces became personified and their attributes became personalities—opposing angelic and demonic identities, part of heavenly versus satanic hierarchies. Surrounding Ahura Mazda were Good Thought, Correct Action, Wisdom, Piety, Salvation, and Immortality. Among the opposition were Evil Thought or Deceit, Pride, Disease, Irreverence, and Desecration.

The struggle between the conflicting forces was manifested in nature in the ebb and flow of seasons, in light versus darkness, in the sown land versus the desert, in life versus death. Men were also involved. Each man was free to choose which side he would support. Every act and thought expressed the individual's allegiance. Zoroastrian myth called men to a life of rigid discipline in support of the good. It recognized the continuing pressure on each individual by the cohorts of Ahriman, but promised that light, truth, and good would ultimately triumph in a final conflict and that the followers of Ahura Mazda would be rewarded. All men would be judged. The wise followers of truth would cross the Separation Bridge to the realm of the righteous, the house of song, the dwelling place of good thought. There they would behold the divine throne of Ahura Mazda. The foolish followers of the lie went to the house of the lie, the place of evil thought, to dwell throughout the ages in darkness, misery, and suffering.

Zoroastrianism thus offered a solution to the thorny problem of theodicy. By projecting rewards and punishments into an afterlife, it gave meaning to the apparently meaningless suffering of the righteous. One

Jewish book, Daniel, written during the persecutions by Antiochus IV in the second century B.C., accepted and used other-world mythology like that of Zoroastrianism. The forces of good on earth were the pious Jews who, despite persecution, followed the precepts of Judaism. The faithful would enjoy the kingdom of Yahweh after the final cosmic battle. Those who had died before the end-time would be resurrected. The writer of Daniel believed that the end-time was at hand.

JEWISH SECTS

During the post-Persian Greek and Roman periods and just before the Christian era, Judaism divided into several sects. In Jerusalem, the temple cult, with its emphasis on sacrificial rituals, was under the control of the aristocratic, conservative Sadducees. These priests, deeply concerned about religious survival, became involved in high-level politics with the Romans, who controlled the country. The Sadducees were committed to freedom, independence, and a theocratic state, as were most Jews, but they viewed themselves as realists so far as cooperation with the Romans was concerned. They stressed observance of Jewish law, but were not particularly troubled by foreign influence in Jewish society. They retained the traditional Jewish belief that divine rewards and punishments were experienced in this life, not in some mythical afterlife.

The Pharisees were laymen, committed to a purified Judaism marked by meticulous observance of moral and ceremonial law. They supported the temple and temple ritual, but were most intimately associated with the synagogues, where local Jewish congregations gathered to pray and to study Jewish scripture. The Pharisees, strongly affected by mythical themes developing from Zoroastrianism, had developed their own myths about the resurrection of the dead and the rewards and punishments to be experienced in a life beyond death. Alliances with foreigners were viewed with suspicion; the Pharisees struggled against foreign influence in Jewish life.

The headquarters of the Essene sect appears to have been the communal center discovered in 1947 at Qumran on the shores of the Dead Sea. The Essenes withdrew from Jewish society to fulfill the Torah requirements in accord with the interpretation of their leader, whom they called "The Teacher of Righteousness." The organization was a highly structured hierarchy governed by strict rules. The Essenes believed that the kingdom of God was at hand and that it would be ushered in by a climactic battle between the sons of light and truth (themselves) and the sons of darkness. The sons of light were marshaled under an angel or spirit of light—perhaps the Jewish angel Michael; the sons of darkness were under the angel of darkness, Belial. Naturally, the myth placed God on the side of light and truth and projected an ultimate victory over the sons of darkness. In the interim before the final cataclysm, the children of light—the Qumran people—although afflicted by the sons of darkness, were given strength to resist by God. The Qumranites were convinced that they were right and the rest of the world, including the other sects of Judaism, were wrong. They were the sons of light; others were under the shadow of darkness.

Ben Sira's Wisdom

Ben Sira, a Jewish sage of the second century B.C., directed a wisdom or scribal school that continued to reinforce Jewish societal mythology.[50] Many of his teachings echo the attitudes of Proverbs, counseling obedience to the law, trust in Yahweh, patience, and subservience to important persons, and noting the benefits derived from aiding the poor. Ben Sira warned his students against recklessness in speech, deceit, slander, and ridicule, and against showing partiality and trusting enemies. He urged them to cultivate social graces, pleasant voices, and friends who were more than table companions—intelligent individuals with insight. The students were also warned against the dangers inherent in becoming involved with loose women, virgins, and female singers.

Young people were to honor their parents, Ben Sira taught, because honoring one's father atoned for sin (Sir. 3:3, 14). To anger one's mother was to be cursed by God (3:16). Children were to serve their parents as masters; parents should chastise their sons regularly and severely:

> The man who loves his son will beat him often
> So that he may be glad about the way he turns out. . . .
> The man who spoils his son will bind up his wounds
> and he will be troubled by every cry. . . .
> Beat his sides when he is young (30:1–13)

Ben Sira expressed grave concern about a daughter's chastity: "If you have daughters be concerned for their bodies (chastity)" (7:24).

> Keep strict watch over a headstrong daughter. . . .
> Keep watch over her roving eye
> And don't be surprised if she offends you.
> As a thirsty traveler opens his mouth
> And drinks from any water at hand
> So she will squat by every doorpost
> And open her quiver to the arrow (26:10–12)

Ben Sira's thesis that individual life-styles developed from individual choices was similar to the teachings of Zoroastrianism:

> It was he (God) who created man in the beginning
> and left him in the power of his own inclination.
> If you want to you can keep the commandments
> and acting faithfully is a matter of your personal choice.
> Fire and water are set before you,
> Reach out for whichever you desire.
> Life and death are before each man
> and whichever he chooses will be given to him. . . .
> He (God) has not commanded anyone to be ungodly
> and he gave no one permission to sin. (15:15–20)

Ben Sira believed that societal patterns were divinely revealed and that although each individual was free to accept or reject the revealed way, violation of the divine pattern would bring judgment.

CHRISTIAN MYTH

Christianity began as a sect of Judaism. Like members of other Jewish sects, the Christians accepted traditional Jewish scripture and composed religious documents of their own. The New Testament, a product of the early Christian community, includes mythic societal patterns that reflect motifs found in some of the earlier societies we have discussed. For example, the Gospel of Matthew portrays Jesus in the role of a new Moses. Like Moses, Jesus came out of Egypt—in Jesus' case, after a flight to avoid persecution and death. Like Moses, he proclaimed societal law from a mountaintop—the Mount of Beatitudes (Matt. 5)—and thereby laid the foundation for a new Israel. In the Gospel of John, Jesus is described as an incarnate deity, just as the Egyptian pharaoh was—the divine dwelling among men, the sacred in the midst of the profane. Unlike pharaoh, Jesus' divinity was neither recognized nor accepted during his lifetime. In some respects, the Johannine gospel parallels the ideas found in Egyptian Ptah myths, with its emphasis on the divine word or *logos* (John 1). Like the Pharisees, the early Christians accepted a messianic mythology, only they claimed that Jesus was the messiah who had come and would return to establish his kingdom. Like the Persians and the Qumran believers, Christians developed an eschatological mythology promising rewards and punishments in an afterlife, the ultimate destruction of the existing world, and a miraculous creation of a new world from which all but Christians would be excluded. Moreover, early Christian myth and ethics seem to have been directly affected by the conviction that the end of the existing world was at hand. This conviction added a note of urgency to societal standards, some of which seem harsh.

In his mountaintop pronouncement, Jesus claimed that certain persons should be happy in the belief that their behavior had divine approval and would earn divine blessings: the poor in spirit, the mourners, the meek, the sufferers for and seekers after righteousness, the merciful, the pure, the peacemakers, and those reviled for their Christian faith. Jesus' social regulations not only reinforced certain Jewish legal concepts, but exceeded some of them in severity. Anger and insult were the equivalent of murder. To look at a woman lustfully was to commit adultery, and the thought appears to have been condemned as heartily as the act. Divorce, except on grounds of adultery, was prohibited, and marriage to a divorced woman was adultery. Deeds of kindness were to exceed the accepted norms, but acts of personal piety should not be performed to gain public approval.

As the Christian movement spread into the Mediterranean world, Jewish food laws and the circumcision requirement were relaxed (see Galatians). Because Christian groups were composed of persons of varied social status and national background, the concept of community tended to be fluid and nondiscriminatory. Relationships within Christian families were to be characterized by love and kindness.

Nevertheless, there were clear status lines. Women continued to be treated as inferior. They were reminded that according to Jewish mythology, woman was created from man. A wife was to be subject to her husband (Col. 3:18; 1 Peter 3:1–6), who was recognized as the head of the household (Eph. 6). Her function was to bear and rear children (1 Tim. 5:14). In church, women were to remain silent (1 Cor. 14:34–36). Church offices held by women tended to be secondary, characterized by service rather than by leadership. 1 Timothy 2 states the position of women in the church succinctly:

> Women must dress appropriately, modestly and sensibly, without fancy hair-dos and not in gold or pearls or costly clothes, but in good deeds as is appropriate for women professing piety. A woman must listen quietly and with submissiveness. I do not permit a woman to teach or to have authority over men. She must keep quiet. For Adam was created first, then Eve, and it wasn't Adam who was deceived, it was the woman who was beguiled and who fell into sin. But she will be saved through childbearing, if she continues in faith and love and holy living with modesty.

Christian teaching did not challenge slavery. Within the Christian community, slaves were recognized as spiritual equals with their masters, but in everyday living they were not social equals.

The few New Testament passages that touch on sexual themes denigrate sexual relationships outside marriage with strong labels: "immoral," "impure," "licentious," "evil desire," and so on (1 Cor. 5:1–7:39; Col. 3:5–8; Eph. 5:5). Even sex within marriage seems to have been thought of as passion that required control. Paul warned his congregation of the dangers associated with sexual passion that might arise during periods of abstinence. Perhaps the virgin birth mythology and the celibacy of both Jesus and Paul contributed to the attitude. Certainly, Paul expressed the wish that everyone could be unmarried, as he was. Homosexuals and prostitutes were unacceptable in the Christian community unless they changed their sexual habits. Those who associated with prostitutes were believed to have defiled themselves (1 Cor. 6:16). The Gospel of Matthew makes it clear that Jesus was sired not by Joseph, but by the "Holy Spirit," who "came upon" Mary and impregnated her. The account provides the basis for the mythical virgin birth, but its implication is clear: Jesus was not the child of Joseph. The Christian church defended Mary against the charge of sex outside of wedlock and Jesus against the label "bastard," but in so doing passed an opportunity to open doors of acceptance to children who were socially unaccepted because their parents were not married and to women who were labeled and castigated because they became pregnant outside marriage.

The tragic arrest, sentencing by a Roman court, and death of Jesus were given mythic significance by Christian interpreters. They held that Jesus' death was required by the deity to expiate for sin. The mystical quality of blood sacrifice released the believer from sin. What is most startling is the rather ugly mythic image of the god engaging in child sacrifice, a practice that the Jews had abandoned centuries earlier. According to the myth, Jesus was the son of God, a divine person—through *logos* mythology in 1 John, virgin birth mythology in Luke and Matthew, or some form of adoptional mythology in Mark. The death of Jesus, the son of God, was essential for the removal of sin. The rewards accruing to those who believed in Jesus would be paid in a mythic afterworld which, according to Paul, was very close at hand (1 Thess. 4:13–18). The descriptions in the book of Revelations of John reveal that only Christians would enter the divine kingdom and receive the rewards; nonbelievers would be punished and destroyed.

MONOTHEISM MYTH

Early Hebrew mythology was monolatrous; that is, the Hebrews believed in their own god, Yahweh, but did not deny the reality or existence of other gods. This belief is clearly expressed in the Deuteronomic code, which received its present form during the late seventh and early sixth centuries B.C. It commanded individual Hebrews, "You shall have no other gods beside me" (Deut. 5:7). The cultic recitation stated, "Yahweh is our god, Yahweh alone . . ." (Deut. 6:4).[51]

During the late sixth century, when King Cyrus of Persia was assuming control of the ancient Near East, a Jewish writer, exiled in Babylon, proclaimed Yahweh as the only god and dismissed all other deities as meaningless. His poetry, which became attached to the book of Isaiah and which comprises at least chapters 40 through 55 of that book, rises to lyrical heights in his exaltation of Yahweh as the sole deity. The antecedents of this new mythology cannot be determined for sure. The recommendation of the prophet Jeremiah to the exiled Jews may have been influential, for in a letter, Jeremiah advised them that they had been placed under foreign control for a definite time period, after which they would be rescued. Certainly, the implications in the letter concerning Yahweh's control and the possibility of worshiping Yahweh while in the land controlled by Marduk of Babylon may have stimulated the development of monotheistic thinking.[52] Perhaps Zoroastrian dualism was filtering into the exiled Jewish community, helping to push Jewish mythology toward monotheism. In any event, from the late sixth century, monotheism entered Jewish thought and became a unique feature of Judaism and the heritage of Christianity and the Western world.

The mythic implications of monotheism were dramatic. First, the multiplicity of gods accepted throughout the Near East was challenged by the unification of all divine processes into one. It was far simpler to recognize one divine cause, one divine law, one divine principle controlling the cosmos, and to address worship to that single deity. The confusion of gods and goddesses became a subject of derision by the Jews and later by the Christians as they pressed out into the Greco-Roman world. Confused mortals, beset by the turmoils of life, were no longer in the plight of the Babylon worshiper who did not know which god he had offended; for Jews and Christians there was only one, a father-creator, who was responsible for the entirety of the cosmos. All worship was directed toward him.

However, the proclamation of monotheism also introduced problems. If there was but one deity, how could Jews and Christians sustain their mythical superiority? Were not all humans creations of the deity? The answer was given in Jewish tradition and later in Christian interpretation of that tradition. Jews were chosen as revealers of the "way of Yahweh"; they were Yahweh's "witnesses," "a light to the nations."[53] Christians, possessing a new revelation through Jesus, saw themselves in something of the same light, and to the Greco-Roman world proclaimed allegiance to one god and salvation through Jesus.

Monotheism also accentuated the problem of theodicy, the justice of the deity. If the one god was good, how to account for the presence of evil by which man was damned? If the one god was just, why did innocent people suffer? Traditionally, Yahweh had been responsible for both the good and the evil that befell his people; good resulted from obedience, evil from disobedience. The suffering of the innocent could be explained by the idea of corporate personality, whereby the sins of the fathers were visited on the children. Now the concept of an anti-god developed, stimulated, no doubt, by Persian dualism. The anti-god or demonic power was variously called Belial, Semaja, Azazel, Lucifer, and Satan, as well as other names. Most present-day Jews do not believe in a devil, but many Christian groups accept the doctrine. Demonic forces were not new in the ancient Near East, but with the centralizing of the concept of the deity into a single figure and the giving of that figure the attributes of goodness, justice, and mercy, it became important to embody the power of evil in a single image. Thus, the mythology of monotheism helped to develop the concept of the devil.

Despite modern mythic proclamations of belief in a single, universal deity, most Western religious organizations continue to operate on the ancient mythic basis of a national or a denominational god. United States citizens describe themselves as "one nation, under God" and imprint on their coinage, "In God we trust." The emphasis appears to be on *this* people under God and trusting in the deity, as opposed to other nations that may or may not be under the same deity and that may or may not trust in him. "We" are on God's side and God is on ours. The British sing "God save our gracious Queen"—not some other ruler. Canadians sing "May Heaven bless the Maple Leaf forever"—not the emblem of some other nation. Each nation sees itself in the mythic context of being uniquely "under God."

The mythic idea is particularly pertinent in time of war. The ancient concept of the holy war, desired, supported, and empowered by the god, who actually participated in battles, has faded, but not completely disappeared.[54] In ancient times, the enemy was the enemy of god as well as of the people. The ways of the enemy were contrary to the revealed ways of the national god, his mythic concepts and rituals odious to those who embraced the national myths and performed the local rituals. The enemy was "bad," "wrong," or "evil." Battles assumed the dimensions of truth versus falsehood, light versus darkness, good versus evil, the forces of order versus those of chaos. Some of the imagery was no doubt related to cosmogonic myths and rituals.

It is only a short step from a holy war to a just war. The definition of what is "just" is vague; those who use the word present it in broad, generally approved social terms. The battle is against enemies who have demonic dimensions. We need only review the depiction of Japanese soldiers in films produced during World War II to see how the enemy was portrayed as something close to nonhuman. Ancient mythic cosmic battle imagery was resurrected. Instead of wearing masks or costumes to depict creatures such as Tiamat, the Japanese were shown with evil, cruel, demonic expressions on their faces. Early in the Vietnam War, the enemy became "gooks." It was easy to understand that there must be moral and social merit in eliminating "gooks" from the world, for the term conveys the image of something less than human.

Before battle, chaplains pray for the soldiers, not for the enemy. The enemy, not our soldiers, commits atrocities. When American military men were charged with violent, unnecessary killing of helpless civilians, many Americans could not believe the accusations. President Nixon defended Lieutenant Calley.[55] There was little outcry against such acts from religious organizations. The mythic concepts of the just war, of soldiers of light versus soldiers of darkness, of right versus wrong, condition social responses. The universal god concept is forgotten.

Nor does the mythic idea of a single god really function among religious communities. The attitude of one God with many avenues of approach to him operates more in theory than in practice, despite the trend toward ecumenism and interfaith cooperation. In 1959, Pope John XXIII modified the Roman Catholic "Good Friday" prayer, which had included the formula, "Let us pray for the *perfidi* Jews" (*Oremus pro perfidi Judaeis*). The term *perfidi,* which referred to nonbelieving Jews, had come to imply perfidy or treachery. The prayer now reads, "Let us pray for the Jews." On the other hand, in prayer, the religious Jew congratulates himself on not being a *goy* —a non-Jew, and the prayer also congratulates the male Jew on not being a woman.

Tighter money and the overnight development of "planned communities" has necessitated a functional ecumenism among the larger Protestant denominations. Developers set aside space for only one or two churches, and denominational leaders meet to decide which particular branch of Protestantism will locate in which community. The older pattern, in which small communities often had four competing churches located on the four corners of the central intersection, is disappearing, and there is a flow of membership between the cooperating denominations. But many communions discourage change of membership, and some require liturgical rites of acceptance for those coming from other denominations, such as rebaptism by immersion rather than by sprinkling.

Intermarriage between members of most Protestant denominations is widely accepted, but not between Catholics and Protestants or Christians and Jews. Some Christians find Jews deficient by their failure to recognize Jesus as Messiah, and Catholics consider Protestants outside the "true" church.[56] Jewish opposition to mixed marriages is related to concern for the survival of the Jewish culture: marriages between Jews and non-Jews tend to weaken the community, because many Jews involved in such alliances ignore their heritage and fail to transmit it to their children. Most clergymen discourage interfaith marriages; many will not officiate them. In June 1973, the Central Conference of American Rabbis (Reformed), meeting in Atlanta, Georgia, voted to oppose rabbis performing mixed marriages. A week later, the Rabbinical Council of America met in Fallsburg, New York, and agreed to pressure Jewish secular and religious organizations to exclude from leadership both those who officiated at such marriages and those who engaged in them. A few days afterward, the New York Board of Rabbis, which includes Reform, Conservative, and Orthodox rabbis in the Metropolitan New York area, declared that their membership was open only to "rabbis who neither officiate at nor make referrals to rabbis who officiate at mixed marriages." Those who perform mixed marriages usually require the "outsider" to take a brief course of study in the faith of the "insider" or require a commitment by the outsider that there will be no interference with the insider's cultic performance and belief and that any children will be raised in the faith of the insider. Students who have interviewed clergy find that the emphasis on a single deity is almost always absent from the conversation.

The result of the adamant position against interfaith marriages and against those who do not conform to doctrinal positions and concepts is exclusion from what many conceive of as their "heritage." Many Jews believe that a child is automatically a Jew if its mother was Jewish. To deny the individual the resources of Judaism in marriage and burial is a form of excommunication. The same can be said for Catholic and Protestant groups that function in the same way. On one hand are those who are convinced that by performing interfaith weddings, the clergy or the religious communion sanctions such marriages and makes them equal to infaith marriages. On the other hand, those who seek clergy to perform interfaith services experience excommunication and rejection because they dare to love someone outside their faith. For the Jew, such excommunication signifies a denial of the heritage into which he was born and which no one should be able to deny him. On both sides there are deep convictions, deep emotions, and often deep hostilities. In Israel, Rabbi Schlomo Goren, chief rabbi for Ashkenazi (Western) Jews, approved the marriages of an Israelis brother and sister who had been considered outcasts according to Orthodox interpretation of ancient Jewish law because their mother had not been divorced from her first husband according to Jewish law (the children were considered to be *mamzerim*—bastards; see Deut. 23:2). The rabbi came under extensive condemnation and was physically attacked by four young men.[57]

Roman Catholics born and raised during the first half of the twentieth century were trained in the Baltimore Catechism and taught to recite, "We know that the Catholic Church is the one true Church established by Christ because it alone has the marks of the true Chruch."[58] Obviously, all other churches and faiths were considered less than "true." Since Vatican II, there has been what can only be called a superficial ecumenism. The Vatican II Decree on Ecumenism noted with regard to other Christian churches that "the Spirit of Christ has not refrained from using them as a means of salvation which derive their efficacy from the very fulness of grace and truth entrusted to the Catholic Church."[59] That same decree also stated, "For it is through Christ's Catholic Church alone, which is the all-embracing means of salvation, that the fulness of the means of salvation can be attained. It was to the apostolic college alone, of which Peter is the head, that we believe our Lord entrusted all the blessings of the New Covenant, in order to establish on earth the one Body of Christ into which all those should be fully incorporated who already belong in any way to God's people."[60] Obviously, other denominations supposedly lack fullness. The myth proclaims Roman Catholic superiority; union with others is possible only if they merge into the "true church."

A group that believes itself superior obviously tries to persuade others of its superiority. Missionary efforts at conversion are proper procedures for the in-group, but often offensive to those who constitute the target. Where religious organizations are in a majority and can affect government attitude, proselytizers and converts can encounter rough opposition. Where no such power structure exists, the group under pressure may react in other ways. In 1972, the Associated Synagogues of Massachusetts, reacting against the influence of a conversion-minded group known as Jews for Jesus, stated that a Jew who converted to Christianity betrayed his people and forfeited his rights to be married to a member of the Jewish faith, to be a member of a Jewish congregation, and to be buried in a Jewish cemetery.[61]

Nor does the myth of a single god function in interracial relationships. In recent years, there has been a movement away from all-white, all-black, all-Oriental schools and communities toward integration. But until 1967, when the Supreme Court ruled them invalid, antimiscegenation laws were still on the books of many States. Marriage between races is still discourged by clergy who proclaim one God. Sometimes they invoke prejudicial myths of racial superiority, but more often the basis for the objection is the "social difficulties" encountered by interracial couples. Belief in a single God does not necessarily imply belief in social equality or in the equal worth of every human being—except in theory. In 1972, when Harold B. Lee was chosen president of the three-million-member Church of Jesus Christ of the Latter-day Saints (Mormon), he reaffirmed the church's policy banning blacks from the priesthood on the basis of divine revelation.[62]

Overtones of the mythic relationship between the god and the state can still be discerned.[63] In England, the church–state relationship is openly acknowledged, and the coronation of the ruler is a religious rite replete with ancient mythic pattern. In the United States, the president takes the oath of office holding a Bible, which symbolizes divine power guaranteeing the authenticity of his pledge and perhaps suggests that to be deceitful at such a moment might invoke divine wrath. A battery of clergy recite prayers in English, Hebrew, and Latin to invoke divine blessing on the forthcoming regime, again suggesting the ancient mythic relationship of the state and the deity. A president may also have a personal religious counselor.[64]

The relationship between church and state is also made explicit in religious services. Many churches display national flags. Prayers are offered for the authorities in power and for the nation itself. The constituents of the religious organization believe their ritual utterances capable of persuading the deity to lend power to the government and to reveal his will and intent to the national leaders.

Both church and state are extremely careful to avoid, wherever possible, church–state clashes. Church organizations, such as the National Council of Churches, have Washington offices. Legislators review all proposals to be sure that the sensitivities of religious groups are not going to be affronted by the wording of a bill or by the bill itself. Numerous church lobby groups in Washington, concerned with the moral implications of pending legislation, unite to shape their strategy in the Washington Interreligious Staff Council, composed of about fifty members, which meets every two weeks. House and Senate chaplains not only utter prayers to begin daily sessions, but are also available for counseling members of their legislative "flock."

For the most part, churches support the government. The strong protests against racial discrimination and against the Vietnam War began outside organized religious communities. Indeed, many churches denounced both protests. When the voices of protest continued and public leaders began to take favorable stands, then church and state belatedly joined forces.

FAMILIAL MYTHOLOGY

The nuclear family, consisting of parents and children, continues to be the core of modern Western society. Despite the continuing influence of ancient mythic interpretations, dramatic changes are in process and new forms of "family" are emerging.

Many marriage ceremonies still include the phrase "till death do us part," and many couples deeply in love cannot imagine a time when their feelings might change. Many marriages do last. In 1972, *Life* magazine published the results of a questionnaire related to marriage. Of 62,000 responses, 80 percent rated their marriages "happy" or "very happy." Nevertheless, a high percentage of modern marriages dissolve, and former partners enter into new alliances. Marriage, divorce, remarriage, custody of the children, alimony, half-brothers, half-sisters, former mate, and visitation rights are all part of the modern vocabulary. There seems to be less stability than ever before in love relationships.

Increased mobility of the population and new travel patterns developed by youth broaden contacts between the sexes in manners unforeseen by ancient mythologers. In their time, marriages were within the community, preferably among relatives, so that young women would not be burdened with the curse of singleness and would fulfill their mythic role as mothers. As we have seen, marriage outside blood lines or racial and religious groups was condemned. Today, more and more marriages are between persons from different communities, different parts of the same nation, and even different nations. Religious and racial lines are crossed and recrossed. A comparison of polls taken in 1968 and 1972 indicates a trend toward less intolerance of interracial and interfaith marriages. Approval of marriages between whites and blacks rose from 20 percent to 29 percent, between Jews and non-Jews from 59 percent to 67 percent, and between Catholics and Protestants from 63 percent to 72 percent. Individual cases indicate the lingering resistance to such marriages. For example, in December 1971, an out-of court settlement was reached in a suit brought by a young man (a Baptist) against the father of a young woman (a Jew) who had promised to pay the young man $10,000 if he would stop seeing the daughter and would marry someone else. Unfortunately, the ancient mythic taboos remain, and those charged with the right to perform marriages often refuse to violate the mythic teachings.

Taboos against divorce still exist but are fading in influence.[65] In September 1972, the National Conference of Catholic Bishops reaffirmed their support of Roman Catholic discipline which barred Catholics "who remarry after divorces without church annulment of previous marriages" from participation in the sacraments. Among Muslims, divorce remains a male privilege. A man may divorce his wife simply by repeating three times, "I divorce you"; a woman may also be divorced *in absentia* when her husband declares his intention before a justice of the peace, the wife not even knowing she has been divorced. The Muslim customs are derived from the mythic authority of the Koran. In some countries, such as Brazil, divorce is impossible for any reason. Brazilian marriages may be broken by *desquite,* official separation, but *desquite* is granted only after a couple has been married for two years and then only on grounds of adultery, cruelty, desertion, or slanderous accusations. Neither partner separated by *desquite* is permitted to remarry; consequently, many legally separated persons live with new partners in relationships that have no validity for wills, property ownership, and the like.

Among Christians, the statement attributed to Jesus that divorce should be granted only on the grounds of adultery may still exert some mythic power, but marriages are frequently dissolved for other reasons. To some, a divorce in the family is an embarrassing symbol of failure. When a forty-five-year-old woman finally dissolved a miserable marriage of twenty-five years, her two children, both in their twenties, expressed amazement that she had waited so long. On the other hand, when she visited her parents—both in their late sixties—in the small midwestern town where she had been raised, they asked her to keep her divorce secret to avoid reflecting on the family and embarrassing her relatives.

The concept of the family is changing. Some present-day families consist of one parent and children. Organizations like Parents Without Partners are composed largely of women, because women obtain child custody in about 90 percent of divorce cases. Some of the 10 percent of divorced males who receive custody have formed Fathers Without Partners groups to discuss problems unique to their family structure.

Ancient social pressures to beget large families are losing their power. Some couples do not want any children; others limit the size of their families. Modern contraceptive techniques and liberalized abortion laws make both choices possible. Some couples capable of producing children prefer to adopt orphans and unwanted children. In California, under the 1970 Family Act, foster parents may be awarded custody of a child in preference to the biological parent when such a judgment is deemed to be in the child's best interests. For example, in 1972 three Oakland, California, children, aged eight, nine, and eleven, were awarded to foster parents over the claims of their natural parents. In another case, a girl who had been under the care of a childless couple as a ward of the courts was adopted by the husband after the death of his wife. Nor does the ancient mythic taboo against homosexuality always prevent custody. In 1972, a California court awarded custody of three children to their mother—a lesbian—over the protests of their father, with the stipulation that the mother's association with her female lover was to be limited to times when the children were absent, visiting with their father or at school.

Many couples living together do not believe in the rites and ceremonies, licences, or contracts which would legalize their relationship. They dwell together because they love one another and believe that religious or government documents are meaningless to their relationship. They may encounter some social problems, but more serious problems concern their children's rights. For example, damages have been refused in court cases involving the accidental death of "illegitimate" children, and "illegitimate" children have been denied damages in a case involving negligence in the death of their mother. Inheritance problems may also arise, for example, if the father dies without leaving a will. Even though he had lived with and cared for his "illegitimate" children, some states accord these children and his "unmarried wife" no legal claims. Even in the Social Security system, which provides for children born out of wedlock, there may be discrimination against "illegitimate" children. In Sweden, labels such as "illegitimate" and the prejudices associated with them have been abandoned, but in most Western countries the stigma remains. It would be difficult to assess the continuing impact of biblical mythology on the degrading of such children (see Deut. 23:2; Heb. 12:8). Unwed mothers and their children often experience social and economic pressures, ranging from the hostility of hospital clerks who fill out birth certificates, to difficulty in obtaining coverage from insurance companies or assistance from public services, to rejection as potential employees. In Chicago, an organization called Mothers Alone, Inc. was formed to assist unwed mothers who decided to raise their children by themselves. In most states, when an unwed mother decides to give up her child for adoption, should the father of the child wish to adopt his offspring, he may find that he has no legal rights. In the case of unwed parents, the mother and child form the social unit—the "family." Public announcements by prominent women that they freely choose to be mothers without marrying may ease some of the negative attitude toward fatherless and motherless families.[66]

For the most part, homosexuals are treated by "straight" society as social misfits. Gay bars and churches exist in large cities throughout the United States. Gay churches are usually ministered to by pastors ordained by church officials unaware of their sexual orientation. For example, the Unitarian Universalist Association's Southwest District officially approved the work of a minister as "specialized minister for gay concerns" in 1973. The clergyman had been a minister of the UUA for eight years before publicly acknowledging his homosexual orientation. In 1972, the United Church of Christ in California ordained an avowed homosexual. Opposition to homosexuality, homosexual ministers, and gay churches reflects deep emotional reaction bolstered by mythic authority. Christian opponents usually quote from Paul's letter to the Romans (1:26–27):

For this reason God gave them up to shameful passions. Their women exchanged natural intercourse for unnatural, and their men also gave up natural relations with women and burned with lust for one another, males engaging in indecencies with males and getting in their own persons the proper payment for their perversion.

This and other passages make it clear that homosexuals are without divine approval; thus, the rejection of homosexuals seems justified by societal myth. Still, homosexuals do fall in love and live together. Some formalize their relationship by marriage ceremonies, which have meaning for those involved but are without legal recognition. Despite the lack of legal and social acceptance, this new concept of the "family" has become part of modern society.

Some communal families are composed of a number of men, women, and children, living together and designating their relationship as a "family." Other groups consist of two or more married couples and their children. Income and familial responsibilities are shared. Because sexual relationships are open and sometimes rotational, any children born into the family belong, as do all members, to the total group. In other groups, males or females may predominate numerically, and members may be married, divorced, or single. Communal families may form haphazardly or may develop out of long associations in which personality differences, attitudes, and responses are deeply probed. Ideally, as in any other kind of family, group relationships are characterized by love, concern, and loyalty among members. Studies of communal living patterns indicate that most groups are short-lived, and that the most stable tend to be agrarian.

The decision to beget and bear a child has generally been accepted as a private matter between the two adults involved. The ancient mythic concept of life as a gift of the deity still prevails in some communities, and certainly operates in some arguments against the use of contraceptives. Recently, the issue has taken new form in the matter of legalized abortion. Various church organizations insist that voluntary abortion, except to save the physical life of the mother, violates the biblical prohibition, "Thou shalt not kill."[67] The official Roman Catholic position was stated in mythic terms in the "Pastoral Constitution on the Church in the Modern World" at the Vatican II Ecumenical Council: "For God, the Lord of Life, has conferred on men the surpassing ministry of safeguarding life—a ministry which must be fulfilled in a manner worthy of man. Therefore from the moment of conception life must be guarded with the greatest care, while abortion and infanticide are unspeakable crimes." In 1968, Pope Paul VI issued the encyclical *Humanae Vitae* (concerning human life), forbidding the use of birth control pills or other man-made devices for preventing pregnancy.[68]

Other religious groups have also taken positions on abortion. The Greek Orthodox Archdiocese of North and South America sanctions abortion only when the mother's life is in danger. The Episcopal and Lutheran Churches in America sanction abortion if the mother's life is in danger; if the pregnancy is the result of rape, incest or other felonious acts; or if there is evidence that the child might be born with serious mental or physical defects. Both these groups and others, such as the United Church of Christ, the United Methodist Church, and the United Presbyterian Church, which press for liberalized abortion rulings and the acceptance of abortion as a medical rather than religious problem, base their arguments on the concept of responsible personhood and individual rights, including those of the woman, the unborn child, and other members of the family or families involved.

The Roman Catholic Church expressed deep concern over public opinion polls that indicated that about two-thirds of the American public—including a majority of Catholics—believe that abortion laws should be repealed and that each pregnant woman, in consultation with her doctor and any other counselor she chooses, should be permitted to decide on an abortion. In October 1972, the Roman Catholic Church sponsored a national "Respect for Life Week" to launch widespread support for the anti-abortion position. Although some attention was given to peace and war, poverty, the problems of aging, and the right of individuals to die with dignity, the major thrust of the publicity was against abortion. Roman Catholic handouts declared that "abortion is murder."[69] The Roman Catholic position was lauded by President Nixon, who wrote to Terence Cardinal Cooke, archbishop of New York, speaking of the "defenders of the right to life of the unborn" as engaged in "truly a noble endeavor." The president rejected the recommendations of his Commission on Population Growth, which called for liberalized abortion laws, "particularly when the child's prospects for a life of dignity and self-fulfillment are limited."

Some medical doctors have taken public stands against abortion, providing physiological data to show that the fetus really is a "person" in process.[70] In America, powerful government voices have been raised against liberalized abortion laws. Some people have appealed to the Fourteenth Amendment to the Constitution of the United States, which holds that no state shall "deprive any person of life . . . without due process of law," claiming that the unborn fetus is a "person." The Constitution holds almost the same authority as the law codes of the ancient Near East, which attributed their authority to various gods.

Early in 1973, in a 7–2 decision, the Supreme Court of the United States ruled that women have a constitutional right to abortion during the first six months of pregnancy. During the first three-month period, the decision is left to the patient and her doctor; during the second three months, because of the increase of potential medical complications, such factors as the "preservation and protection of maternal health" must be considered.[71]

Individual state interpretations of and reactions to the ruling varied, and new anti-abortion legislation was immediately projected. That Justice William J. Brennan, Jr., a Roman Catholic, voted with the majority provoked the Society for a Christian Commonwealth, a conservative Catholic lay association, to call for Brennan's excommunication.

In the spring of 1972, two communities adhering to differing societal myths came into conflict. After the ten-month struggle of the Bengalis to secede from Pakistan, hundreds of Bengali women, many in their early teens, who had been raped by Pakistani soldiers, faced the problem of their pregnancies. As Muslims, the Bengalis accepted the local societal mythic norm that once a woman lost her virginity outside marriage, she became a social outcast, no matter who was to blame. Moreover, the woman's family would also suffer economic and social boycott by the community. Married women raped by Pakistanis were cast out by their husbands. The children of the rapes would be unacceptable in local society and would suffer other burdens because they had been fathered by the Pakistani enemy, a people hated and despised by the Bengalis. Nor could the Bengali women solve the problem by entering into hasty marriages, claiming that their children were born prematurely, for their were real possibilities that the children would inherit identifiable Pakistani characteristics, becoming heavier in build and fairer in complexion than the Bengalis. The woman faced a traumatic decision: to have abortions, forbidden by the Muslim faith but which would spare them from ostracism; to bear the children and suffer together with their families and the children the societal pressures; or to commit suicide. The Muslim government of Bangladesh, which opposed abortion on the basis of religious societal myth, nevertheless supported Mrs. Nabi, a Muslim Bengali social worker, in her efforts to abort the unwanted fetuses. But medical personnel, supplies, and accommodations were limited. The largest and best-organized relief organization, the only one with facilities to meet the situation, was operated by the Roman Catholic Church under the direction of Mother Theresa. However, Roman Catholic social mythology forbade abortions. Mother Theresa offered to shelter the women during pregnancy and to arrange for the children to be adopted, possibly in Europe. However, the village people could not run the risk of having neighbors discover the truth. Several hundred of the women died each week by suicide or from self-inflicted abortions. A third group —a team of five trained abortionists from America, England, and India— entered the situation and without proclaiming any specific societal myth, expressing only concern for the pregnant women and their families, performed some 1,500 abortions and introduced to local paramedics simplified but effective methods of medical abortion.

ANCIENT MYTH AND THE ROLE OF WOMEN

One of the most dramatic modern departures from ancient mythic societal concepts is occurring in the role of women. In ancient cultures, the role of women was in terms of wife-mother-housekeeper, an image reinforced with societal myths whose effects ranged from legislation to wisdom teaching, from stories of goddesses such as Isis to divine pronouncements. A woman was "unfulfilled" if she was not married and had not borne children. Biblical women are often pictured as frustrated if they could not produce children for their husbands. For example, Hannah sulked (1 Sam. 1:7) and Sarah, in desperation, gave her maid Hagar to Abraham to bear a son (Gen. 16:2–4). The ideal wife was a homemaker (Prov. 31:10ff). Some women went into business or were active in military forays (Deborah, Judg. 4–5) or espionage (Judith), but by and large the accepted place of the woman was in the home. New Testament teachings encouraged women to think of themselves as inferior to men. Women of Corinth were reminded that they were secondary, made from men for men (1 Cor. 11:8). They were told to keep silent in the churches and to recognize their subordinate rank. Should they wish to know anything, they were to ask their husbands at home (1 Cor. 14:33ff). The husband, not the wife, was the head of the household.

The mythic role of women is reinforced in cultic ritual. Marriage was supposedly blessed by Christ, who attended the wedding in Cana (John 2; Jesus actually participated as a wine-maker). Couples are warned that unions not in accord with mythic doctrine are not really blessed. The bride is given away—like property—by her parents, the change of relationships often characterized by the father placing the bride's hand in the hand of her husband-to-be, just as one would hand over the reins of a horse or the keys of a car. In some marriage ceremonies, the woman still promises "to love, honor, and obey" although the word *cherish* is often substituted for *obey.* The couple are usually united "till death do us part," although some have changed the phrase to "so long as we both shall love." The closing cultic rubrics contain implicit warnings such as "What God has joined together, let no man put asunder."

Acceptance of the ancient patterns is still wide-spread, but the power of the ancient myth is being broken as new roles for the liberated woman emerge. Many women combine the homemaking with a career, refusing to give up the years when their children are small and their "duty" as mother-homemaker "requires" them to be constantly at home with the child. Nursery schools and day care centers release such women to pursue their interests, so that although a small setback in their careers may occur during these years, the effect is not nearly so devastating as it is on women who suddenly discover that their children have grown, their home responsibilities are diminished, and they are without training or background to enter the commercial or professional world.

Numerous marriages are now begun with the understanding that husband and wife will share household responsibilities. Why should the wife be required to clean the bathtub after the husband and children have used it? Why should the wife alone be responsible for preparing food and for housecleaning? Release from sole responsibility for such chores has given women the time and freedom to pursue interests outside the home.

Business and the professions are gradually opening to women on the basis of equal pay for equal work. Women's organizations are winning accession to their demands that discrimination against hiring women for management and professional occupations, including university teaching, be abandoned and that hiring, salary, and promotion for women be on an equal basis with men. The ultimate goal is that women be accepted as equals, as companions rather than as inferiors or second-class household help. The mythic stereotype of divinely and biologically predetermined roles has begun to fade as new life-styles for women emerge.

Some women continue to discover their identity in terms of their husbands' achievements, but this, too, is changing. A number of famous women are known for their creative work. For example, Agatha Christie is acknowledged throughout the world as a magnificent writer of detective stories. Most of her readers are unaware of or not particularly concerned with the career of her husband, the eminent archaeologist M. E. L. Mallowan. Christie is an exception, but the exception may become more and more the rule. The use of *Ms.* to designate a woman without labeling her as married or unmarried is spreading, as many women insist on being accepted for themselves rather than because they happen to be married to a certain individual. The designation gives them the same freedom as *Mr.* gives a man in terms of social relationships.

Sexual myths and the taboos that developed from them are losing influence in some instances and retaining power in others. Some people still consider female virginity until marriage important, but statistics taken among youth indicate that premarital sexual experiences are common and generally accepted as normal.

Ancient myth appears to operate in unperceived ways in cases involving rape. In ancient times, judgment was in the man's favor: if the woman was raped in the city, she was considered guilty, for she might have summoned help; the assumption is that she received what she wanted. The descriptions of woman as seductress, and indeed, Eve's role as the one who violated Yahweh's command in the garden of Eden myth, have created the feeling that a woman who is physically violated has in some way been a willing partner. Surveys have shown that unless the unfortunate woman is bruised and beaten, unless she appears in court in somber clothing, devoid of makeup, and with an air of meekness and humility, she is judged negatively because of her clothing and her physical attractiveness. Moreover, the alleged rapist's attorney often seeks to demonstrate her complicity with such questions as "Did you enjoy the act?" or "Did you resist physically?" Protests that the woman was passive because she feared for her life are mocked, unless it can be proven that a weapon was indeed involved. Of 3,490 cases of forcible rape reported in Los Angeles County in fiscal 1970–71, only 1,380 suspects were arrested, and of these, only 320 were convicted. Of the 320, less than half were sentenced to prison on felony convictions; the remainder negotiated lesser pleas and were sentenced on misdemeanor charges such as fraudulently obtaining money, lewd conduct, or sexual perversion. The FBI estimates that only one rape in ten is reported. The Los Angeles Commission on Assaults Against Women, formed in 1973 by a group of women, established a twenty-four-hour "crisis line" to provide aid and counsel to rape victims.

Myths associated with the menstrual period are fading as more and more men and women come to consider menstruation as a natural body function, neither clean or unclean. Some people still conform to biblical taboos concerning the uncleanness of a woman and the need for refraining from sexual relationships during the menstrual period, but increasing numbers of men and women, liberated from the mythic teachings of more than two thousand years ago, reject such restraints in favor of modern evidence that there is no medical reason why sexual intercourse cannot or should not be performed during the menstrual period. Some may refrain for personal, aesthetic reasons, but such restraints seem to result from social conditioning. Nor do many present-day men and women believe that there is something unclean about the act of intercourse or the semen.

Attitudes toward adultery have not changed perceptibly: sex outside marriage tends to be a secretive affair. The penalties for adultery have changed. Social ostracism, a form of social or economic death, has replaced the physical death prescribed by Hammurabi and others. On the other hand, wife-swapping, "swinger" parties, and other noncommittal forms of sex are accepted and practiced by many married persons as nonthreatening, even enhancing, to the marriage.[72] Incest taboos remain, although a recent French film, "Le Souffle au Coeur" ("Murmur of the Heart"), written and directed by Louis Malle, dealt with the sexual relationship between a mother and son in a tender and understanding manner.

YOUTH AND AGE

Changes in the way in which children are raised have produced important social changes. Some parents still adhere to the guidance of the ancient sages, preferring wisdom such as that of Ben Sira to that of the more modern Ben(jamin) Spock.[73] Such parents reprimand their children regularly to warn them against deviant behavior. Parents influenced by Spock and other modern counselors value the power of love and concern over the power of the rod, seeking to encourage children to express themselves and find their own life-style. As a result, the voice of youth is being heard and heeded throughout the land.

During the 1960s, the cult of youth grew, shattering many long-accepted cultural patterns. The music of youth now dominates radio and television commercials. Youthful hairstyles and beards, once the subject of ridicule, are now common among young and old. With the lowering of the voting age, youth have gained a more powerful voice in government. The Gilgamesh search for whatever retains or renews youthfulness has driven individuals to take up health spas, vitamins, health foods, and encounter groups, among other fads. The impact of youth is felt in almost all social settings.

There is still great concern over "rebellious youth," for the mythic labels remain: the mark of "good" is obedience to the norms; "bad" is deviation. The labels reflect belief in a universal code for judgment, a divinely revealed pattern of good and bad, of "thou shalt" and "thou shalt not." Where the labels are accepted, disobedience produces guilt, which more often than not induces conformity and stifles personal initiative toward change.

There seems to be less tendency to categorize individuals by age, although newspapers still report that "a thirty-seven-year-old woman . . . ," "a nineteen-year-old man . . . ," "John Doe, age 59 . . ." as though the age was important. Elected officials at all levels of government now include men and women who would in other times have been considered too young and immature for office. As officials, they hold equal authority and carry equal weight with other elected authorities, despite age differences. Youthful scientists abound. Marriages between men and women of widely different ages are becoming more common. The moving French film "Mourir d'Aimer" ("To Die of Love"), written and produced by Andre Cayette, is based on a real-life tragedy of the love between a thirty-one-year-old teacher at a Marseilles lycee and her sixteen-year-old male student. Another film, "Harold and Maude," treats the love between a teen-aged male and an eighty-year-old woman.

The pendulum of social attitude about age has swung to a new extreme. In ancient times, youth was made to feel insecure, unimportant, and without wisdom. Old men, and in family settings old women, were persons of importance. Communication was primarily verbal. Only the upper-class elite could read and write. Today, the accumulated knowledge is available to the masses through libraries, film, radio, and television. In ancient times, however, the elders were repositories of experience and tradition. They could look back on their experiences and sift out the essence of life, phrasing their observations in maxims and parables which they transmitted to youth.

Today we react ambivalently to the aged. Some see their guidance as a stumbling block, because the world has moved rapidly through many phases of growth, and the wisdom of the old is perhaps less relevant than before. Computers store and retrieve data, systematically organizing information to project patterns of action. The young and the vigorous are needed for animating the present and forging new models for the future. People retire at sixty-five or before, the assumption seems to be that they have no more to offer to society. Many older persons, isolated in retirement homes and communities, actually deteriorate and wither mentally, physically, and socially. They have been made to feel useless, and the feeling has become a reality. On the other hand, some people believe that useless old age is a mental attitude, that important reminiscences and insights can be gained from the past. Fixity of attitude and life-style are associated with age; some people's patterns of living become frozen very early in life. Others remain flexible and able to accept changes in thought and ways of living without becoming disturbed, critical, antagonistic, or threatened. Thus, the idea of being young or old might be better expressed in terms of how one responds to life, rather than according to the number of times the earth has circled the sun during an individual's lifetime.

History books record events which have affected masses of people. However, archeologists and historians are aware of the frustration associated with the recovery of artifacts or public records without any knowledge of what the item or the official action meant to the people alive at that time. Hammurabi's law code describes Hammurabi as he wanted people to think of him and lists the laws he believed essential to keep order in his land. But what of the people who lived in his time? What did they think about Hammurabi's portrayal of himself as chosen by the gods? How did his laws affect them? Today we have oral history programs: tape recorders permanently store conversations with outstanding poets, performers, government officials, military leaders, Nobel Prize winners, and other famous people. Other data need to be recovered, too: the memories and impressions of those who experienced World War I, the Great Depression, the internment of Japanese, and so on—the "ordinary" citizens. Family data is important so that members of a family can sense their continuity and perhaps gain a deeper awareness of their personhood. The recollections, evaluations, and insights provided by older persons revive older societal patterns in which the experiences and wisdom of the past are accepted as having some relevance for the present and the future.

Despite the teachings in Jeremiah and Ezekiel concerning individual responsibility, and despite the denial of the validity of the proverb, "The fathers have eaten sour grapes, and the children's teeth are set on edge" (Jer. 31:29; Ezek. 18:2), the judgmental pattern remains. The prophets were addressing themselves to a mythic theme—divine justice and divine judgment. Today's societal judgments do not carry the same mythic content. The responsibility of parents for their children is most obvious when the child of a prominent social or government leader becomes embroiled with the police. Newspapers report that "John Doe, the son of . . . ," and thus John and his total family become implicated. If the individual had not been the child of a well-known family, no such pronouncement would have been made. A university professor accused of indecent behavior resigned his post rather than fight the charges, which he stated were not true, because his children were at the point of establishing their professional reputations and he knew that to fight the case publicly would be to involve them indirectly in the scandal, to the detriment of their careers. Mythically, each individual might be said to be judged by the deity and punished or rewarded; socially, the family is affected, and the ancient concept of corporate personality continues to operate.

NOTES

[1] This is clear in the fifteenth century writings of Thomas à Kempis, *De Imitatione Christi.*

[2] "The Moabite Stone" *ANET,* p. 320.

[3] "Nabonidus' Rise to Power" *ANET,* pp. 308ff.

[4] "Lamentation over the Destruction of Sumer and Ur," *ANET,* pp. 611ff.

[5] Lam. 2.

[6] John Wilson, *The Culture of Ancient Egypt* (Chicago: University of Chicago Press, 1951), pp. 236ff.

[7] "Results of a Trial for Conspiracy," *ANET,* pp. 214f.

[8] Adolph Erman, *The Ancient Egyptians* (London: Methuen, 1927; reprint ed., New York: Harper & Row, 1966), pp. 278f. Similar feelings are expressed in the accession hymn of Ramesses IV, *ibid.,* pp. 279f.

[9] John Wilson, "Authority and Law in Ancient Egypt," *Journal of the American Oriental Society,* Supplement 17, "Authority and Law in the Ancient Orient," July–September 1954, 1.

[10] Wilson, *The Culture of Ancient Egypt,* p. 48.

[11] E. A. Wallis Budge, *The Book of the Dead* (New York: University Books, 1960; reprinted from the Medici Society version, 1913), p. 587.

[12]James H. Breasted, *A History of Egypt* (New York: Scribner's, 1905; reprint ed., New York: Bantam, 1964), pp. 104ff.

[13]E. O. James, *Seasonal Feasts and Festivals* (New York: Barnes & Noble, 1961), p. 53.

[14]Margaret Murray, *The Splendor That Was Egypt* (New York: Hawthorne, 1963), pp. 100ff.

[15]For possible identifications, see note 1, p. 415 in *ANET,* where A. Scharff suggests that the king was Wah-ka-Re Khety II of Heracleopolis. For a different identity, see the introductory note on p. 180 of W. K. Simpson, ed., *The Literature of Ancient Egypt* (New Haven, Conn.: Yale University Press, 1972).

[16]A similar point is made in Luke 11:5–13.

[17]John Wilson, in Henri Frankfort et al., *Before Philosophy* (Baltimore: Penguin, 1949), pp. 41f, 45ff.

[18]For a discussion of the cruel injustices and vicious treatment of the helpless common man, see S. N. Kramer, *The Sumerians* (Chicago: University of Chicago Press, 1963), pp. 79ff. Texts relating to the situations are translated on pp. 317ff.

[19]E. A. Speiser, "Authority and Law in Mesopotamia," *Journal of the American Oriental Society,* Supplement 17, "Authority and Law in the Ancient Orient," July–September 1954, 8.

[20]*Ibid.,* p. 9.

[21]"The Edict of Ammisaduqa," *ANET,* p. 526.

[22]*Ibid.*

[23]Speiser, "Authority and Law in Mesopotamia," p. 13.

[24]"Sumerian Laws," *ANET,* p. 525.

[25]"Treaty Between Niqmepa of Alalakh and Ir-dim of Tunip," items 5, 6, 7, *ANET,* p. 531; "Treaty Between Idrimi and Pilliya," *ANET,* p. 532.

[26]For examples, see "Litigation and Inheritance," *ANET,* pp. 543–44, item 7.

[27]Violent punishment for theft is still practiced. For example, in 1972 the Revolutionary Command Council in Libya introduced an Islamic law that states that a thief will lose his right hand and a highway robber his right hand and left leg.

[28]"List of Date Formulae of the Reign of Hammurabi," *ANET,* pp. 269ff., item 31. Compare with the Christian hymn "Onward Christian Soldiers," which states that "Christ, our royal master, leads against the foe."

[29]*ANET,* p. 270, item 37.

[30]An Assyrian marriage contract from the nineteenth century B.C. includes a stipulation that if the bride failed to provide the man with offspring within a two-year period, she would purchase a slave woman to produce a child by him. See "Marriage Contract," *ANET,* p. 543.

[31]*Ibid.,* p. 544.

[32]"A Trial for Murder," *ANET,* p. 542.

[33]See "A Babylonian Theogony," *ANET,* pp. 517f. The text is known only in a late Babylonian version.

[34]"Counsels of Wisdom," *ANET,* p. 426.

[35]"The Words of Ahikar," *ANET,* pp. 427ff. See also R. H. Charles, ed., *The Apocrypha and Pseudepigrapha of the Old Testament* (Oxford: Clarendon Press, 1913), pp. 715–834.

[36]"Man and His God," *ANET,* p. 589; Kramer, *The Sumerians,* pp. 125ff.

[37]"Prayer to Every God," *ANET,* p. 391.

[38]"I Will Praise the Lord of Wisdom," *ANET,* pp. 596ff; W. G. Lambert, *Babylonian Wisdom Literature* (Oxford: Clarendon Press, 1960), pp. 21ff.

[39]"A Pessimistic Dialogue Between Master and Servant," *ANET,* pp. 437f.

[40]The same pattern appears in Gen. 5. By ascribing long lives to ancient heroes, early writers covered long periods of time concerning which they had no information.

[41]*ANET,* pp. 72ff, 503ff; Alexander Heidel, *The Gilgamesh Epic and Old Testament Parallels* (Chicago: University of Chicago Press, 1946; reprinted, 1963); N. K. Sandars, *The Epic of Gilgamesh* (Baltimore: Penguin, 1960).

[42]It is possible that this Hebrew myth is a terse reworking of a Canaanite myth in which El copulates with two women and produces offspring that proceed to devour everything in sight. Unfortunately, the conclusion of the Canaanite myth is lost. For a somewhat different interpretation of this god–human relationship, see the Book of Enoch, Chapter 5.

[43]"The Moabite Stone," *ANET,* p. 320.

[44]For a modern parallel, see Walter Goldschmidt, "The Brideprice of the Sebei," *Scientific American,* July 1973; 74–85.

[45]In more recent times, some biblical interpreters have identified Ham with black-skinned people; thus, the condemnatory myth was and still is directed against blacks. Perhaps the report also accounts for myths of black sexuality. See H. Shelton Smith, *In His Image, But . . . : Racism in Southern Religion, 1780–1910* (Durham, N.C.: Duke University Press, 1972).

[46]The forceful sexual use of one male by another—a form of rape— was viewed by the Assyrians as humiliating and demeaning. Homosexual rape was the kind of treatment to be wished on vassals who dared to violate treaties. See "The Vassal-Treaties of Esarhaddon," *ANET,* p. 540, Item 91(616).

[47]"Marriage Contract of a Former Slave Girl Who Is Subject to *Paramonē,* 420 B.C.," *ANET,* p. 548.

[48]Others questioned the claims of revealed precepts. In the eighth century, the oracles of Isaiah were mocked, scoffers demanding that Yahweh quit threatening and deliver the terrible fate that Isaiah predicted. Only then would they be convinced (Isa. 5:18–19). Two centuries later, Jeremiah faced similar opposition from those who laughed at his oracles and who claimed that Yahweh would do nothing and thus the emptiness of the prophetic word would be disclosed. For those who believed in prophetic oracles, the confusion must have been great when two prophets claiming to speak in the name of Yahweh produced conflicting oracles from the same deity (see Jer. 28).

[49]This attitude would seem to make pointless the motto emblazoned on the philosophy building at the University of Southern California: "Know the truth and the truth shall make you free."

[50]His sayings, known as Ecclesiasticus or The Wisdom of Jesus the Son of Sirach, are included in the Bibles of the Roman Catholic and Eastern Orthodox churches, but placed in the Apocrypha by Protestants and Jews.

[51]Since no verbs are given, variant translations are possible, including "Yahweh our god, Yahweh is one," "Yahweh is our god, Yahweh is one" and that which is most commonly used today, "Yahweh our god is one Yahweh."

[52]Jeremiah 29. See also Psalm 137:4.

[53]Isa. 43:10ff, 48:17f, 49:6, and so on.

[54]In October 1973, Sheik Abdel Halim Mahmoud, the Grand Mufti of Cairo's Al Ashar Mosque, labeled the war with Israel a "jihad" or holy war, and stated that any Muslim country that did not participate would not be in conformity with the teachings of God and his Prophet (UPI report published in the *Los Angeles Times,* Oct. 13, 1973).

[55]Wayne Greenshaw, *The Making of a Hero: The Story of Lieut. William Calley, Jr.* (Louisville, Ky.: Touchstone, 1971); Seymour Hersh, *My Lai 4* (New York: Random House, 1971).

[56]For a sensitive, scholarly statement on the attitude of a Jewish scholar toward Jesus, see Samuel Sandmel, *We Jews and Jesus* (New York: Oxford University Press, 1973).

[57]According to an AP report in the *Los Angeles Times,* Nov. 21, 1972.

[58]*A Catechism of Christian Doctrine: Revised Edition of the Baltimore Catechism, #2,* lesson 12, item 153.

[59]Walter M. Abbott, ed., *The Documents of Vatican II* (New York: Herder & Herder, 1966), p. 346.

[60]*Ibid.*

[61]Various newspaper reports have noted the tensions created by the Jews for Jesus movement, both in the United States and Israel. See Kenneth Turan, " 'Jews for Jesus' Fly in the Face of Orthodoxy," *Los Angeles Times,* Nov. 16, 1972; Harry Trimborn, "Christian Missionaries Pose Israeli Dilemma," *Los Angeles Times,* Feb. 26, 1973.

[62]*Los Angeles Times,* July 8, 1972.

[63]There are practical advantages to the relationship, so far as the Church is concerned. For example, the Church, with its various properties and other holdings, is exempted from taxation. Nino Lo Bello, in *Vatican U.S.A.* (New York: Trident, 1973), has estimated that the Roman Catholic Church is exempted from taxes on holdings valued at $44.5 billion each year. The tax exemptions for other Christian and Jewish religious organizations are proportionately large.

[64]For analysis of the ties between President Richard M. Nixon and the Rev. Billy Graham, see Lowell D. Streiker and Gerald S. Strober, *Religion and the New Majority* (New York: Association Press, 1972), and Charles P. Henderson, Jr., *The Nixon Theology* (New York: Harper & Row, 1972).

[65]Instant divorce became available in Sweden in January 1974, when the twelve-month waiting period was abolished. The new laws also permitted persons over eighteen to marry without parental consent, and sanctioned marriages between half-brothers and -sisters.

[66]Carole Klein, *The Single Parent's Experience* (New York: Walker, 1973).

[67]This was the opinion expressed by the Southern California Orthodox Presbyterians at a presbytery meeting in 1972. On numerous occasions, Pope Paul VI has declared that abortion is murder under any and all circumstances.

[68]For a discussion of the issue of birth control, see Frederick S. Jaffe, "Public Policy on Fertility Control," *Scientific American,* July 1973.

[69]The Soul Assurance Prayer Plan, Chicago, called on the laity to "fight abortion with prayer" and announced that "abortion is murder."

[70]For example, blood cells form at seventeen days and the heart as early as eighteen days, with irregular pulsations beginning on the twenty-fourth day and becoming regular at thirty days. The nervous system begins to develop at eighteen

days and the brain, spinal column, and entire nervous system begin to form on the twentieth and are completely formed by the thirtieth day. By then the embryo, with forty pairs of muscles and millions of cells, is approximately one-quarter inch long and has a distinctly human appearance.

[71]For a discussion of some medical problems, see Carl Djerassi, "Fertility Control Through Abortion," *Bulletin of the Atomic Scientists,* January 1972.

[72]See Rustum Roy and Della Roy, "Is Monogamy Outdated?" *The Humanist,* March–April 1970; William Tucker, "Four in a Bed, Will You Hate Yourself Afterward?" *New Woman,* July 1971; Morton Hunt, "Future of Marriage," *Playboy,* August 1971.

[73]For a discussion of the role of schools as conveyors of social myth, see Ivan Illich, "Schooling: The Ritual of Progress," *The New Yorker Review,* 1970.

four

Myths of the End
of the Age

Some people were inclined to disobey the revealed rules given by the gods, and a certain tension was created between the secular and the divine, between the profane and the holy. The myths taught that mankind had been created as servants of the gods, and that when individuals or groups balked at this arrangement, the entire people suffered divine retaliation because of the concept of the corporate nature of the group. Men's actions were constantly judged and the gods were intolerant of deviation from established patterns. Eschatological mythology struggled with this tension.

Eschatological mythology is concerned with "last things" or "end-time," with the termination of a period, an age, or an entire topocosm. Such myths describe a time when "former things are passed away" and new things—a new era, a new world, a new topocosm—emerge. Some eschatological myths look backward for an explanation of the present. They assume a "historical" perspective, depicting the termination of periods of divine–human relationship. Certain moments become watersheds marking clearly defined time sequences and separating epochs. Each eschatological myth symbolizes the breakdown of divine–human working relationships because of man's failure to live up to divine expectations. In each case, the gods acted against mankind. With each eschatological event, with each closing of the time period, changes occurred and new contractual arrangements developed or a new era was inaugurated with altered life patterns.

Other eschatological myths are futuristic, projecting visions of a period when the harmonious existence of men and gods experienced in "beginning time" would be realized in "end time," when the chasm that had developed between the sacred and the profane would be closed, when the time circle would be complete and the beginning would be realized at the end. All persons could not be included in the utopian end, for there would always be rebels. Thus, eschatological myths were ultimately compelled to move beyond communal ethics, stressing instead individual commitment to divinely established rules, at which time they assume apocalyptic dimensions which we will discuss later. Myths of past eschatological events contributed to the descriptions of anticipated future events: by describing the actions of angry deities who punished mortals for rebellious acts or other misdeeds, they implied that present or future disobedience to the divine will could bring disaster.

For example, the Egyptian myth of man's attempt to subjugate the gods explained why the gods were separated from mankind, how pharaoh as an incarnate god came to the sole representative of the sacred in the world of the profane, and why men celebrated their deliverance in the Hathor festival. The ancient Sumerian flood myth and its modified adaptation in Babylonian and Hebrew mythology stated that at one time, all living things were almost eliminated. Only through the efforts of a heroic savior —Ziusudra (the priest-king of Sumer), Utnapishtim of Babylonia, or Noah of the Hebrew myth—were various life forms preserved. From the rescued specimens, all present life developed. Hebrew mythology contained a promise that never again would a flood destroy the world, but there was no guarantee that destruction might not come by other means or that individual nations or groups might not be eliminated. Such myths explained the termination of a particular age and the beginning of a new period that accounted for present conditions. Punishments meted out in ancient eschatological events ushered in new relationships that continued to affect humans and their topocosm, making a return to former patterns impossible. Moreover, man could never be completely safe from divine actions that might trigger further change. Cultic observances and recitals of past eschatological events served to reinforce accepted behavioral patterns, lest a new era marked by disaster be ushered in.

Some eschatological myths project the hope that somehow, someday an ideal divine–human relationship might come about. This dream placed responsibility squarely upon the community's ability to fulfill its responsibilities to the gods, thereby earning blessing and favor. Both short- and long-term goals appear to have been involved. Short-term eschatological hopes focused on the coming year and appear to have been part of certain new year festivals. Long-term hopes embodied concepts such as the "kingdom of (the) god(s)," or more precisely, the "kingdom of believers."

During new year festivities, cultic rites were performed so that their power would affect the coming year positively. However, negative prognostications might also be made, using past *eschatons* or end-time periods to forecast the future. For example, it now seems very probable that the eighth century Judean prophet Amos, who prophesied at the royal shrine of Bethel in the Kingdom of Israel, was involved in new year rites. He made repeated reference to the Hebrew Exodus tradition, which had marked the end of the period of enslavement for the Hebrews and the beginning of nationhood—an eschatological mythic interpretation of the past, for Yahweh was the enabler (see Amos 2:10, 3:1, 4:10). Now, Amos warned, because of sin and disobedience, a new age would replace the present state and Israel would again be enslaved—this time under Assyria. Israel's identity as a free people would be lost (see Amos 3:9, 5:2–7, 6:8). Amos depicted the widely anticipated "Day of Yahweh" as a time of horror (5:18–20, 8:9–14) from which only a tattered remnant would survive to enter the new age (3:12, 5:3).

One myth could be used for either positive or negative eschatological prediction. The prophet Isaiah, who began to prophesy in Jerusalem about a decade after Amos's journey to Bethel, used the Exodus tradition to encourage the king and Hebrew people to trust Yahweh to deliver them from Assyrian power, just as he had rescued them from Egyptian bondage (Isaiah 10:24–27, 11:15–16). Two centuries later, when the Jews were captives in Babylon, an unknown prophet whose oracles have become attached to those of Isaiah of Jerusalem (he has been called Isaiah of Babylon) used Exodus imagery to predict deliverance and a new age (Isaiah 51:10–11, 52:11–12). For Isaiah of Jerusalem, failure to trust in Yahweh would bring unspeakable horrors like those predicted by Amos (Isaiah 7:18–20, 23–25), from which only a remnant would survive. The unknown prophet "Isaiah" of the Exile offered deliverance from bondage to Jews who would heed his words (Isaiah 40:21–31, 41:8–10, 43, and so on). Eschatological mythology, therefore, might embody threatening or hopeful anticipations. In either case, the new age which began after the termination of the present age would mark a complete change of life patterns.

Eschatological mythology involves a number of presuppositions. First, there was the assumption that undergirded societal myth: that the gods were concerned with and involved in human affairs, judging and evaluating human behavior patterns. Failure to conform to divinely approved or ordained behavior codes could result in punishment by annihilation or in some other tragic event that completely altered the present state. Second, eschatological myth presumed some kind of dissatisfaction with the present age. The myths anticipated an age when the existing situation would be changed, for better or for worse. Third, the concept of the future was sometimes drawn from past eschatological myths. The new age might reflect an earlier state in which conditions were more or less ideal than the present. Fourth, the end-time period might involve a remnant, the few faithful or chosen ones within the group, or a haphazard collection of individuals who would manage to escape the holocaust. Fifth, the new age was near, but its coming might be altered by human behavior; the people determined whether they would follow the dictates of the deity or their own inclinations. In either case, they were judged, and the judgment could start a new era. Finally, eschatological myth in its pre-apocalyptic period was not concerned with individuals but with groups, with nations. The individual as part of the corporate group would be involved, but individual actions were not weighed and judged and rewarded or punished.

ESCHATOLOGICAL MYTH IN EGYPT

Apart from the Ra myth which we discussed earlier, very little Egyptian writing seems to have been eschatological and futuristic. One after-the-fact writing may be cited. The prophecy of Nefer-Rehu purports to recount the visions of the future with which Nefer-Rehu entertained the fourth dynasty monarch Snefru (middle of the third millennium). Actually the account was composed during the twelfth dynasty (early second millennium) to laud the accomplishments of King Amen-em-het I, who was instrumental in restoring order to troubled Egypt. Our earliest versions of the story are schoolroom copies from the eighteenth and nineteenth dynasties (fifteenth to twelfth centuries). Because the composer of the narrative wrote after the disruptive period in Egyptian history, he was able to make Nefer-Rehu, the prophet, "foretell" the future. Amen-em-het I is described in messianic terms as conqueror of Egyptian enemies—Asiatics and Libyans—and one through whom "justice will come" and evil will be expelled.[1] There is no promise of permanence, only the immediate transformation of a period of trouble to a time of prosperity and peace.

ESCHATOLOGICAL MYTH IN MESOPOTAMIA

Samuel Noah Kramer has written that, so far as we can tell the Sumerians did not develop utopian visions of the future. Instead they cherished the past, clung to the present, and wanted to be remembered in the future. They were without anticipations of human betterment and progress and without the dreams that accompany such anticipations.[2] However, they did have a deluge myth, and although only fragments remain, scholars believe that the Babylonian and Hebrew flood myths developed from the Sumerian account. The partial texts suggest that the Sumerians, too, believed in a time when an era was terminated by divine action and a new epoch began. We have no way of determining how the flood myth was used in the Sumerian cultus, nor what impact the myth had on the people. The flood did cause societal change, for the Sumerian King List itemizes the pre-flood kingships and states that after the flood, "kingship was again lowered from heaven."[3] The flood marked an eschatological event.

Within the Babylonian and Assyrian empires, the deluge myth was included in the eleventh tablet of the Gilgamesh epic. When the flood-storm broke and engulfed the earth, the goddess Ishtar cried out:

> Truly former times are returned to mud
> Because I predicted evil in the divine Assembly.
> How could I portend evil in the Assembly of the gods
> and declare war for the destruction of my people—
> I who gave birth to my people?

Clearly, Ishtar blamed herself for the flood, but the factors that led to the call for the destruction of living things are not so clear. Perhaps the goddess's fickleness and quick temper were involved. The account only suggests that her fury had somehow been aroused. After the flood, when Utnapishtim made offerings to the gods, Enlil was identified as the deity who sent the flood. As the gods gathered for the banquet, Ishtar raised her jeweled pectoral and said:

> O gods now present. By the lapis lazuli
> Around my neck, I will not forget
> or disregard these days. I will never forget.
> Let the gods gather about the offerings,
> but do not let Enlil come . . .
> For he without reason, caused the flood
> and committed my people to destruction.

Enlil arrived, furious. According to the plan agreed on in the divine assembly, no individual was to have escaped destruction. Ea, who had disclosed the plan and enabled Utnapishtim to avoid destruction, stated that there were better ways than the flood to diminish the number of humans, although he did not elaborate. Enlil then granted Utnapishtim and his wife immortality. Thus, all human and nonhuman life descended from Utnapishtim's family, the craftsmen, and the creatures that had been aboard the boat.

We can gain some insight into the causes of the flood from a different flood story, preserved only in fragments, popularly known as *Atrahasis*.[4] This account relates that the gods were angered by the continuing clamor of humankind, which disturbed their rest:

> The land had become broad and the people numerous . . .
> The god was upset by their clamor.
> Enlil . . . said to the great gods:
> Mankind's noise has become oppressive
> and their racket prevents sleep.

Perhaps some of the "better ways" to reduce the human population, mentioned by Ea in the Gilgamesh epic, were those used by the gods in the Atrahasis epic. The gods decided to diminish the number of noise-makers by famine. After six years of drought and crop failure, the people become cannibals:

> They prepared a daughter for a meal. . . .
> One household devoured another.

Apparently Atrahasis, guided by Ea, did whatever was necessary to terminate the drought and bring rain. Because of the poor condition of the text, Atrahasis's actions are not known. At any rate, cannibalism ceased and life returned to normal. The clamor of humans again reached the heavens.

Next, the infuriated gods sent a plague to decimate the population. Aches, fevers, and chills beset the people and their noise again subsided. Again, Atrahasis, in consultation with Ea, was able to bring an end to the situation. When nocturnal noises began again, the gods decided to eliminate life by a flood. As in the Gilgamesh account, Ea decided on the preservation of life forms, and the ship was built.

On the basis of the Atrahasis account, we can perhaps assume that it was noise that angered the gods in the Gilgamesh flood story, and that Ishtar was the chief complainant. The accounts may have been designed to convey concern about excessive noise in shrine areas during the night hours, for in a prayer addressed to the gods of the night, the worshiper noted that the great gods Shamash, Sin, Adad, and Ishtar were asleep in heaven and that the holy places were quiet and dark.[5] Peaceful, unbroken sleep was important to the gods. In the Atrahasis account of the rebellion of the gods, Enlil was asleep when the revolt began. It has also been suggested that the myth was related to problems of overpopulation and methods to control particular groups within a society.[6] Certainly, the concluding portion of the text explains why many infants died and why some women were barren:

> Henceforth only a third of the people will come into existence—among humans (there shall be) the woman who bears and the woman who does not bear. Let the *pashittu*-demon exist among the people; let her snatch the infant from the woman who bears.[7]

The flood accounts marked the close of one period of human history and the inauguration of a new time.

The annual new year rite enacted in Babylon (the Akitu festival) may have had eschatological overtones. Each year was in a sense a new epoch. The existing year terminated with kenotic and mortification rites: the king, the symbol of the nation, was deposed. The new year was inaugurated with plerotic and invigoration rituals: the king was reinstated. A new period, guided by auguries, was introduced. In Hammurabi's time, it was customary to designate each year according to principal events occurring during that year, including canal building, temple building, and war. Each year had a unique identity. In one new year's rite, when Irra-mitti, ninth king of the Isin dynasty, was ritually dethroned and before the reenthronement ceremony had been enacted, a gardener, Bel-ibni, was appointed "substitute king." Irra-mitti died before the re-inauguration rite and Bel-ibni remained on the throne. This event was clearly the beginning of a new era.

Apart from deluge mythology and what may be implied in the short-term eschatology of the Akitu rites, there appears to have been no developed eschatological mythology in Mesopotamia.

BIBLICAL ESCHATOLOGY

A number of eschatological themes appear in biblical mythology. The garden of Eden myth is eschatological, in that it marked the termination of the paradise age and thrust humans into a hostile world to fend for themselves. The myth of the sons of Elohim having sexual intercourse with women who gave birth to sons who were mighty warriors, followed by the flood myth, is eschatological, in that it describes the end of the age of the long-lived antediluvians and semidivine supermen and the beginning of a new postflood epoch. The Hebrew flood myth, which includes the mythic interpretation of the rainbow as a reminder to the deity that he promised not to send another deluge (Gen 9:13–16), is eschatological, as we have noted. After the flood, a new age began in which all human inhabitants of the earth were said to be descendants of Noah. This age closed with the myth of the tower of Babel, which explained how men began to speak diverse languages. Thus, the Old Testament describes a series of past eschatons which explained facets of the succeeding ages.

Eschatological myths associated with national identity, such as the myths marking new beginnings with Abraham and Moses, must have had great significance for the Hebrew people. Each hero introduced a specific age in the mythical or real history of Israel. Abraham marked the beginning of peoplehood, an age which terminated with enslavement in Egypt. Moses marked the desert sojourn that closed just before the invasion of Palestine. These eschatons were commemorated by cultic rites. Participants were enabled to understand themselves and their nation–deity relationships in terms of the eschatological events of the past, as they shared ritually as members of a community of faith.

The age in which the Hebrews existed as a nation was, according to the mythology, part of a new era. The Hebrews looked back on past stages and past ages and thanked Yahweh for having brought them to peoplehood and national identity. The covenant relationship with Yahweh may have been renewed annually at the new year's rites, when the people participated in rituals of topocosmic renewal for the coming year.[8] Such rites hopefully committed the nation and the god to continuing divine–human relationships marked with the blessings of peace and well-being. During such renewal rites, the prophets, including Amos and Isaiah, forecast the proximity of the end of the present age.

The eschatological predictions of the prophets were fulfilled. The northern kingdom of Israel ceased to exist after 721 B.C., when the Assyrians absorbed the Israelites into their empire. Judeans were made captives in Babylon when Nebuchadrezzar and his armies took control of the nation in 597 and again in 586. The collapse of Israel and the fall of Judah were both eschatological events in that they marked the end of eras. Both events were given mythic overtones, because the people believed that their plight was not just the result of human struggle, but constituted divine punishment.

During the Exile, new voices projected mythic eschatological visions of new nationhood and new peoplehood. Ezekiel, whose prophetic oracles between 597 and 586 were negative, produced hopeful predictions after the destruction of Jerusalem. He interpreted the Exile as an interim between the past and the future. The eschaton would mark the end of the captivity and the new beginning of nationhood. Ezekiel's projected new age was the divinely ordained kingdom of the Jews, governed by a monarch of the Davidic line (whose living members were royal hostages in Babylon) in paradise-like environs in Palestine. The envisioned nation would be populated only by those faithful to the legal requirements of the faith (see Ezek. 34–37). The temple would be rebuilt in new and more wondrous splendor, and from its precincts all but the faithful would be barred (Ezek. 40–46). Other nations would be powerless against the Jews, and those who had previously despoiled the nation would be plundered by the Jews (Ezek. 38–39). It was to be a time of peace, because no people would be powerful enough to dare to attack.

Just before Cyrus of Persia assumed control of the Babylonian empire (539 B.C.), the unknown Jewish prophet, "Isaiah of Babylon," also made eschatological mythic pronouncements. For him, the day of Yahweh was at hand, to be introduced by Cyrus of Persia who was, whether he knew it or not, an anointed messianic deliverer under Yahweh's control (Isa. 45). The eschatological predictions envisioned a miraculous exodus from Babylon over a divine highway across the desert (Isa. 40:3–5, 43:18–21). From all parts of the Near Eastern world, the prophet envisioned scattered remnants of the Judean and Israelite nations returning (43:3–7). From foreign countries, wealth would pour into the Jewish kingdom (45:14). The prophet's emphasis on the nearness of what was to happen, the proximity of

Yahweh's day, and the newness of the event and of what was to be created gave the eschatological mythology a sense of historic immediacy that is stirring and exciting. The restoration of the Jews to their homeland was to mark the beginning of the new age, in which the Jewish nation would be given a new destiny as a "light to the nations" (Isa. 42:6, 49:6), Jewish people would be exalted (Isa. 49:23), and Jewish religion and law would provide guidance for the whole world (Isa. 51:4). The new age would be safeguarded by a new covenant that guaranteed Yahweh's continued protection and compassion:

> "For this is like the time of Noah to me,
> and as I swore that Noah's waters
> would not flood the earth again,
> so I have sworn not to be angry with you
> nor rebuke you.
> Even if the mountains are moved
> and the hills shaken,
> my loyal love will not leave you
> and my covenant of peace will not fail,"
> says Yahweh, who has compassion for you.

About the same time, Jewish scholars were restudying the work of earlier prophets, perhaps looking for words of hope. Since the eschatological predictions of doom had been fulfilled, then, if words of hope could be found, these too might be fulfilled. Most modern scholars find little to suggest that the eighth century prophets and their immediate successors looked beyond their immediate concerns to produce a second eschatological myth that promised restoration after punishment. Instead, they emphasized changing the direction of societal thinking and the patterns of living to bring national attitudes and behavior into conformity with what was conceived to be Yahweh's will. Failure to do so would bring the end of the nation. Therefore, the numerous oracles portending a day of peace and restoration are generally taken to be the work of writers living in the closing days of the Babylonian Exile, under the influence of the same kind of thinking found in the work of "Isaiah of Babylon."

One such eschatological oracle is found in both Micah 4:1–5 and Isaiah 2:2–5. It is believed that neither prophet composed the oracle and that it was a "floating" poem attached by different groups of Jewish savants to the two individual prophets' works. It echoes some of the motifs found in the restoration mythology of the Exilic Isaiah.

> And it will happen in the last days,
> that the mountain of Yahweh's house
> will be the most prominent of mountains

and will be elevated above the hills
and all nations will come to it.
Many people will come and say,
"Come, let's go to Yahweh's mountain
to the house of Jacob's god
that he may teach us his ways
and we may walk in his paths.
For the law will go forth from Zion
and Yahweh's word from Jerusalem.
And he will settle disputes between nations
and decide issues for many people,
And they will beat their swords into ploughpoints
and their spears into pruning hooks.
Nation will not raise sword against nation,
neither will they study war any more.
And every man will sit under his vine or fig tree
And none will make him afraid.

The eschatological myth extended peace and goodwill to the whole world, but left no doubt that the way of peace and accord stemmed from Jewish law.

Two passages associated with the Davidic kingship appear among the collected oracles of Isaiah of Jerusalem. Some scholars argue that Isaiah might have prepared them for the celebration of a coronation rite, perhaps that of King Hezekiah; others believe they are exilic. Isaiah 9:2–7 and 11:1–9 describe an ideal monarch of the Davidic line in messianic terms. Every monarch, at his accession, may have been viewed with idealistic hope; certainly every Judean monarch was supposed to be an anointed representative of Yahweh (Psalm 45:7) and could even be referred to as the son of Yahweh (Psalm 2:7). However, the second poem moves beyond the confines of the Davidic kingdom and provides the ideal monarch with judgmental authority over the earth (11:3–5). This poem closes with an eschatological myth envisioning the return to paradise, as when humans and animals lived harmoniously in Eden:

The wolf will live with the lamb,
the leopard will lie down beside the kid,
the calf and the lion will be friends
and a little boy will lead them.
The cow and the bear will feed together
and their young will lie down together.
The suckling infant will play over the asp's lair
and the weaned child will put his hand on the viper's den.
They will not hurt or destroy
anywhere on my holy mountain
for the land will be filled with knowledge of Yahweh
as the waters cover the sea.

The paradise situation, restricted to Mount Zion and its environs, would become a model for the world.

The eschatological mythic imagery of Isaiah 24–27—a collection of oracles from the post-Exilic period—is centered in the destruction of Judah as punishment for violation of the divine law. Although some translations read "Lo, Yahweh will lay waste the earth and make it desolate" (24:1), in view of the focus on Jerusalem and Judah in subsequent verses, the passage probably should read "Lo, Yahweh will lay waste the land . . ."— the Hebrew supports either translation. The emphasis would then be on Judah, rather than on the world.

Few futuristic eschatological myths were concerned with universal themes. However, cosmic destruction was introduced into the eschatological mythology of the seventh century Judean prophet Zephaniah. The book is generally recognized as a composite of oracles from different periods, composed by different authors. The opening, which may have been added by an editor, suggests that Yahweh would destroy all living creatures (Zeph. 1:2–3). The real focus of the book was on Jerusalem and Judah, although surrounding nations were also included: the Philistines, Cretans, Moabites, Ammonites, Ethiopians, and Assyrians—in other words, all of the world that had direct impact on Judah. Thus, the day of Yahweh—the eschatological day—included the whole world, according to one set of oracles which seem to have been added later (1:2–3), but according to Zephaniah, only Judah and the nations directly affecting Judah were involved. Like other prophetic oracles with eschatological motifs, Zephaniah believed the day of Yahweh to be at hand. The universalistic thrust, which we will discuss later, has a sense of immediacy because of its setting. Futuristic cosmological motifs appear in apocalyptic mythology, which seems to have been developed first in Zoroastrian religion.

APOCALYPTIC MYTHOLOGY

Even during the most ordinary times, but particularly during periods of deep frustration and dark despair, people are most open to visions of an ideal world close at hand, in which all the troubles that beset them will miraculously vanished, when the vanquished will be victors, the outcasts will be the accepted, and the persecuted will be blessed or perhaps become persecutors. We have identified some aspects of this dream in eschatological myths, but the concern was never with the individual—only with the nation, the group. Those who managed to escape the prognosticated holocaust were the lucky ones, who just happened to make it—not a selected group. Among the Jews taken into captivity in Babylon, some began to see themselves in a new light. They were spared by Yahweh for a purpose: to reconstitute the Jewish nation, to be a light to the nations. With the development of apocalyptic mythology, eschatological thought assumed new dimensions.

The term *apocalyptic* means to uncover or disclose or reveal. Apocalyptic writing purports to expose events associated with the final end of the age and to make clear the meaning of life and living. Apocalyptic myths differ from other eschatological myths in that they envision the new age ushered in by a cosmic cataclysm, not simply occasioned by human evil, but as the culmination of the divine plan, concerning which humans had nothing to say. The end of time was very near according to apocalyptic thought, and wise individuals were encouraged to link themselves with the forces of good, so that when the eschaton arrived, they would be among the blessed who survived to participate in the divine kingdom. The emphasis on individual survival as contrasted with group or national survival is an important factor in apocalyptic thought.

Apocalyptic myths were not revealed in the oracular form of prophetic utterances, nor in the legalistic or ritualistic patterns of priestly lore, nor in the maxims of wisdom schools. They were special revelations to selected individuals of the hidden secrets of the future. Angelic mediators might transport the apocalypticist physically or in a vision into the presence of the god, where hidden mysteries were made known. The apocalyptic myth unfolds as a narrative that discloses the inner meaning of history—past, present, and future. The accounts are often written in biographical form (for example, parts of Daniel) or in autobiographical form (as in Revelation).

Apocalyptic myths seem to have been most popular in times of persecution. Despair was heightened as the perversity of the wicked seemed to thrive unchecked and the righteousness of the pious brought only suffering. Apocalyptic myth sought to transcend the present unhappy situation, enabling individuals to function adequately and overcome feelings of confusion, despair, and anxiety. The apocalypticist projected a new age when the situation would be reversed and the righteous rewarded for their fidelity and perseverance. The myth made sense of the non-sense of human suffering. It gave strength to the righteous sufferer, for unlike Job, he knew why he suffered and had secret information that promised an end to his sorrows. He could develop a utopian mind-set which could break the power of existing reality and link him to a new, mythically organized world that existed apart from the external chaos. It enabled him to be strong, for he knew that the final answer lay outside this world.

Apocalyptic myths envisioned time as a series of epochs, each worse than the one before. There was cosmic decline. Those to whom the apocalyptic myth unfolded the future understood that they were living in the final period, the last and worst days, and that the new kingdom, the new world, the new cosmos was about to begin. Sometimes weird symbolism, cryptic numbers, and vague allusions added to the mystery, but the faithful could understand, for they had the key to the mysteries of the sacred scriptures, given to them by enlightened individuals who had access to divine knowledge through angelic mediators or even directly from the god.

Individuals were helpless to affect the final end of "history," for such matters were of cosmic proportions, beyond the realm of the human. Men and women could only align themselves with good and live by the will of the god. At the time of the final destruction, the faithful would be saved to dwell among the blessed forever. Should an individual die before that day, the apocalyptic myths provided varying solutions: a final resurrection when all humans would be judged, or through the myth of the existence of a human soul, continuation after the body perished. Some myths combined the two, so that the soul was said to exist after death, and at the end of time the body would be resurrected.

Zoroastrian Apocalyptic Mythology

According to most scholars, Zoroaster or Zarathustra is believed to have lived during the sixth century B.C. in eastern Iran, near Lake Urmia. Hero legends tell of his miraculous escapes from enemies who would have destroyed him. He was supposedly led by the angel Vohu Manu or Good Thought to an assembling of spirits, where he was instructed in the true or pure religion by Ahura Mazda. Even though Zoroaster acknowledged Ahura Mazda as the supreme and only god, dualism developed in the religion.

Zoroaster's teachings postulated a cosmic polarity in which the powers of Ahura Mazda, the all-knowing creator and sustainer of the world of good, struggled against the power of evil, symbolized by the Persian epitome of demonic malevolence, Ahriman. Truth struggled with falsehood, light with darkness. About the two main figures there grew up a hierarchy of angelic and demonic cohorts. After creation, time was divided into three-thousand-year epochs. At the end of twelve thousand years, the creation process would be complete, and the time of the final consummation would be at hand. A savior called Saoshyant would purify the world, remove all traces of evil, regenerate the world, and recreate it in purity. The dead would be resurrected. The righteous and those who had been cleansed of their sins—and, according to some interpreters, even the wicked, who had been purged by suffering—would enter the kingdom of the righteous and live forever in paradise.

Man had absolutely no involvement in this mythic pattern; the four ages and the final outcome were predetermined. During the twelve-thousand-year period, Ahura Mazda and Ahriman would struggle for power and for the allegiance of human souls, but the final outcome was known: Ahura Mazda would triumph.

Daniel

Only one Old Testament book, Daniel, can be properly classified as apocalyptic literature. It is set during and immediately after the Exilic period, but on the basis of literary analysis and internal evidence, most scholars believe that it was written in the second century B.C., probably about 167 B.C.

By the second century, the empire that Alexander the Great had established 150 years earlier had been subdivided among his successors, and Palestine had become a buffer state desired by the Ptolemies of Egypt and the Seleucids of Syria. Both were ardent enthusiasts of Greek culture who sought to bring Greek ways into all parts of their kingdoms. Many Jews favored adopting the Hellenic life-style, but others, who came to be known as the *Hasidim,* the "loyal or pious ones," resisted adamantly and kindled a conservativism committed with zealous vigor to the retention of the old ways. When Judah came under the control of the Seleucid Antiochus IV, the pressure on pious Jews to abandon their faith and ritual-cultural patterns became almost unbearable. They were subjected to inhuman torture, humiliation, and death (see 1 Macc. 1:41–64; 2 Macc. 6–7). Pig flesh was offered to Zeus on Yahweh's altar, rendering it unclean and unfit for cultic usage—an act called "the desolating abomination" (Dan. 12:11). At this time, the book of Daniel was written to encourage resistance, to fortify the pious in the face of suffering and torture, and to assure them of vindication for human wrong in an afterlife.

Daniel and his friends were portrayed as heroic models of resistance to change in Jewish mythic patterns. Arrested and sentenced to die for their faith, they were, according to the mythic accounts, miraculously preserved by the deity. Of course, in real life, the pious Jews who underwent excruciating torture and died horribly for their faith enjoyed no such deliverance.

To justify uncompromising adherence to the faith, the author of Daniel divided history into a series of ages. Because the story was set in the Babylonian period, this era became the first age, the age of gold. But the path of history was on a decline; after the ages of silver (the Medes), bronze (the Persians), and iron (Alexander's empire), there came the final stage of corruption—the intermingled bronze and clay age, the time of the Seleucids. Now the god of history would act. The end was at hand! History would cease! God would intervene! Pious Jews whose names were recorded in "the book" would be rewarded, and all others would be punished. Those who were dead at the moment of the end would be resurrected:

And many who sleep in the dust of the earth will awaken, some to everlasting life and some to shame and everlasting reproach and contempt. The wise ones will shine like the brightness of the firmament and those who have led men in the right like the stars for ever and ever. (Dan. 12:2–3)

The author of Daniel provided the Jews with a new mythic answer to the problem of theodicy: if the righteous suffer on earth despite their goodness and fidelity to the law, they will be rewarded in the afterlife. Should evil people seem to prosper and grow in power and wealth and authority, the pious knew that in the afterlife they would be punished in proportion to their evil deeds, and that all the power, wealth, and authority gained in this life would matter nothing in the world to come, where only fidelity to the divine will was counted. The righteous knew, too, that the time of the end was at hand.

Christian Apocalyptic Literature

New Testament literature is dominated by apocalyptic expectation of the end of the age. Jesus is portrayed as the central vehicle for divine action. His miraculous birth through a divinely impregnated Jewish virgin marked the beginning of "end-time"—"in the fulness of time God sent his son, born of a woman . . ." (Gal. 4:4). In other mythic terminology, Jesus was also a preexistent divine being (John 1:1–18) who emptied himself of his superhuman power to become man dwelling among men (Phil. 2:5–7), but like the Pharaoh, he could be interpreted by some followers as an incarnate god (Heb. 1:3; John 1:10–13; Col. 1:15–17). During his lifetime, he manifested his divine power through miraculous acts. His death, in terms of human mind-set, came as a tragic miscarriage of justice (Acts 7:52, 13:27–29), for he died the death of a criminal or a sinner among sinners (Matt. 27:38 and parallels). However, his death had mythic implications, for his shed blood atoned for human sin (1 Pet. 1:13–25). In Christian myth, Jesus became a human scapegoat, like the sin-bearer at the ancient Akitu festival; he was the lamb of god that removed the sins of the world (1 Cor. 5:7; John 1:3a), just as in Jewish ritual, animal blood cleansed the nation of sin. Moreover, Jesus' death eliminated the need for any other sacrifice; being for all men and for all time (Heb. 10:12). One needed only to accept the mythological interpretation as reality to obtain the blessings.

The resurrection, the Christian mythology suggested, marked the beginning of a cosmic catastrophe, the end of history. An era had ended and something new was in process. The power of death was abolished (1 Cor. 15:55f; 2 Tim. 1:10); the demonic had been rendered powerless (Matt. 10:1 and parallels); the risen Christ had taken his rightful place in the seat of

honor at the right hand of the father God (Heb. 1:3; Acts 2:33, and so on).
It was expected that he would return soon—in the lifetime of some of those
who wrote—to complete his redemptive task. At that time, the resurrection of the dead would take place and the living and dead would be judged
and rewarded or punished (1 Thess. 4:13–5:10; 2 Thess. 2). The key word
in this mythic pattern was *soon:* the kingdom of believers was at hand (Rev.
22:20).

For believers, a new age was in process and a new people with a new
identity had emerged. As 1 Peter 2:9 stated, "But you are a chosen race,
a royal priesthood, a holy nation, a people for his (God's) possession. . . ."
Ancient eschatological mythic patterns were discarded or were in the process of reversal. The old covenant had been replaced by a new and better
covenant (1 Cor. 11:25; Heb. 7:22, 8:6ff). The old covenantal symbol of
circumcision had become meaningless (1 Cor. 7:19; Phil. 3:3). A new people
had been chosen to replace the old Abrahamic election (1 Pet. 2:9). The
myth of the Tower of Babel (Gen. 6), which explained the variety of
languages, was reversed in the Pentecostal myth, according to which a
multitude of persons from diverse parts of the world miraculously heard
the preaching of Galilean disciples in their individual native tongues (Acts
2). The inversion of two other Hebrew myths was also anticipated: the
flood was to be paralleled by a final holocaust that would completely
destroy the world, and a new paradise—a new heaven and earth—would
come into being, surpassing the old. Once again, the deity would dwell
among men as in Eden.

The fullest expression of apocalyptic hope in the New Testament is
found in the book of Revelation. Here an unknown Christian seer, "John,"
envisioned the end of the age and the coming of the divine kingdom.
Scholars believe that this volume was composed near the end of the first
century A.D., when the Roman government was exerting excessive pressure
on Christians, especially in the region of Asia Minor, the area to which this
volume was addressed and from which it may have come. Pliny the
Younger, governor of Bithynia and Pontus, corresponded with the emporer
Trajan in 112 A.D. concerning the punishment of those who admitted to
being Christian. Clearly Christians were suffering for their beliefs and their
allegiance to the Christian movement.

In a vision, the seer, John, was permitted to enter the court of heaven
and witness that which was to occur, as the scroll of destiny was unsealed
by Jesus, "the lamb" (Rev. 5). As the seven seals on the scroll were broken,
horrendous catastrophes occurred. The breaking of the seventh seal introduced a completely new cycle of devastating events. However, the end was
predetermined, and as in all apocalyptic mythology, the kingdom of believers would come. Evil, personified by Satan, was overcome, the devil
sentenced to be "thrown into a lake of fire and brimstone" to be "tor-

mented day and night for ever and ever" (20:10). The dead were judged according to entries made opposite their names in the "book of life"; those whose names were not found in the book were "thrown into the lake of fire" (Rev. 20:12–15). Individuals who had succumbed to Roman pressure, bowing down to Caesar as god and forsaking Christianity, were to be tortured "with fire and brimstone in the presence of the holy angels and in the presence of the Lamb. And the smoke of their torment ascends for ever and ever; and they have no rest, day or night . . ." (Rev. 14:10).

After the nonbelievers were sentenced to torture, a new creation would begin:

> Then I saw a new heaven and a new earth for the first heaven and the first earth had passed away . . . And I saw the holy city, a new Jerusalem, descending out of heaven from God . . . And I saw no temple in the city for the Lord God Almighty and the Lamb are its temple. And the city doesn't require either sun or moon to illuminate it, because God's glory is its light and the Lamb is its lamp. And the nations will be guided by its light . . . But nothing unclean will ever enter it, nor anyone who indulges in abominations or lies, but only those who are recorded in the Lamb's book of life. (Rev. 21:1–2, 22–24, 27).

The new kingdom was to come quickly—it was at hand. Unlike the Zorastrian religion, the Christian myth offered no hope for those who had failed to measure up to Christian standards during their earthly life: they suffered eternally. Only the "saved" enjoyed paradise.

MODERN ESCHATOLOGY

For the most part, we have moved away from eschatological thinking, but reminiscences of ancient patterns remain. We often observe rites that mark the transition from one period or epoch of personal living to another. For example, modern rites of passage are observed at graduation from high school or college, at the time of marriage or retirement from a job, and at other stages where we leave one phase of living to move into another. The past becomes a time unit: for example adolescence, pre-voting age, pre-employment period, or pre-marriage years.

On a larger scale, the same concept is observable in government patterns. The Soviet Union at one period introduced a series of five-year plans, each with specific achievement goals, to facilitate the socialization pattern. In democratic countries, periodic contests among political parties to win the popular vote and gain victory and the power to govern also involve echoes of short-term eschatons. Government is by Liberal or Conservative parties, Republicans or Democrats, Socialists, Christian Democrats, or whatever other labels mark groups with various philosophies of government. In the United States, as in the time of Hammurabi, periods of control are labeled, for example "The Great Society," "The New Deal," "The Fair Deal," "The Square Deal," and so on. Each period had a beginning and an end-time and was characterized by specific emphases. Each was introduced and terminated by transition rites involving campaigning, which pointed to the end of the time period, voting and election, which marked the time of change, and inauguration, which symbolized the new beginning. Dramatic changes in personnel are usually involved, and inauguration speeches hold forth hope for the new age that is dawning. Past "eschatons" are often labeled to indicate "good" or "bad" periods: "The Roaring Twenties," "The Great Depression," World War II, and so on; reference is often made to these past epochs to provoke uncertainty or fear of return to past life-styles.

Much more prominent are the ancient apocalyptic myths that still exercise conditioning power in modern society. Some Christians continue to accent the polarity of good and evil, a good God versus an evil devil. In 1972, Pope Paul VI claimed that the "devil" was dominating entire communities and societies through sex, narcotics, and doctrinal errors. He is reported to have discarded arguments that the devil was a mythical being and to have stated, "This obscure and disturbing being does exist." Hal Lindsay, a popular apocalypticist, and the Rev. Billy Graham also believe in the reality of the devil. Lindsay has apparently analyzed the diabolic strategy and has reportedly claimed that about 1967, Satan began to promote occultism, Satanism, witchcraft, astrology, and so on.

Many groups adhere to the New Testament mythology of the end of the age, of the Parousia or second coming of Jesus, of a final judgment and a new heaven and earth to replace the present world. These themes receive unequal emphasis in the various groups, but all of them are present. A new dimension has been given to Christian apocalyptic thought among the youth by some members of the so-called "Jesus Movement," who have produced mini-comic(?) books with titles such as "This Was Your Life," "The Beast," "Creator or Liar?," "Somebody Goofed," and "The Fool."[9] These groups, like the early Christians, believe that only the "saved" will be part of the heavenly kingdom—the rest will suffer in hell. The continuation of this ancient mythic pattern, may reveal a deep unrest and dissatisfaction with modern life and living, and an archaic hunger for something more than mere survival. Perhaps the issue of theodicy is involved; certainly, for many people there is little justice, mercy, or kindness in this life, and if existence has any meaning, it must lie in preparation for something beyond the grave. On the other hand, the movement may only result from conditioning by the cults that keep alive ancient myths and program modern behavior.

A new form of apocalypticism has emerged from the sciences. Demographers have created new "horsemen of the apocalypse" in the form of fears about population explosion and an overcrowded earth; with reports of environmental pollution and its effects on present and future generations and life forms; with threats of nuclear war and the destruction of all life; and, perhaps most destructive and distracting, with the confusion of data which destroy ancient myths but create no substitutes.

The population explosion can possibly be contained with planned families, birth control, and abortions. Demographers contend that a balance can and must be maintained between what the earth can support and births and deaths. Pollution of the environment must be controlled; creative use of human and industrial wastes must and will be found. Without a doubt, the most fearsome apocalyptic vision of the twentieth century is the potential annihilation of all human life by manmade radioactive weapons. They are capable of destroying advanced animal life, leaving only certain simpler forms such as cockroaches and ants, which seem to resist radioactivity. Intense radioactive release could affect plant life and make the earth sterile. The world would then return to its pre-life barrenness, to its pre-creation nakedness. Waves would beat on a lifeless shore and dust clouds would sweep over the earth. Life processes and the evolutionary stream might begin again, but what forms would develop after billions of years cannot be imagined. Like the apocalyptic myths of two thousand years ago, the end would mark a new beginning, "for former things are passed away." With the weaponry already in hand, and new and more devastating armaments in process, a balanced and calm approach to human conflicts becomes imperative. Unfortunately, the manufacture of nuclear weapons is no longer secret, and any nation or individual able to acquire the proper ingredients can produce destructive tools. The number of "beserk" killings by individuals, who possess small arms—those who kill indiscriminately with no regard or concern for their own survival—is enough to cause some insecurity about the potential of a single act triggering a nuclear holocaust.

Most confusing of all for those who seek to understand themselves, their world, and their history is the maddening pace of the production of new knowledge. Over one hundred new journals appear each year, each containing a collection of articles which are only part of those written and submitted. Thousands of new books appear each year, along with films documenting facets of civilization. Complete volumes can be stored on a single sheet of microfilm. Computers store and rapidly retrieve data. For the average person, there is simply too much to understand. Because we have no new myths to interpret our human nature, we are reluctant to discard the old myths. The pace of living seems to accelerate uncontrolled. Many people believe that we will overextend ourselves and collapse under the weight of our knowledge. They study the old apocalyptic myths for signs of the end of the present age, for "where there is no vision the people become unstrung" (Prov. 29:18).

NOTES

[1]"The Prophecy of Nefer-Rehu," *ANET,* pp. 444ff.

[2]S. N. Kramer, *The Sacred Marriage Rite* (Bloomington: Indiana University Press, 1969), p. 22.

[3]"The Sumerian King List," ANET, pp. 265f.

[4]The term *Atrahasis,* meaning "exceedingly wise," was an epithet applied to several Mesopotamian heroes. The Babylonian title for the account was *Enuma ilu awelum*—"When god man . . ."—which are the opening words of the account. See the creation account from Atrahasis in the chapter "Cosmological Myths," ANET, pp. 104f.

[5]"Prayers to the Gods of the Night," *ANET,* pp. 390f.

[6]W. F. Albright, "From the Patriarchs to Moses," *BA,* Vol. 36, No. 1 (Feb. 1973), 25.

[7]Ibid.

[8] See Murray Newman, *The People of the Covenant* (Nashville, Tenn.: Abingdon, 1962).

[9]Published by Chick Publications, P.O. Box 662, Chino, Calif. 91710.

five

A Time to Die:
Myths of Death and Dying

Death is the normal termination of all plant and animal life. The process of aging and the journey toward death begin at birth. When the moment of death comes, in youth or old age, by accident or deliberate act, by sickness or deterioration, there is no known way to restore life. Death is final, or so it seems in light of present knowledge. So far as we can tell, only man, of all living creatures, is conscious of the fact of death and is troubled by it.

The concept of not living, of being dead, of nonexistence is terrifying for many. For others, death is a reality to be accepted. How one contemplates death may affect how one lives life. One who believes in an afterlife involving judgment for acts done during life on earth may be deeply concerned about conforming to life-patterns that will guarantee rewards in the afterlife. One who believes that this life is all that there is, might treat living as a cup to be drained rather than as a measure to be filled. Both beliefs were current in the ancient Near East, and some of the mythic patterns associated with death that developed there continue to affect present-day life.

What the earliest human beings believed about death cannot be known. But at some time, humans found it essential to cope with the reality of death. Life was precious. Rules to protect communal life were formulated and given mythic power. "You shall not murder" is an almost universal edict, but there have always been exceptions to the rule. For example, killing has been approved in time of war and to protect personal safety, family, and property.

When death came, the body had to be disposed of. We surmise that there was perhaps a time when corpses were left where they died to decompose or be devoured by carrion-eating creatures. At some point, men found it necessary to try to come to terms with the cessation of life and the frightening finality of death. Graves investigated by archeologists reveal human concern for the deceased. Tombs were dug in the soil and lined with rocks; heavy stones were placed on the burial mound to protect the corpses from wild animals. Caves were carved into hillside bedrock. Bodies were placed in positions that held significance for individual cultures: some were tightly flexed with knees drawn up beneath the chin, suggesting the prenatal position; some were gently flexed in what has been called the sleep posture and placed on the right or left side; some were stretched out and laid on their backs. Bodies were arranged facing the east, the direction of sunrise, suggesting hope for a new life, and facing the west, where the sun descended into the underworld, suggesting that the dead also made such a journey. Artifacts were often buried with the deceased.

Carmel man, who lived in Palestine more than fifty thousand years ago, buried his head beneath the floor of the cave in which he lived. Some bodies, like the ancient skeleton found at Rehov har Bashan in Tel Aviv, were buried beneath the floors of dwellings. This practice created a continuum—the dead were separated from the living, but occupied the same space. Grave furnishings were buried with the dead in eras before man recorded his thoughts in writing, so we can only surmise what the living had in mind. Did the dead require the utensils, weapons, jewelry, and food for an existence in or beyond the grave? Were the items personal possessions of the deceased and therefore touched or contaminated by his essence or his spirit? Were the furnishings funerary gifts, marks of respect and affection, like the flowers deposited on graves today? Or were they efforts to alleviate the sense of aloneness associated with death? We cannot know for sure, but the custom suggests beliefs about the influence of personality on objects, about life after death, or about appeasement of the dead by gifts.

As communities developed for the living, corresponding communities developed for the dead. The necropolis was usually at the outskirts of the village or city, often in the hillside below the city. Burial patterns varied with geography. In areas where there was a substratum of limestone which could be easily cut, burial caves were common. Where there was deep alluvial deposit, graves were dug in the soil and lined with matting or stone. Graves, however, are only containers for the dead, telling us little about mythic patterns and the funeral rituals that dramatized the myths. For this data we depend on written sources.

Death myths often reflect the frustration experienced by sensitive humans when confronted with the reality of death. There is no way to stop death, no help to be given to restore the dying person, no way to revive the dead. At times, bafflement became associated with fear, and fear of dying was linked to fear of the dead, to fear of their power to do mischief to the living, and to a variety of beliefs concerning the afterlife. Some mythic beliefs about death and resurrection or life after death may have developed from the observation of death-rebirth sequences in seasonal cycles and/or of perennials in plant life.

We noted earlier the life–death polarity in both seasonal and apocalyptic myths. For example, in the Canaanite myth of Ba'al, life-providing and life-denying powers came into violent conflict in the battle between Ba'al and Mot. The fertility god, Ba'al, died and was revived in accordance with the patterns of the seasons. Mot, however, did not die; he waited with open gullet to receive candidates for membership in his kingdom of the dead. Some may have desired to become involved in the life-death-resurrection pattern of Ba'al and the forces of nature. The burial of the body may have been equated with the planting of a seed. Clearly, men did not grow again, but the mythopoeic response to concern about death, to concern about the physical remains, and to observation of patterns in nature gave rise to myths about death and dying. Dreams about the dead may have encouraged people to think of the dead as having continuing existence, because it is not clear how much distinction was made between dream and reality. Should the dead in the dream seem hostile or angry or express malevolence, genuine fear of the dead might induce the living to act to appease the unhappy deceased. In Egypt, letters to the dead demonstrate that there were beliefs about the way in which the dead could affect the living.

EGYPTIAN MYTHS

The earliest Egyptian texts concerning the dead are the Pyramid texts from the third millennium B.C., which are believed to incorporate much earlier concepts. They include hymns, prayers, and incantations with innumerable mythic themes. Clearly, the Egyptians believed in an afterlife. Two distinct mythological patterns were dominant: one, Heliopolitan, was linked to the sun god Ra, and the other, from Abydos, was Osirian. The two patterns not only existed side by side but at many points melded into one another.

Great emphasis was placed on the preservation of the body. The art of mummification was highly developed as part of the priestly responsibilities in the cult of the dead. Through an incision in the left side, the vital organs—liver, lungs, stomach, and intestines—were removed and placed in separate canopic jars, each organ under the protection of one of the sons of the god Horus. The heart, believed to be the center of the intelligence, was left within the body. During the Middle Kingdom (ca. 2000–1780 B.C.), it was customary to withdraw the brain through the nostrils by means of an iron hook. Body cavities were filled with linen balls or mud to preserve the physical features. The embalming process, which required seventy days, involved the dessication of the body by soaking it in natron, the preservation of the tissues by anointing them with oils and resins, and the

wrapping of the corpse with linen bandages. Later, during the New Kingdom (sixteenth to eleventh centuries), the internal organs were left intact
and the canopic jars were symbolized by figurines of the gods. The greater
the wealth and position of the deceased individual, the more elaborate and
costly were the embalming preparations.

In Heliopolitan myth, the pharaoh was the incarnation of Horus the
Elder, the physical son of Ra, and therefore a divine being. According to
Ra mythology, the sun was born anew each morning, attained major
strength at noon, and in the evening became old, died, and passed into the
underworld, where it was called Auf. As Auf, it passed through the twelve
provinces (hours) of darkness, successfully battling serpent-like demonic
powers to be born again the next morning. Upon his death, the king joined
or at times was identified with Ra. The story of the king's translation to
the heavens took varied forms. In one, he crossed the Lake of Lilies, ferried
by a boatman to whom he was compelled to prove his royal identity. In
other texts, the pharaoh became a falcon and winged his way to the
heavens. In still others, he ascended a ray of sun as if it were a staircase,
to take his place among the immortals. The story of Si-nuhe, composed
during the twentieth century B.C., records the death of King Amen-em-het
I about 1960 B.C. and states that the divine monarch "ascended to heaven
and merged with the sun disc, the divine body became one with his
creator."[1] Upon arriving in heaven, a king underwent lustration rites in the
sacred celestial lake, perhaps to be completely purified for his life among
the gods. Food was obtained in various ways: from perpetual offerings
made at sepulchral shrines, by suckling the breasts of the goddesses associated with Ra, or from the harvests of the celestial fields.

Intermingled with the Egyptian solar beliefs were stellar concepts,
equally as old but proposing a different interpretation of the afterlife. The
multitude of stars became associated with the dead who had risen to the
heavens. The entrance to the Great Pyramid of King Cheops was designed
so that it pointed directly toward the polestar, perhaps to guide the stellar
flight of the monarch.

The Osirian cult, with its completely different mythological pattern,
fused with the solar-stellar rites and ultimately dominated them. The most
complete and unified form of the myth has been preserved by Plutarch
(first century A.D.), who was handicapped, however, because he could not
read Egyptian and had to depend on priests who were not particularly
interested in ancient traditions and thus gave him interpretations current
in their time. However, the analysis of mythic references in ancient texts
suggests that the Plutarch account is substantially accurate.

According to the myth, Geb, the earth god, and Nut, the sky goddess,
were the parents of Isis, Osiris, Set, and Nepthys. Set and Nepthys were
paired, but Nepthys remained barren until one night when she managed

to get Osiris drunk and embraced him sexually. The result was a child, Anubis, the jackal god who presided at embalming rites and was popularly known as the "master of mummy wrapping." Set was represented as the adversary, the embodiment of evil. He is said to have been born prematurely, emerging from his mother's womb through an opening he tore in it. He had white skin and red hair, an abomination to the Egyptians, who believed it resembled the hide of an ass. In jealousy, Set plotted the death of his brother Osiris. Perhaps Set is to be identified with the fringe area of the desert. Like Anubis, he may have been a god with a separate and distinct function before his incorporation into the Osirian myth.

The key figures in the myth are the divine triad, Isis, Osiris, and their son Horus. According to Plutarch, the love between Isis and Osiris was expressed even before their birth: they are supposed to have had intercourse within the womb of their mother. Isis became the symbol of the Egyptian ideal in womanhood. It was she who imparted the essence of domesticity to women, revealing the techniques of grinding grain and weaving linen. She domesticated men by educating them to the concept of marriage, and she taught them the divine secrets of the cure of illness and disease. When her husband Osiris, the king of Egypt, was away, she ruled in his place. When he was murdered, she sought his dismembered body, reconstituted it, and with the help of Anubis, mummified it. Throughout Osiris's life, Isis, his loyal companion sought to guard him against evil; when he was killed, her mourning rites provided a model for mourning women in Egypt. She was the magician goddess, the sourceress, and she represented the rich alluvial plains made fertile by the inundation of the Nile (Osiris).

Osiris may have been a historical king who was raised to heroic ranks as a symbol of an ideal ruler and ultimately deified. In the earliest texts, he is represented as a fertility god and identified with the soil and vegetation—with the corn that springs into life from a dead seed—and with the Nile, which was depicted as flowing from his penis. He was associated with regenerative and life forces. He thus combines the responsibilities of fecundity and kingship. However, it was as a god of the dead that Osiris made his greatest impact on Egyptian life. He was supposed to have been born at Thebes on the first of five intercalary days created by Thoth for the sky goddess Nut. At Osiris's birth, a voice in the temple cried out that a great and good king had been born and that the lord of all was entering into the world of light. Osiris was supposed to be tall, handsome, and dark-skinned. When his father, the god Geb, "retired," Osiris became lord of Egypt. His queen was Isis. He taught men agricultural skills—the growing of grain and grapes and the manufacture of implements—and he instituted the cult of the gods and created statuary. Because he desired to spread his divine gifts among all mankind, he left his throne in the control of his wife Isis and with his grand vizier, the god Thoth, set out to conquer Asia. An advocate of nonviolence, he overcame by gentleness and won allegiance from people of various countries by music, singing and playing various musical instruments until he had spread civilization everywhere. Upon his return, he fell a victim to a plot devised by his brother Set, who desired Osiris's wife and throne. The details of the plot as described by Plutarch are not reflected in any Egyptian sources, although it is clear in those sources that Set killed Osiris.

According to Plutarch, Set and seventy-two co-conspirators planned a huge banquet to which they invited Osiris. The centerpiece was a magnificently wrought casket, designed to fit the form of Osiris. Set offered to give it to anyone whose body would conform to its pattern. One by one, the seventy-two guests tried the coffin and failed to fit. When Osiris lay in it, it received his body perfectly, and the plotters clapped the lid shut and sealed it. The chest was hurled into the Nile and carried to the sea through the Tanaitic mouth of the Nile. It floated to the shore of Byblos, where a giant tamarisk grew around it.

Meanwhile, Isis had learned of Osiris's death. In mourning she cut off a lock of her hair, donned mourning apparel, and began to search for his dead body. From little children, whom the Egyptians seem to have thought were good observers and knew many things about natural mysteries, Isis learned where the box had gone. She journeyed to Byblos and recovered the chest, returned it to Egypt, and concealed it in the Nile marshes. There it was discovered by Set, who dismembered the corpse into fourteen parts and scattered them throughout the land. Isis recovered all the parts except the phallus, which had been devoured by the Oxyrhyncus crab. She modeled a clay penis, made the body whole, transformed herself into a vulture, and animated the corpse by beating her wings. She then copulated with the resuscitated Osiris. According to Plutarch, the phallic symbol was part of the rites of veneration in the Osirian cult. The pyramid texts record the event:

> Isis, your sister, comes to you, joyous in her love for you
> You have placed her on your penis
> Your seed is ejaculated into her . . .
> Horus-Soped comes out of you as Horus who is in Sothis.

(Sothis is the Dog Star, which is associated with Isis). From this necrophilic sexual union, Horus is said to have been born. The basis for this myth may lie in Osiris's origin as a fertility god through whom the inert earth received the seed which became a living plant. In the early dynastic era, corn kernels were placed in Osiris boxes within the tombs of the dead; hence there was a long association in Osirian mythology between fertility and death.

The Osirian mythology fused with the Heliopolitan myth. The dead king became Osiris, monarch of the realms of the dead. His son Horus reigned on earth as the king. When the living king (Horus) died, he became Osiris in death, and his successor became Horus on earth. The myth preserved the divinity of the king as established in Ra mythology, but extended it into the afterworld in a different way than in the Heliopolitan cult.

Originally, only the king was believed to become one with Osiris or Ra in the afterworld. During the First Intermediate Period of Egyptian history (ca. 2250–2000), when nobles and lesser princes ruled, the privilege was extended to the nobility, and during the New Kingdom, when merchants, artisans, and farmers—the common people—acquired wealth, they too enjoyed the immortality once reserved for the monarch.

The emotional appeal of the Osirian myth is obvious. Osiris had lived as a human—a king, to be sure, but human. He was a good person, betrayed to death by the envious conspirator Set. Osiris's wife and sister had mourned him, just as in all ages the living have mourned the beloved dead His son had sought to avenge his death. But Osiris had conquered death and had achieved immortality, and to his followers he offered the same victory over the grave. In addition, the Osirian myth provided models for all people. For the monarch, the myth pointed backward to the ideal ruler For the citizen, the myth portrayed ideal family relationships and the responsibilities of husband and wife, parent and child. Finally, the myth offered the believer identity with Osiris, the god. Death and decay represented the onslaughts of Set and his companions, perhaps considered to be demons; these had to be overcome. The mummification of the body paralleled Isis's reconstitution of Osiris's body. As Osiris overcame death and was portrayed as a mummy-wrapped form with a green or black visage, so the beloved dead, wrapped as a mummy with darkened skin, would transcend death and achieve immortality.

Inscriptions carved within the pyramids (pyramid texts) and hieroglyphs painted on coffins or included in papyrus scrolls placed within coffins (coffin texts) have provided information about the spells, incantations, and rites essential to guarantee safe entry into the joy-filled life beyond death. The study of papyruses has revealed that the so-called Book of the Dead or Chapters of Coming Forth by Day contained 190 sections, which were recensions of earlier coffin texts.

The form assumed by the deceased in the afterlife is not completely clear. The *ba,* often interpreted as the soul, seems to have come into being at the moment of death, with both material and immaterial form. It is usually depicted as a human-headed falcon or as a stork, but it could

assume the form of other creatures if it wished. Although it had freedom
of movement, it often sought the protection of the tomb at night. The *ka*
was much more closely related to the physical body. It came into existence
when the individual was born and seems to have been regarded as the
protective genius. It was represented in the tomb by statues that were
almost life-size. At the moment of death, the *ka* separated from the body
and did not die, but traveled to the west, where it was welcomed by
Hathor, the sky goddess, and strengthened before returning to the
mummy. The tomb was known as the house of the *ka*. Offerings made at
the tomb sustained the *ka;* when offerings ceased, the *ka* perished.

Funeral rites were closely associated with the mythology. The embalm-
er-priests were identified with the deities involved in the preservation of
Osiris's body, including Anubis. Female mourners included the deceased's
next-of-kin, but professional mourning priestesses represented Isis and
Nephthys. As the coffin was moved to the tomb on a sledge drawn by oxen
and men, two women knelt on the sledge at the ends of the coffin, again
representing the two goddesses. Male mourners preceded a second sledge
on which the canopic jars rested. Then came professional female mourners
and servants bearing the accouterments for the tomb: food, clothing, utensils, furnishings, and so on. The entourage was transported to the western
bank of the Nile. Renewal rituals designed to magically impart "life" were
performed, including the opening-of-the-mouth rite, associated with the
revitalization of the individual. Offerings were made. After the priests
finished reciting the funeral liturgy, the tomb was sealed.

From this point onward, the individual was on his own in the afterworld. Armed with spells and talismans to protect against evil or to influence the gods, and with the passwords and statements of the Book of the
Dead, the deceased traversed the space between the living and the dead
and was led by Anubis before a tribunal of deities in the Hall of Two
Judgments. Various gods presided at the judgment at different times, but
during the eighteenth dynasty (sixteenth to eleventh centuries), Osiris
became the chief justice. He sat on an elevated throne, the dais symbolizing
the primeval mound. He was garbed in white feathers, symbolic of righteousness, and had a green face, a reflection of his fertility role. Behind him
stood Nephthys and Isis. Forty-two judges representing the forty-two
nomes sat around the hall, each in mummy form and each holding a knife.
In addition, there were the gods and goddesses of the Heliopolitan hierarchy, each seated on a throne. Thanks to the Book of the Dead, the deceased
knew the proper address to be made to each deity and the "negative
confession," a denial of guilt, evil action, and sin. A second judgment
involved the weighing of the heart—the seat of volition—against the
feather of truth. Beside the balances stood Thoth, with a scribal palette to
record the verdict, and the fearsome devourer—a creature part crocodile,

part hippopotamus, and part lion. Presumably, those who failed to pass the test were consumed on the spot. Having passed the second judgment, the deceased was led by Horus to the throne of Osiris and was then enabled to enter eternal bliss as an *akh*—a glorified being—enjoying the association of friends and sustained by regular funerary offerings.

Rites in the Osirian cult varied from time to time and according to the individual's ability to pay. The myth of Osiris gave the individual's earthly behavior eternal significance; Egyptians could look forward with hope and anticipation to a life after death that exceeded the joys of earthly existence. When the "perpetual mortuary care" failed, inscriptions were added to tombs imploring passersby to make offerings to the dead and promising that the deceased would commend the donor to the gods. Magical formulas were also employed. Violation of tombs prompted inscriptions threatening curses against robbers. Another reaction to the plundering of tombs has been found in the fourteenth century B.C. "Song of the Harper."[2] After commenting on the desecration of the tombs, the harper noted that no one ever returned from the dead to discuss what was needed in the afterlife, and until the individual joined the dead, he had no way of knowing what lay beyond. The harper stressed the enjoyment of the earthly sojourn, after the fashion of the ale wife in Gilgamesh and the writer of Ecclesiastes:

> To fulfil your desire,
> let your heart forget
> the performance of funerary rites for you—
> Yield to your desires during life.
> Put myrrh on your head,
> wear fine linen . . .
> acquire earthly goods,
> don't restrain your passions
> until the day for mourning you arrives.

Despite the emphasis on the practical enjoyment of life, there is no real denial of the mythic concepts—just skepticism.

Animal Burials in Egypt

Because the gods could be represented in animal form and because some animals were considered to be sacred, the preservation of certain animal bodies was practiced in Egypt. Like humans, the animals were mummified before burial. After the shriveled remains were padded to return them to something of their original shape, the whole body was wrapped in linen. Animals which were mummified include the cat, which was sacred at Bubastis; the bull, which was sacred to Osiris and which was buried with its horns protruding from the ground; the ibis, the symbol of Thoth, which was usually buried at Hermopolis; and the crocodile. Animal funeral rites apparently included all the pomp which accompanied a human burial.

MESOPOTAMIAN MYTHS

To the best of our knowledge, Mesopotamian people viewed death with fear and horror. As we have seen, the very insecurities of survival led them to mythological concepts and cultic expressions by which the topocosm was revived annually. Failure to perform the rites and ceremonies properly could bring famine and death. Eschatological myths reinforced the sense of insecurity. Siduri, the barmaid in the Gilgamesh epic, may have best summarized the Sumerian and Babylonian attitude toward death when she discouraged Gilgamesh in his search for eternal life:

> When the gods created man,
> they ordained death for man
> and kept immortality for themselves.

There is nothing in Mesopotamian mythology to parallel the Egyptian belief in pleasure and the continuing existence of earthly luxuries in the afterlife. According to the Mesopotamians, man lived his brief span in the service of the gods. When that time was completed, he went to the land-of-no-return. Enkidu dreamed of his impending death, envisioning the frightening transformation of the human in entering the place of the dead (the text is fragmented in part):

> Heaven and earth moaned . . .
> . . . and I stood alone
> . . . [before a creature] whose face was gloomy
> . . . [and he came at me] with eagle-like claws
> . . . and he overpowered me . . .
> . . . and smothered me . . .
> . . . and I was transformed—
> my arms became like a bird's [wings]
> and he stared at me and took me to the Dark Palace,
> to Irkalla's home,
> to the house from which no one departs,
> along the road of no return
> to the house where the inhabitants are without light,
> where they have dust and clay for food.
> They are clothed like birds with wings for covering
> and they have no light but live in darkness. (Tablet VII, col. iv)

As he looked about in the gloom, Enkidu realized that in the underworld those who had held high office on earth—princes and temple personnel—now were slaves to the gods of the House of Dust. His entrance was challenged by the recorder, who held a tablet from which she had been reading: "Who brought this one here?" Unfortunately, the remainder of the dream sequence is missing. Because dreams revealed hidden realities and conveyed information from or about the gods, it can be assumed that Enkidu's report depicted common beliefs.

The death of Gilgamesh is recounted on three tablets found in Nippur, dating from the early second millennium.[3] Unfortunately, large portions of the text are missing. The dead monarch is pictured lying on a multicolored bier surrounded by mourners. As S. N. Kramer has indicated, it is possible that human sacrifice was involved and that Gilgamesh was accompanied into the underworld by a large retinue of palace personnel. That such customs were practiced by the Sumerians is clear from Sir Leonard Woolley's excavations at Ur.[4] In the royal graves which were uncovered, in addition to the body of the king or queen, the bodies of servants, richly garbed, and of soldier-guards, together with provisions, were found in the huge death pits. Because there was no sign of violence and because the bodies did not appear to have been specially prepared for burial, Woolley concluded that they had been alive during the festivals and were either drugged or simply lay in their appointed places until the earth covered and smothered them. It is possible, as Woolley has suggested, that the monarchs were deified.[5] Apparently, the Sumerian rulers believed that they, at least, could "take it with them" by transferring their earthly status to the grave and perhaps also into the nether world.

On the other hand, the image of the dead in the Gilgamesh account suggests that the physical grave was linked to the underworld, where there was clay for food. The place of the dead was therefore a locale, not simply a grave, and it was under the control of the goddess Ereshkigal and her consort Nergal. There was a special route to the kingdom of the dead. In the underworld existed a court complete with royal amenities, just as such courts existed in heavenly and earthly regal circles.

Further insight into mythic concepts of death and the world of the dead are provided by the Sumerian myth of Inanna's descent into the nether world, and its counterpart in Babylonian myth, Ishtar's descent into the nether world. Both goddesses were fertility deities, and in both instances the disappearance of the goddess resulted in sterility on earth. The myths have been associated with a seasonal festival or with the disappearance of the planet Venus, the stellar symbol of Ishtar, from the heavens. The Sumerian myth is, of course, the older, and the Babylonian version is an adaption of it to Babylonian settings.

The reason for the journey to the underworld is not told. It has been surmised that Dumuzi (Sumerian) and Tammuz (Babylonian), the consorts of the goddesses, may have been dead and that the goddesses were attempting to rescue them, but there is no evidence for this conclusion in the texts. The Inanna text, which comes from the early second millennium B.C., is based on thirteen fragmented tablets found at Nippur.[6] How much older the myth might be is not known. The Semitic myth comes in two versions that differ only slightly. The older, from Ashur, dates from the end of the second millennium, and the other, from Nineveh, is from Ashurbanipal's library (seventh century B.C.).

Before departing to the nether world, Inanna instructed her loyal messenger Ninshubur in the procedure for bringing about her return. Entry to the underworld was through seven portals in a lapis lazuli mountain. As she passed through each gate, the guardian, Neti, removed some of Inanna's apparel and adornments, and she arrived naked before her sister Ereshkigal, queen of the nether world. Beside the throne of Ereshkigal stood the seven judges of the dead. When they gazed upon her, Inanna was turned into a corpse and hung on a peg in the wall. The presence of judges in the nether world may indicate that some sort of evaluative process was believed to occur in the realm of the dead. When the goddess failed to return after three days and three nights, Ninshubur began to follow the instructions of her mistress. She gashed herself in mourning ritual and pleaded with the gods for Inanna's release. Enki responded, fashioning from earth two sexless creatures—perhaps so that they would not succumb to Ereshkigal's beauty—and dispatching them to the underworld with the magical food and water of life. The food and water were to be applied to Inanna's dead body sixty times. This rite was accomplished, the goddess revived and returned to the upper world accompanied by the *galla,* demonic creatures who were to guarantee that she would send a substitute to take her place in the underworld. As her servant, Ninshubur, and then Inanna's sons, Shara and Lulal, approached in mourning garb, the *galla* prepared to seize them, but were dissuaded by Inanna. When Inanna arrived at her sacred city, she discovered much to her hurt and anger that her husband, Dumuzi, was not in mourning, but arrayed in splendor and seated on the throne. So Dumuzi was given to the demons. They tortured him in preparation for his entry into the nether world, and Dumuzi cried to Utu, the sun god. Utu helped him escape to the home of his devoted sister Geshtinanna. But there was no safe refuge from the *galla*. Ultimately, it was decided that Dumuzi would spend part of the year in the nether regions and then be resurrected, and that during the second half of the year Geshtinanna would substitute for him.

Like Inanna, in the Babylonian version Ishtar approached the entrance to the nether world, but it was blocked by a huge door. At her threat to smash the gate, the gatekeeper reported to Ereshkigal. The queen of the nether world was deeply disturbed by the presence of Ishtar, but granted permission for her entry. As Ishtar passed through the seven guard stations, she was stripped of her ornaments and clothing, entering nude into the land of no return. Ereshkigal, furious, caused various illnesses to attack Ishtar, thus making her prisoner. On earth, all fertility ceased. The text reads:

> The bull does not mount the cow, the ass does not impregnate the jenny
> and the young man in the street does not copulate with the young woman.
> The young man lies alone in his room
> and the young woman lies alone on her side.

The serious situation was brought before Ea, who created a eunuch, Asushanamir. Like Inanna, Ishtar was freed when Asushanamir sprinkled her corpse with the animating water of life. As she returned through the seven portals, her jewels and possessions were returned to her. The myth concludes with a rather obscure reference to Tammuz, her husband.

To the Mesopotamian peoples, death was not simply a stasis, a condition opposite to life. As there was an entry to the world of the living, so there was an entry to the world of the dead. The seven portals may have represented developmental stages in death parallel to those in life; or, as the ancient zigurrats which linked heaven and earth had seven stages,[7] so the link between earth and the underworld may have been conceived as an inverted ziggurat with seven stages.

The Story of Kumma

A seventh century B.C. text found at Ashur provides a vision of the nether world granted to a prince named Kumma.[8] He saw himself before Nergal, god of the underworld and lord of the plague. Fifteen other deities were present, most of whom had human bodies and weird animal heads. For example, Namtar, the vizier, had a dragon head and his consort Namtartu the head of a *kuribu*;[9] the Sustainer of Evil had a bird's head and wings; and the boatman had the head of the mythic *Zu* bird. Nergal was furious at the invasion of the underworld and spared Kumma only when his counselor Ishum intervened. Kumma was commissioned to inform mankind of Nergal's power. The scene is one of terror, the forms grotesque and frightening. Certainly the nether world was a place to be avoided so long as possible.

Monarchs of the Underworld

In the underworld, as on earth and in heaven, the queen had a male counterpart. It has been suggested that in the Sumerian period, Ereshkigal ruled alone in the nether regions, but that when the myth came into the Semitic world, the idea of a woman in the sole position of leadership was unacceptable. Hence the Semitic myth provided a consort, the dread god of pestilence, whose sacred city was Cuthah.[10] According to the myth, Ereshkigal was unable to leave the realm of the dead to participate in a festive gathering of the gods. When her messenger arrived before the divine assembly, all the gods except Nergal paid homage to the queen's representative. To compensate for the insult, Nergal was dispatched to the underworld, but he was warned by Ea, god of wisdom, who had secret knowledge, not to mount the throne, eat the food, or drink the water or to succumb to the physical beauty of Ereshkigal. Having passed through the seven stations[11] of the nether regions, Nergal came into the presence of the goddess. In conformity with Ea's instructions, Nergal refused the throne, the food, and the water, but was unable to resist Ereshkigal's seductions. Six days of passionate embracing followed, and on the seventh Nergal was permitted to climb the long staircase to heaven and to reassure the gods of his safety. However, Ereshkigal desired the god as a husband and threatened to release the dead to overpower the living—apparently the forces of death and sterility to overcome the powers of life and fecundity —should Nergal not be given to her. Nergal returned to the nether world, seized the goddess by the hair, pulled her from the throne, copulated with her for six days, and became, by divine decree, king of the underworld.

CANAANITE MYTHS

The mythic material found in the excavation of Ugarit, which is assumed to be representative of Canaanite thought, demonstrates the polarity of life and death, the tension between existence and nonexistence. As life and life-giving powers were personified in Ba'al, the fertility god who expressed himself in refreshing and renewing rain, so death was symbolized by Mot, the god of life-robbing power and lord of the underworld. Ba'al dwelt in heaven, Mot ruled the nether world. Mot was not an inert god, merely the epitome of not-living. He was active, issuing invitations to his dark domain. His wide, animal-like mouth was open to accept guests into his gullet.

The approach to Mot's kingdom was through mountains at the rim of the world. When Ba'al's messengers were sent to Mot, they were instructed to lift or open these mountains to enter the realm of the dead.[12] Mot's regions were known as the "pit", but his underworld city apparently had a name: Hamriya. As king, Mot sat on a throne and received envoys from the upper regions. The ravenous god of the dead was dangerous, and Ba'al's representatives were warned to keep their distance lest they be crushed like lambs in Mot's powerful jaws. Mot was to be respected, approached in humility and reverence.

When Ba'al descended into the realm of death, according to the mythographers, "the breath of life was missing from the earth"—a concept that recalls the lack of life-producing activity and the sterility that the Babylonians associated with Ishtar's descent.

In the Canaanite myth of Aqhat, when the young hero was slain, his life-force (*nephesh*) left him like breath from the nostrils. In Canaanite thought, life and breath were one: when the breath ceased, death came; when death came, the breath ceased.

Funeral rites suggest the existence of a cult of Mot. El, the father-god, mourned for Ba'al, sitting on the ground in dust and ashes and then in a desperate mood wandering like Gilgamesh, crying and gashing his face, arms, chest, and back. Anat, too, began a search for the missing god. As she hunted the countryside, she gashed herself as her father had done. When Ba'al's body was recovered, it was buried in a niche in the earth. Sacrificial rites included the slaughter of numerous animals to honor Ba'al. In the Aqhat myth, funeral rites for Aqhat included ritual wailing by professional women mourners who beat their breasts and slashed their bodies, sacrificial offerings to the gods of the underworld, and a limping dance that was associated with death rituals.[13]

The resurrection of Ba'al suggests that the Canaanites believed that the powers of Mot and the reality of death could be overcome, at least in the case of Ba'al. There is no evidence to indicate that the myth conveyed any hope for revival for humans. However, the mocking dismissal of the eighth century Hebrew prophet Isaiah's warnings of disaster suggests that rites were performed by Hebrews and Canaanites to hold off the actions of Mot. After denouncing the leaders in Jerusalem, Isaiah warned of impending disaster. He recorded the reply of those who rejected his oracles:

> We have cut a covenant with Mot
> and we have an agreement with Sheol (the underworld)
> so when the surging flood passes through
> it won't reach us. (Isa. 28:15)

Isaiah's prediction contradicted their feeling of security:

Your covenant with Mot will be annulled,
your agreement with Sheol won't stand up
and when the surging flood passes through
you will be battered down by it . . . (Isa. 28:18)

There can be no doubt that the Canaanite cults were part of the religious scene in Jerusalem. The shrines at Shechem dedicated to Ba'al of the covenant (Judg. 8:33, 9:4) or El of the covenant (Judg. 9:46) suggest that agreements were sealed before these gods (see Josh. 24:25), or perhaps covenants were made with them. Certainly the Hebrew people described their relationship to Yahweh in terms of a covenant (Gen. 9:15–18; Exod. 34:27; Deut. 29:1; and so on). It is reasonable that because Mot was also a god, covenantal relationships might have been established with him so that when death passed through the land in the form of a plague, a war, or some other general catastrophe, those who had entered into such an agreement might expect to be spared. However, so far as the Canaanite texts are concerned, no evidence of covenantal rites with Mot has been found.

ZOROASTRIAN MYTHS

Zoroastrian mythology placed upon individuals the responsibility for choice among actions that were reckoned as positive or negative, good or evil, ritually pure or impure. Merits accruing from right actions and right attitudes included the acquisition of self-control and rewards from Ahura Mazda. However, material rewards did not always come during one's earthly life. As with the righteous Babylonian and the biblical Job, so with many of the faithful followers of Zoroaster hunger, disease, violence, and other forms of distress often seemed to be in control. Zoroastrian mythology projected divine rewards and punishments into the afterlife. A person's actions followed him beyond the grave with no escape from divine retribution, evil for evil, good for good.

On the fourth day after death, the soul was believed to cross the bridge of separation which linked the physical world to the unseen world. The righteous entered the realm of the blessed, a place of beauty and endless joy. The wicked went to a place of woe and suffering. At the end of time, all souls would pass through a river of molten metal. For the righteous, it would be like bathing in warm milk. For the evil, it was a journey marked by intense suffering for sins not yet requited. After this final rite of purification, the formerly wicked joined the righteous souls to share in the reconstituted world of the pure.

Zoroastrianism offered salvation for all: some reached it through living a righteous life on earth, others through purging their sin by suffering in the afterlife. In paradise, all adult men would be forty years old and all children fifteen. Each man received a wife, but there was to be no begetting of children.

Zoroastrianism, like other religions, was based on the belief that there was but one way, one truth, one faith. Zoroastrianism differed from others in its mythic promises of salvation for all in the afterlife. It was unique also in that despite male dominance, women were spiritually on a par with men. Every human being, male or female, made choices between good and evil, and each was judged impartially at the bridge of separation without regard for sex or status.

HEBREW MYTHS

In Hebrew thought, the individual was a psychosomatic entity, not separated into what some people today analyze as body and soul. As the J creation myth implied, the flesh (*basar*) was composed of earth, animated by the breath of Yahweh to become a living *nephesh,* a living unit. At death, the person was not merely dead flesh (*basar*), but a dead *nephesh.* [14] Apparently, so long as some part of the body remained—bones, for example— the person continued to be considered a *nephesh.*

Human remains were important and deserving of burial. A corpse left unburied and consumed by carrion eaters was an unspeakable horror, a fate to be wished upon those who had violated the mores of the people or offended the deity (1 Kings 14:11, 16:4, and so on). Nonburial was a desecration of the individual. The bodies of Saul and his three sons, fastened to the walls of the city of Beth-shan by the victorious Philistines, were removed by the citizens of Jabesh-gilead, cremated, and given proper burial (1 Sam. 31:8–13). When David had seven of Saul's sons hanged at Gibeon, Rizpah, Saul's concubine, protected the corpses from being devoured by birds and animals until David provided proper burial (2 Sam. 21:1–15). The concern for dead bodies went beyond sanitary interest and included respect and love for the persons in addition to mythic belief about the importance of burial.

The dead were entombed, sometimes in the houses where they had lived. According to one tradition, Samuel was buried in his house at Ramah (1 Sam. 25:1), although another account simply notes that internment was in the village of Ramah (1 Sam. 28:3). Whenever possible, those who died away from their community were returned for burial. The aged Barzilai refused a comfortable and honorable political appointment in Jerusalem to remain in Rogelim where his parents were buried, so that at death he could be buried near them (2 Sam. 19:37). Family sepulchers appear to have been common; thus it could be said that the dead were gathered to their own people. The bodies of Abraham, Sarah, and their descendants are said to have been buried in a cave at Machpelah (Gen. 49:29–32).[15] Archeologists have uncovered numerous multiple burials in caves that might have been family burial sites.

A grave was more than a hole in the ground or rock; it was part of the total realm of the dead, part of Sheol, which had spatial identity. Just as heaven, earth, and the oceans made up the world of living man, so below the earth was the dwellingplace of the nonliving—Sheol. Nor was the grave an isolated, individual, private space, any more than an above-ground house could be isolated from the total community and the environment of the living. The grave and its occupant were part of Sheol. As the heavens marked the highest reaches above ground, so Sheol marked the depths below (Isa. 7:11). Above the heavens were the waters of the primordial sea, and below Sheol were these same waters.

The Hebrews, like the Mesopotamians, did not consider the realm of the dead a pleasant place. It was the land of no return (Job 7:9, 10:21, 16:22), a place of darkness and gloom (Job 10:21), where

> . . . the wicked stop rebelling
> and there the weary rest
> and there prisoners lie quietly together
> for they do not hear the demands of their overseers.
> Both small and great are there
> and the slave is free from his master. (Job 3:17–19)

There was equality in Sheol, yet the individual appeared to retain his identity and some of the power associated with his role on earth. For example, when Saul, in desperate loneliness and frustration, asked the necromancer to raise Samuel from the grave, the woman described what she saw as an *'elohim*—a divine figure—and in relating to Saul what the *'elohim* wore, indicated clearly that her vision was of Samuel. Moreover, Samuel was still able to provide Saul with an oracle, just as he had during his earthly life (1 Sam. 28:8–20). After Elisha was buried, his bones retained the life-restoring power that the prophet had had during life (see 2 Kings 4:18–37, 13:20–21). Death was not complete extinction: so long as the bones remained, the individual seems to have had identity.

Three different attitudes toward death can be discerned in the Old Testament. One, seemingly drawn from Canaanite mythology, pictures Sheol as a realm under a ruler who actively sought candidates for his kingdom. Most of the information concerning such beliefs must be drawn from the prohibitions in the Hebrew cult and from prophetic comments that point to unacceptable mythic beliefs and practices. The second attitude, associated with the Hebrew cultus, eschewed all contact with the dead. A third attitude, stemming from Persia and coming into Jewish society during later Old Testament history, introduced the myth of rewards and punishments in a future life beyond the grave.

Despite cultic protestations, some form of cult of the dead appears to have had popular following in ancient Israel. Sheol was personified as a greedy monster whose mouth opened wide to receive the living (Isa. 5:14; Prov. 1:12). The descent into the grave constituted a rite of passage from the world of the living to the world of the dead. In Sheol, the dead were under a new dominion, the power of death.

Death was personified. The Hebrew term *mawet* corresponds to the Canaanite Mot. Death was believed to come in through the windows and to enter the palaces, and in the streets to cut off life from the young (Jer. 9:21). As the grim reaper, it stacked the bodies of the dead like sheaves in the field (Jer. 9:22). In the Exodus mythology, death was personified as the destroyer who robbed the Egyptians of their first-born children; through the magic of the blood smeared on the lintels of Hebrew homes, death passed over those dwellings. Although the destroyer was linked to Yahweh's determination to punish the Egyptians, the separate identity of death remained. When David offended Yahweh by taking a census, the angel of destruction brought death to the people (2 Sam. 24:16). A psalmist wrote of his rescue from death's snares by Yahweh (Ps. 18:4–5). As we have noted, there is evidence that during the eighth century some residents of Jerusalem believed that it was possible to enter into a covenant relationship with the god of the dead, so that as the destroyer passed over the Hebrews in Egypt, so Mot would not take his covenanted ones in Jerusalem. When the third-year tithe was paid at the temple in Jerusalem, the worshiper made a confession in which he stipulated that he had not "offered any part to the dead" (Deut. 26:14), which suggests the custom of sharing food with the dead.[16]

Mourning rites reflected Canaanite rituals (Jer. 41:5, 47:5). The prohibitions against such rites, which included cutting the flesh for the dead, reveal that such activities were not acceptable in the Hebrew cult (Lev. 19:28, 21:5f). Incense was burned for the royal dead (Jer. 34:5), but whether this practice was associated with Hebrew or Canaanite rites is not clear. On the other hand, death was sometimes accepted rather unemotionally, as an occurrence which could not be remedied. During the illness and until the death of his first child by Bathsheba, King David fasted and performed rites of repentence in the hope that Yahweh might be persuaded or be moved to compassion and lift the sentence of death from the infant, who was suffering, so said the mythic beliefs, because of David's theft of

Uriah's wife Bathsheba and the ruthless murder of Uriah. When the child died, David appears matter-of-factly to have renewed normal life patterns without mourning for the dead infant (2 Sam. 12:22f).

Tension existed between those who were drawn to Canaanitish mythology and those who were associated with the Hebrew cult. Hebrew cultic law forbade any association with the dead, dead bodies, or rites of mourning that echoed Canaanite practices. The dead were unclean; any contact with them rendered one unclean for seven days (Num. 19:11ff, 31:19). Animals that died a natural death or were not killed ritually for food were also unclean and could contaminate anything they touched or fell into (Lev. 11:31–40).[17] A contaminated individual was separated from the clean and had to perform cleansing rites (Num. 19:1ff). Priests and Nazirites (sacred persons under an oath) were particularly enjoined not to come in contact with the dead, even when a close relative had died (Lev. 21:1ff; Num. 6:6ff). Yahweh was a god of the living, not of the dead. Those who died moved beyond the orbit of Yahweh's cult and hence out of Yahweh's interest. Death marked separation from Yahweh. A psalmist who, in his misery, felt separated from Yahweh, wrote:

> I am counted as one who has descended into the Pit [grave],
> I have become like a man devoid of strength.
> My bed is in [the realm of] Death,
> my couch is in the grave
> where you [Yahweh] no longer remember them
> for they are cut off from your concern. (Ps. 88:4–5)

Another writer noted that the dead do not worship Yahweh (Ps. 115:17); the liturgical hymn associated with the illness of Hezekiah makes the same observation and concludes: "The living, the living; he shall praise you [Yahweh] . . ." (Isa. 38:19).

The distinction between life and death is somewhat blurred by the belief that sickness, infirmity, imprisonment, and oppression by enemies were associated with death. Thus, a writer might exclaim that he had entered into Sheol and Yahweh had rescued him (see Pss. 28:1, 88, and so on). Like the Babylonian who composed "I Will Praise the Lord of Wisdom," such Hebrew worshipers declared that Yahweh could deliver his followers even from Sheol (Pss. 16:10, 18:4ff, and so on). Should Yahweh forsake the individual or the nation, the result was the equivalent of death. In Ezekiel's vision of the dry bones, the exiled Jews living in Babylon in the sixth century complained: "Our bones are dried, our hope is lost. . . ." Ezekiel promised the renewal of life to the nation (Ezek. 37). Nevertheless, despite the extension of the physical reality of death to illness and exile and the reassurance that Yahweh could and did rescue from "the grave," cultic myth separated Yahweh from the realm of the dead and emphasized his role as the god of the living.

Then what of the dead? Were they forgotten and discarded? The dead were remembered through the living. To have one's line completely wiped out was as if one had never been. Levirate marriage protected from obliteration the man who married and died without offspring: the male child born to his wife through her brother-in-law would bear the name of the dead man (Deut. 25:5–10). Because Absalom, David's son, had no offspring to continue his name, he set up a pillar (*massebah*) so that his name would be remembered (2 Sam. 18:18).[18] Sheol was the place where men were forgotten and entered ultimately into a state of nonbeing. Only among the living could the identity of the individual be preserved. A man was called "the son of his father," and in family genealogy the dead were kept alive in memory.[19]

The J creation myth explained that mortality was the natural condition of mankind. Disobedience of Yahweh had resulted in a death sentence (Gen. 3). Only two men had been able to avoid death and, like the Babylonian Utnapishtim, gain immortality. The terse statement in Genesis 5:24 stipulates that "Enoch walked with Elohim and he was not for Elohim took him." Elijah was taken to heaven in a whirlwind (2 Kings 2:11). Nothing is related of the two men after their translation, but later generations developed mythic traditions about them.[20] The ideal was to die in ripe old age, like Moses (Deut. 34:5–7; see also Gen. 25:8, 35:29; Job 42:17; and so on).

With the development of apocalyptic literature, death and dying assumed new connotations among some Jewish sects. Death was objectified, recognized as an enemy that would be overcome by Yahweh. One writer envisioned a triumphal day when Yahweh would prepare a feast for all people and would "swallow up death" forever (Isa. 25:6–8). The Book of Daniel introduced the concept of resurrection, which was borrowed from Zoroastrian mythology. Believing that the "last days" were in process, the writer encouraged those who suffered persecution under the reign of Antiochus IV (second century B.C.) to take courage. He promised that the angel Michael, whose special assignment was the care of the Jews, would engineer the deliverance of the nation. The dead would be resurrected and those whose names were listed "in the book" would enjoy everlasting life. The others would suffer everlasting shame and contempt (Dan. 12). For the first time in biblical mythology, the individual who was pious but unrewarded in his earthly life was assured of the justice of the deity and promised full payment in the afterlife.

Not all Jews accepted the myth of an afterlife. The Sadducees maintained the earlier belief that death was a termination point. The Pharisees and Essenes embraced the myth. When Christianity developed, it inherited from its Jewish environment a fully developed mythology of death and the afterlife which was given new meaning and interpretation in the developing church.

NEW TESTAMENT MYTHS

Death–resurrection–eternal life are dominant themes in New Testament literature. The prime example of the mythic concept is, of course, the divine-human hero figure, Jesus. The tragic death of Jesus as a common criminal, condemned by a Roman court, was mythologized by the early Christian community and interpreted as a triumphant conquest over death —a victory that would be shared by believers. Of course, the myth of the descent into and return from the realm of the dead by a divine being is at least as old as the Sumerian myth of Inanna's journey to the underworld, but never before had there been any effort to give the myth a historical reality.

Jesus had been a man living among men, known to his followers and to his detractors. A Jew, he lived in Palestine during the period of Roman occupation in the first century of the common era. Letters written by Saul of Tarsus, who had been hostile to the Christian movement and was later converted to Christianity to become the apostle Paul, state that Paul knew people who had known Jesus personally (Gal. 1:10–2:14). It is extremely unlikely that this former opponent of Christianity would have been swayed to accept the historicity of Jesus if there had been any doubt of Jesus' existence as a person;[21] nor has there been any real challenge to the authenticity of Paul's letters.

According to the myth, Jesus was physically resurrected from his tomb after his death and burial, and was experienced as alive by chosen individuals among his followers (Acts 10:41). Reports of the experience varied. Jesus was visible only through eyes of faith; hence those who believed him dead did not, initially, recognize him when he was resurrected. Mark 16:1–8, the earliest Gospel account, reports that three women who went to the tomb did not see Jesus, but were told by "a young man" seated within the tomb that Jesus had risen and that he would be "seen" by his followers in Galilee. According to Luke 24, the announcement was made to the women by two men clothed in "dazzling" garb. Two of Jesus' followers, walking toward the village of Emmaus, were joined by a third person whom they did not at first recognize but who was finally revealed as the risen Jesus. At the moment of recognizance, Jesus suddenly vanished (Luke 24). Subsequent experience reported in Luke and in John 20–21 are characterized by mysterious appearances and disappearances of Jesus, by a lack of immediate recognition, and by fear. Matthew 28:11–15 records an accusation that Jesus' disciples had stolen his body to validate the story about a physical resurrection. The Gospels in the form that we have now appear to have developed some forty years or more after Jesus' death; they demonstrate that a number of mythic interpretations of Jesus' death had developed.

Paul's experience of Jesus was hallucinatory. Clearly, what Paul experienced was not a resuscitated corpse. He wrote of having "seen" Jesus (1 Cor. 9:1), although his personal recounting of the experience is vague (Gal. 1:13–17). The description provided in Acts 9 suggests an auditory rather than a visual experience, although a "light" was seen (compare Acts 22:4–16 and 26:9–18 for variant accounts). Whatever the experience, Paul became an adherent of the Christian cult.

Obviously, Christians found it necessary to explain what had happened to the risen body of Jesus. The ascension myth explained that forty days after the resurrection, Jesus ascended into heaven, which, according to the cosmological concepts of the period, was a place above the earth. Two men informed those who had watched Jesus disappear into the sky that he would return in the same manner (Acts 1:1–11). Ascension mythology became part of the preaching of the early church (Acts 2:32). Jesus had entered his "glory" (Luke 24:26) and was exalted on a throne at the right hand of the deity (Acts 2:33).

The myth of the messianic return promised that as Jesus had risen to heaven, so he would return (Acts 1:11). The return would be marked by a cry of command and a trumpet blast, and those who had died within the Christian faith would be resurrected, ascending from the earth to meet Jesus in the air, together with those who were still living at his return (1 Thess. 4:16–17). The moment of return would bring vindictive judgment of eternal destruction and exclusion from the Christian paradise for nonbelievers (2 Thess. 1:7–10). The precise time of the messianic reappearance was not known (2 Thess. 2:2), but Paul and his contemporaries expected that it would be during their lifetime. Indeed, there is evidence of some impatience with the delay in Jesus' return. The brief document known as 2 Peter, generally conceded to be one of the latest books in the New Testament collection and dated in the second century A.D., points out that much time had passed but nothing had happened.

In the developing mythology, Jesus' death became a sacrificial offering (1 Cor. 5:7; John 3:16), and his resurrection a public manifestation of the divinity of Jesus as "son of God." Hence, through Jesus, both sin and death were overcome (Rom. 5:6, 8:1–2). Paul could mock, "Death, where is your victory? Death, where is your sting?" (1 Cor. 15:55). Jesus was the "first fruits" of the resurrected dead. What had happened to Jesus would happen to the believer (1 Cor. 15:12–28).[22]

The nature of the resurrected person—the beliefs about what happened to the dead person—is at best obscure. Philippians 1:23 seems to suggest a belief that the dead entered immediately into the presence of the resurrected Jesus. In 1 Corinthians 15:51 and in 1 Thessalonians 4:13, Paul depicted the dead as asleep and awaiting a trumpet blast to signal a general resurrection. In very obscure language, Paul discussed the "body" with which the believer was clothed at death: a "heavenly body" or a "spiritual body" which apparently maintained the identity of the individual (1 Cor. 15:35–50; 2 Cor. 5:1–4).

The cultic celebration of Jesus' triumph over death was observed on "the Lord's day," the first day of the week, Sunday, which followed the Jewish Sabbath and differentiated Christians from Jews (1 Cor. 16:2). The ritual seems to have included prayer, the reading of scripture and other writings, preaching and teaching, singing of hymns and psalms, and a fellowship meal. The participants evidently believed that the risen Jesus was with them at the cultic rites.[23]

Death to the Christian was a transition from one world to another, where the believer would be with Jesus and with other believers.

MODERN MYTHS

Despite the passage of thousands of years and the changes in cosmological outlook, many facets of ancient mythology continue to affect our thinking. One need only listen to any of the radio or television programs sponsored by "conservative" religious groups to hear references to an afterlife in heaven or hell, and to the "second coming" of Jesus. About the time of the vernal equinox, Easter services reflect the quickening of life in nature and echo ancient concepts about death and rebirth with specific reference to the Jesus resurrection myth. The ancient myth is given cultic reinforcement.

Baptismal rites in some Christian services are related to death and resurrection, particularly in immersionist churches. Although the rite is supposed to imitate John the Baptizer's baptism of Jesus, certain overtones of dying and reviving are present. The individual is "buried" beneath the waters and "resurrected" into the new life in Christ (an interpretation based on Paul's comments in his letter to the Romans [Rom. 6:3–5]). Because sin is often treated as akin to death, according to Roman Catholic mythology, to die without baptism eliminates the possibility of entry into the kingdom of heaven. The baptism rite, which involves the sprinkling of the individual's forehead with water and the pronouncement of the incantation, "I baptize you in the name of the Father and of the Son and of the Holy Ghost," carries magical properties that release the individual from one kind of death.

It is in funeral rites that we gain the clearest insight into continuing mythic beliefs. In ancient times, most citizens (except for nobility and royalty) were responsible for the disposal of their own dead. Today we depend almost completely on morticians, the official preparers of bodies for final disposal. Special acreage is set apart for the dead. Individuals may arrange for elaborate funeral and burial arrangements, even before their death. The forgotten elderly, the indigent, and the unclaimed dead are disposed of according to local government policies. In Los Angeles, for example, such bodies are cremated and the bones placed in individual cardboard boxes. When a number of boxes has accumulated, all are buried simultaneously in one large, unmarked grave. In recent years, the city chaplain has said a prayer before the burial.

Most present-day Jews express belief in the immortality of the soul but do not pretend to dogmatize about the meaning or implications of the concept; that is left to the deity. Orthodox Jews believe in the immortality of the soul and the resurrection of the dead; Conservative, Reform, and Reconstructionist Jews leave these subjects open to individual interpretation. Some Jews state that they do not know whether there is a soul that continues on after death, and others completely reject the idea. Jewish funeral rituals emphasize what the individual was during his life, rather than immortality and afterlife or heaven and hell. In the Orthodox community, the body must be buried within twenty-four hours unless a holy day intervenes. In Conservative and Reform communities, this regulation is often relaxed. Funeral and memorial rites are simple. The body is washed, clothed in white linen, and buried in a plain wooden coffin, without embalming. A mourning period of seven days follows the funeral. During this period, the next-of-kin do not leave their home except to attend Sabbath services.[24] Three times each day the Kaddish is repeated, an affirmation of faith in the laws and ways of the deity. Neighbors bring food and condolences. A general mourning period continues for one month, and memorial services are held during the remaining eleven months of the year following the death. The Kaddish is recited each day in some communities, only on the Sabbath in others. Before the end of the year of mourning, a grave marker is placed over the tomb. From this time on, on the anniversary of the death, the family recites a prayer and lights a candle to honor and memorialize the deceased person. On special holy days, prayers are recited in synagogue services and the names of the dead are recalled.

Christian church members believe in the immortality of the soul, and some promise the resurrection of the body. Because of this belief, some, like the Roman Catholics, tend to refuse cremation, although cremation is practiced by Catholics in some areas. Some Christians believe that the soul of the Christian goes immediately to paradise, while others, like the Roman Catholics, believe that some souls must be purified, before entering heaven, in a mythic place of purgation called purgatory. Still others believe that the dead are asleep, awaiting a final resurrection. Most Christian churches believe that nonbelievers and other sinners go to hell for eternal punishment, but some admit to the possibility of divine mercy overruling this mythic dogma.

Christian funeral rituals vary. Usually, the body is embalmed by a mortician, dressed in whatever clothing the family deems appropriate, and buried in a grave in a casket of whatever value the family can afford to pay, from wood to steel and bronze. The bones of those who are cremated are often crushed into small fragments and placed in a metal urn, buried in a cemetery, placed in a burial vault, or scattered at sea or on land.

Protestant burial rites reflect belief in an afterlife. For example, graveside services often contain the lines, "We therefore commit his/her body to the ground in sure and certain hope of the resurrection to eternal life through Jesus Christ our Lord, who shall change the body of our low estate until it become like unto his glorious body." A somewhat less specific form is also used: "The body returns to the earth as it was, and the spirit to God who gave it; for as we have borne the image of the earthly, we shall also bear the image of the heavenly"—a statement obviously related to the apostle Paul's mythic comments about the "spiritual" body. The function of the minister and the congregation in Protestant funerals is to comfort the living.

Within Roman Catholicism, a rite once known as extreme unction but now called anointing of the sick is designed to provide an ill or dying person with spiritual comfort. The rite, performed by a priest, offers the individual the opportunity to make a final confession of sin, to express sorrow and repentance, and to become resigned to the will of the deity. Obviously, its intent is to help purify the individual for entrance into the afterlife. Oil consecrated for the purpose is used to anoint the eyes, ears, nostrils, lips, hands, and feet. During the anointing the priest recites, "Through this holy unction and his most tender mercy may the Lord pardon thee for whatever offenses thou hast committed by sight [for the eyes] . . . by hearing [for the ears] . . ." and so on. After death, the eyes are closed and the body is prepared by a mortician for burial. Before interment the body is brought to the church in a closed casket for services. From the church, the body is taken to the cemetery and buried in consecrated ground. The emphases throughout the services are on the sorrow experienced by the living, the plea for divine mercy for the soul of the dead person, and confidence in the resurrection of the dead. Nonbelievers are not accepted for burial from the church, nor are they permitted to be interred in consecrated ground. Baptised infants are believed to be assured of heaven, for the baptismal rite has removed the stain of "original sin" and they have not (ostensibly) committed any sins on their own.

Some individuals reject death mythology, insist that there be no funeral services or memorial rites for them, and even object to the placing of death notices in obituary columns. Instead, they direct that their bodies be delivered to a mortuary for disposal, usually by cremation. Such persons are convinced that all that matters is what happens while they are alive. Those who are closest to them will know of their death, and the rest of the people do not matter. This practice is frustrating for persons who wish to participate in expressions of mutual concern and friendship; often the individual has been dead for a considerable period of time before his acquaintances become aware of the fact, and by then it may be too late to mourn.

One need study only a few tomb markings to become aware of the deep psychic trauma that accompanies death. Somehow in the face of death it becomes important to give worth to human existence and to testify that the life of the dead person had meaning. In general terms, tomb markers can be classified as follows:

1. Those that specifically refer to belief in an afterlife. Such markers often incorporate biblical quotations, such as "I am the resurrection and the life." Others simply state, "Not dead, just resting," or something of this nature, expressing that the dead are not dead in a final sense, but are temporarily separated from the living, who will join them in another life. Belief in the ongoingness of life lifts even the most empty and fruitless life above futility.

2. Those that emphasize the individual's family role as beloved father/ son/mother/daughter/brother/sister or combination of these. Sometimes there is a statement about the deceased or a notice that the person is "sorely missed." Such markings reassure the community of the living that one can be important to others even after death by way of remembrance among the living.

3. Those that emphasize the individual's worth to society, for example, as a physician or serving humanity in some cause. In recent years, those who lost sons in Vietnam seem to have needed to make sense of what might be thought to be senseless deaths in a senseless war. Tomb inscriptions often note that the individual died for freedom, democracy, or his country.

4. Those that seek to give the individual an identity beyond his name on the marker. For example, a personal touch is achieved by inscribing the individual's signature. Lodge memberships or religious identity are often indicated. Pictures of the deceased are sometimes mounted under glass or plastic. Through such efforts to personalize, the individual's grave is differentiated from the endless lines of anonymous flat bronze markers, so common in modern cemeteries, which enable custodians responsible for "perpetual care" to mow the lawns with power vehicles. In older cemeter-

ies, individual identity was expressed through the use of a variety of tombstones. For example, some family crypts take the form of pyramids modeled on ancient Egyptian structures and bearing Egyptian symbols, or fashioned after a Venus temple. Massive obelisks, crosses, angelic figures, and other structures tower over individual and family graves in what must have been some societal attempt to excel in uniqueness.

Special cemeteries segregate the dead into communities. Burial places are reserved for veterans, for Jews and individual Jewish congregations, for Catholics, and, until recently, for white persons only. Evidently even in death some like to be with their own kind.

Remembrance of the dead is often marked by the flowers placed on their tombs on the anniversary of the death and on other special occasions. During the Christmas season, cemeteries are studded with small ever-greens—living, dead, and plastic—decorated with ornaments and even with Christmas cards and erected over the grave of some loved one. On Memorial Day, usually observed on May 30 in the United States, dead servicemen are honored. However, it is also a day when people visit and leave flowers on the graves of those who were not in the armed forces.

Animal Burials

Like the ancient Egyptians, some people today honor dead animals. Animal cemeteries are to be found in all large communities. Within the graveyards are "family" plots where pets of a particular family are interred. That the animals were part of the family is clear from nameplates which carry both the animal's and the family's names—for example, "Kitten Smith." Grave markers, statuary, and inscriptions reflect the religious identity of the humans, and hence of the animals! The Jewish Star of David and a variety of Christian cross forms, including the Greek cross and the Roman Catholic crucifix, are common. Statues of St. Francis of Assisi, noted for his love of animals, are plentiful. Many graves have containers for candles. At times, national identity can be determined from the language used on the marker. That some believe in the immortality of the animal soul is clear from inscriptions that state that the animal is awaiting its master in the afterworld.

Some people visit the graves of their beloved animals regularly, even bringing living animals to "visit" the final resting spot of former pets. During the festive seasons, particularly at Christmas time, special orna-ments are placed on the graves. Dead animals, like dead people, are often remembered.

DEATH AND THE GODS

Sometimes gods died. Because the cyclic patterns in nature were my-thologized and specific aspects of nature were personalized and personi-fied, it appears to have been normal to think of the death and rebirth of certain god figures. Moreover, in the sense that the chief god of a group often became the projection of the life-power of the group, what happened to the god happened to the group: when the god died, the group died (topocosmically), and when the god was revived, the group was rein-vigorated. Thus, Ba'al of Canaan could be completely eclipsed by Mot during a period of drought. Similarly, during the Lenten season and partic-ularly on Good Friday, the Christian community is involved in mortifica-tion rites, and on Easter Sunday celebrates resurrection and new birth, because Jesus, the incarnate god, was killed and was resurrected and, leaving the secular world, returned to the divine realm.

In some myths, gods were killed and not revived. Tiamat and Kingu were killed by Marduk. Tiamat became the basic "stuff" of the universe, and Kingu's blood was mingled with clay to form man. Thus, man and the topocosm were of divine substance, but of divine substance that had lost its peculiar power of immortality.

In more recent times, a "death of God" movement has developed. Be-cause of monotheistic mythic beliefs, there is an absoluteness in this new myth. In the ancient Near East, when a god died, there were always other divinities alive and functioning. Even when Jesus, as the incarnate god, died, the Father was alive and in control of the universe. Now some people argue that the mythic concepts entertained in Western tradition are ended, and God is dead: the god idea fostered by Christians and Jews has no relevance. For the Jewish scholar Richard L. Rubenstein, we live in the time of the death of God. The death is a cultural event and a cultural fact. For Rubenstein, God died at Auschwitz. When millions of Jews went to death chambers calling on the traditional God of history to intervene and to save, and the only response was silence, the Jewish God became alien to the Jewish community—God was dead.[25] Of course, this is a symbolic state-ment marking the drift of society away from the sacred toward the secular. According to Rubenstein, the implications are tragic: man is left alone in the wasteland. Perhaps the only response to Rubenstein can be to quote the maxim of a Jewish sage:

There is no quality and there is no power of man that was created to no purpose. . . .
But to what end can the denial of God have been created? This too can be uplifted through

deeds of charity. For if someone comes to you and asks your help, you shall not turn him off with pious words, saying: "Have faith and take your troubles to God!" You shall act as if there were no God, as if there were only one person in all the world who could help this man—only yourself. (Rabbi Moshe Leib of Sasov)[26]

From some Protestant death-of-God theologians have come expressions of joy at liberation from mythic restrictions.[27] The moment of death is different, according to them. For example, Thomas Altizer believes that God died on the cross with Jesus, literally. His death freed man, because so long as God was God, man was a slave or servant to the deity, as ancient mythology had proclaimed. Hence Altizer moves into the realm of Christian secularism and Christian atheism. The significance of the freedom to be experienced in a secular society was outlined by Harvey Cox (who is not part of the death-of-God movement) in his book, *The Secular City.* Given the anonymity of the city and the mobility of our age, the individual is freed as never before to pursue personal interests and life-styles, to meet persons from varying communities. He is freed from community pressure to conform, and from the threat of exclusion. Individuals can come together to structure their own communities and develop their own behavior patterns. Truly, the reasoning continues, it is the dawning of the Age of Aquarius. Hence, unlike Rubenstein, some Protestant death-of-God followers find nothing tragic in the new myth, but only cause for rejoicing in freedom.

To what degree the death-of-God mythology has penetrated society cannot be determined. Few people question the surge toward the secular life, but many of those who live as if there is no God prefer to remain open to the possible existence of a deity. Such belief in a God seems to have little relationship to life and living. Perhaps the religion of Hathor has come covertly into being again, without temples and formal rites and without recognition of the goddess in the new-old emphasis on love and joy, by which her shrines were known. The sacred beverage is what it has always been, alcohol. If reactions to the recent war are any indication, there seem to be few who are enthusiastic about rousing ancient gods who may have provided humans with a sense of destiny in doing battle and killing others. Perhaps the growth of some of the religious and spiritual groups investigated by Robert Ellwood, Jr., points to the development of new myths that will help man cope with the stress of living.[28] Strangely enough, when one god dies or when certain myths fail, new gods are born or old gods are resurrected, and new mythologies begin to emerge. Man seems to require myths to cope with his world.

NOTES

[1]"The Story of Si-nuhe," *ANET,* pp. 18ff.

[2]"A Song of the Harper," *ANET,* p. 467.

[3]"The Death of Gilgamesh," *ANET,* pp. 50–52.

[4]L. Woolley, *Excavations at Ur* (New York: Barnes & Noble, 1954), chap. 3, and *Ur of the Chaldees* (Baltimore: Pelican, 1938), chap. 2.

[5]L. Woolley, *The Sumerians* (New York: Norton, 1965), pp. 30f.

[6]For the text of the Inanna myth, see *ANET,* p. 52; and S. N. Kramer, *The Sacred Marriage Rite* (Bloomington: Indiana University Press, 1969), chap. 6.

[7]Herodotus wrote that there were eight stages.

[8]"A Vision of the Nether World," *ANET,* pp. 109f.

[9]The *kuribu* was a guardian figure often depicted with an animal body and a human head.

[10]H. W. F. Saggs, *The Greatness that Was Babylon* (New York: Hawthorn, 1962), pp. 337f.

[11]See also *ANET,* p. 103, where fourteen portals are mentioned in the el-Amarna texts, and pp. 509f, where the Neo-Assyrian version records seven gates.

[12]*ANET,* p. 135, col. viii.

[13]The Canaanite priests of Ba'al were reported to have performed such a dance in the rites recorded in 1 Kings 18:26. See also Theodore H. Gaster, *Thespis: Ritual, Myth, and Drama in the Ancient Near East* (New York: Harper & Row, 1950; rev. ed., 1968), pp. 306ff, n.

[14]See Num. 19:11, 13, where the corpse is called a "dead *nephesh.*"

[15]The Muslim Mosque of Ibrahim in Hebron, which is built over Herodian (first century B.C.) masonry, is supposed to contain the patriarchal burial site. Cenotaphs within the shrine mark the purported location of the individual bodies. Because of the sanctity of the shrine, archeologists have not been permitted to make scientific appraisals.

[16]This interpretation has been rejected by some scholars, who deny that any such custom existed in ancient Israel. See G. E. Wright, "Jeremiah: Exegesis," in *The Interpreter's Bible,* Vol. 2, p. 487.

[17]There was practicality in the cultic legislation. For example, if a mouse fell into a clay vessel, the vessel had to be smashed, but should the mouse fall into a cistern, the cistern was not considered unclean and was therefore not destroyed. Obviously, the water supply in the cistern was essential for survival, and it was easier to replace a pot than a cistern.

[18]The futility of expecting to be remembered through erecting great monuments or through spectacular achievements is expressed in Ecclesiastes 2:18ff.

[19]Esarhaddon, King of Assyria, acknowledged this concept in treaties with vassal states, cursing those who would violate the agreement and hoping that just as a mule produced no offspring, so might the violators' names, offspring, and descendants disappear. It would then be as if the individuals had never existed (*ANET,* p. 539, item 66 [537]).

[20]For the story of Enoch, see Ecclesiasticus 44:16, the Book of Enoch, and Jude 14. For the story of Elijah, see Malachi 4:5; Ecclesiasticus 48:10; Luke 1:17; Matthew 11:14, 16:3f, 16:10–13.

[21]The debates about the historicity of Jesus are long past. For a summary of some of the discussions see Albert Schweitzer, *The Quest of the Historical Jesus* (New York: Macmillan, 1948). Subsequent discussions of Jesus' historicity have sought to penetrate the mythic layers that obscure the "real" person and his teaching. For example, see James M. Robinson, *A New Quest of the Historical Jesus* (London: SCM Press, 1959 [Studies in Biblical Theology, No. 25]).

[22]Jesus' power over death was demonstrated by his resurrection of Lazarus (John 11).

[23]See Oscar Cullman, *Early Christian Worship* (Chicago: Regnery, 1953).

[24]The period is called *Shivah*, which means "seven," but the Sabbath day is excluded.

[25]Richard L. Rubenstein, *After Auschwitz* (Indianapolis: Bobbs-Merrill, 1966).

[26]For a slightly different translation, see Louis I. Newman, *The Hasidic Anthology: Tales and Teachings of the Hasidim* (New York: Scribner's, 1934), p. 494. See also I. Berger, *Esser Tzachtzochoth* (Piotrkov, 1910), Hebrew, p. 53; and Chaim Bloch, *Gemeinde der Chassidim* (Vienna, 1920), German p. 189.

[27]For a succinct discussion of the death-of-God movement, see Thomas W. Ogletree, *The Death of God Controversy* (Nashville: Abingdon, 1966), and the sources listed there. See also Gabriel Vahanian, *The Death of God* (New York: Braziller, 1957); Lonnie D. Kliever and John H. Hayes, *Radical Christianity* (Anderson, S. C.: Droke House, 1968). Thomas J. J. Altizer, ed., *Toward a New Christianity* (New York: Harcourt Brace Jovanovich 1967) is a useful collection of writings on the theme.

[28]Robert S. Ellwood, Jr. *Religious and Spiritual Groups in Modern America* (Englewood Cliffs, N.J.: Prentice-Hall, 1973).

six

Implications
for Human Identity

Myths were communal literature and as such, they affected communal mores and life patterns. They pointed to potentials for harmonious relationships between gods and people. They enabled the community to live amid cosmic and sociological tensions and pressures. They gave meaning to group existence. But they also related to the individual, and in this sense, all myths functioned to some degree as identity myths. Myths enabled the individual to understand his place in the world, to grasp the dimensions of being human, to comprehend limits and purpose and perhaps to give meaning to human existence. The myth told the person who listened to or who was involved in the myth who he or she was. If the myth tended to confine and restrict human endeavor, if it limited human imagination or dreams, if it hindered the potential for human adventuring in new realms or the exploration of new concepts or the living of diverse life-styles, it can be said to have had a life-denying impact on those who might have moved away from established patterns. For those who accepted the myth and who were able to expand as individuals within the context of the myth, it can be said to have had a life-affirming quality.

Information from the ancient Near East about individuals seeking personal identity or self-meaning is limited. As we have seen, there are elements of such a search in the Gilgamesh epic, but if our interpretation is correct, the final emphasis of the narrative was on conformity to given patterns, not on encouraging others to adventure into the search for self-meaning. Similarly, the author of Ecclesiastes did not suggest a radical break with societal patterns, but accepted what was current and suggested that one could best adjust to life by eating, drinking, and making merry. The individual had to find himself within the context of social norms, and there must have been many who did just that. Ecclesiastes, in denying the validity of finding meaning in work, wealth, and status, implies that some people did discover their human worth in those very pursuits. One would be most satisfied if one could adjust to the acceptable standards of society and refuse to do as Gilgamesh had done—embark on a desperate search that led nowhere except back to the norm.

The ancients, like many persons today, tended to think of themselves in terms of group relationships; hence, ancient myths elucidated human identity in terms of human belonging. Whatever personal psychic tensions an individual may have experienced were alleviated to some degree through myths about the group of which he was a part. Just as mysterious powers were at work within the world, so there were mysterious purposes known only to the gods. The gods had reasons for what they did, and what they did affected the group and hence the individual. Myths made sense out of what occurred by suggesting or stating that an occurrence was the will of the god(s). Thus, both group and individual success and suffering had meaning, even though that meaning might not be known to the group or the individual.

Cosmogonic myths explained the topocosm and informed individuals that they were the result of divine creative acts and that they had specific responsibilities within the topocosm. All aspects of being human—joy, suffering, life, and death—stemmed from beginnings when cosmic patterns were established. When turmoil and trouble came, myths gave promise of divine help if proper procedures were followed, and threatened punishment if rules were violated.

Cosmogonic myths established basic identities. Creatures were divided into male and female life forms and were segregated and named. Creation was not completed until identities were established. To be without a name was to lack identity. Among humans, names revealed something about individuals. In Egypt, the king had three names: a Horus name that identified him with the god, a Nebti name which symbolized him as the unifying factor of Upper and Lower Egypt, and a Nesu-bit or throne name which he assumed when he took power. In Israel, monarchs sometimes changed names when they were enthroned. When Pharaoh Necho placed Eliakim on the throne of Judah, he changed his name to Jehoiakim (2 Kings 23:34). A change in name marked a change of status or destiny. Thus, Jacob, the patriarch, became Israel, the nation (Gen. 32:28), and in the New Testament, Simon, the disciple of Jesus, became Peter (the rock) (Matt. 16:17–18).

Names often characterized individuals. The name *Adam* means "man." *Eve* is related to a Hebrew term meaning "life" and refers to woman as the life-bearer (Gen. 3:20). The name *Jesus*, which is related to *Isaiah* and *Joshua*, and which means "Yah(weh) is salvation" or "Yah(weh) saves," is given special significance by the author of the Gospel of Matthew, who notes, "You will call his name Jesus (Yahweh *saves*) for he will *save* his people from their sins" (Matt. 1:21).

When a man's name perished, so did he. He was alive so long as his name remained alive. When Akhenaton effaced the name of the sun god Amon, he was in reality destroying the identity of the sun as Amon. When Tuthmosis III effaced the image and name of Hatshepsut from her shrine, he was in effect effacing the queen. To remove a man's name from his tomb was, in Egyptian eyes, to affect his existence in the next world.[1] Similarly, in Israel, to cut off a man's name was to render him extinct. David promised Saul that he would not cut off his descendants or destroy his name (1 Sam. 24:21f). According to a psalmist, Israel's enemies said, "Come, let's eliminate them as a nation; let Israel's name be remembered no longer" (Ps. 83:4). So long as the name was remembered, the individual identity was intact.

Name-giving is still important. In the Christian church, infants are "christened": the name of the child is pronounced, ensuring Christian and personal identity. "John Doe" is everyman and no man. Among Jews, an infant boy is given a name at the time of circumcision, generally on the eighth day of his life. A baby girl is usually named on the first Sabbath following her birth. Jewish boys often receive two names—a Hebrew name and an English counterpart (for instances, Moses and Maurice).

Secular identity moves away from mythic significance. Social security numbers are individually unique in that they provide for no duplication and they fit more easily than names into a computerized society. Despite the impersonality of such an identity, numbers are being used more and more for educational and medical records (together with the individual's name). Ultimately, complete individual inventories will probably be stored in a computerized memory bank for retrieval for whatever purposes.

Societal myths were group myths which defined boundaries of nations and organizations within nations. They treated humans in groups rather than as individuals. The individual was immersed in the group. What happened to the group happened to him, just as in some degree what happened to him affected the group. Those who accepted the group myth achieved identity through membership in the group—through belonging to a family, a clan, a tribe, a city, a nation. The god of the group was the god of the individual. The individual mattered only as a group member and existed only by virtue of belonging. Separation from the group meant extinction.[2]

The Moabites were "the people of Chemosh" (*'am Chmsh,* Num. 21:29); the Hebrews were "the people of Yahweh" (*'am Yhwh,* Judg. 5:11). Election mythology assured the Jews that they had been chosen,[3] and covenant mythology explained the nature of their relationship to Yahweh.[4] Because Christianity began in Judaism, it seems natural to find similar motifs in Christian mythology. A new election myth[5] and a new covenant myth[6] developed. The new myths were deemed to be superior to the old, rendering the old void and meaningless for those who accepted the new. The new myths were as separative as the old and characterized by the same kind of expressions of group superiority.

Nor has the process ceased. Racism, cultism, and nationalism continue to construct barriers between communities. Within the separating walls, the individual acquires identity. He is in, others are out. He knows where he belongs and where he feels comfortable. Others are strange, different, dangerous. Societal myths are alienation myths, linked to insecurity that requires mythic reinforcement. They proclaim that "our god is better than your god, our way is superior to your way, our individuals are more significant than yours." Slogans develop to support the claims: "the true faith," "one way." To accept or tolerate outsiders or other "ways" is to weaken the validity of the claim to superiority and exclusiveness. Ostracism becomes a powerful weapon.[7] In the past, members of one faith have had little or no contact with those who believed differently and supported variant mythologies. In some Christian churches, those who are not members of a particular denomination are barred from participating in sacral communion rites.[8]

Similar barriers are easily discernible on national levels. To pass from one country to another, one must have a passport. Individuals are citizens of a certain country, not of the world. The Berlin Wall is a divisive structure, just as the Maginot Line was a protective and divisive barrier before World War II.

In secular society, divisions are maintained in social clubs that admit no Jews or blacks and that demand certain dress codes for dining room service.[9] Clothes separate the blue-denim subculture from white-collar or blue-collar people. Slogans proclaim that "*black* is beautiful"—not brown or yellow or white. Black Panthers, Brown Berets, Minute Men, Weathermen, and the Ku Klux Klan subdivide men still further.

Groups may develop distinctive markings, clothing, or symbols that further distinguish members from nonmembers. Egyptian priests were depilated. Circumcision became a special mark for the male Jew. Amulets found in tombs suggest that individuals wore the symbol of the god whose help and influence they coveted most.

The pattern remains, sometimes with mythic overtones, sometimes without. Christians still wear crosses, ICHTHUS pins (the symbol of the fish standing for "Jesus Christ [son of] God, our savior"), and other symbolic jewelry. Jews wear Stars of David and Muslims wear the sacred name of Allah. Lodge members wear membership pins, and married persons often wear rings to signify that status. Hair has also become a cultural symbol; long-hairs versus the army crew cut, "naturals" versus nonnaturals. Circumcision is now so broadly practiced that it is no longer a symbol of Jewishness. Certain Chicano groups have developed tattoo marks that convey messages of belonging to other initiates.

The mythic divisions of religious groups extend to all parts of the culture; rather than uniting individuals in a fellowship that stresses individual worth, their emphasis is on group identity, and the individual finds personal identity within the group. Not to belong often symbolizes not to be. Close group identity isolates others from group association. Often the isolated ones form their own identity group.[10]

Apocalyptic mythology streamed out of Persia and flowed into Judaism and Christianity, giving individuals assurance of personal worth. The Zoroastrian worshiper enjoyed the privilege of free choice—to support good or evil. Zoroastrians knew that they were involved in a continuing struggle with aggressive, demonic powers of evil that called for endurance and personal commitment. Prayers requested strength from Ahura Mazda to face the demands of daily living successfully.

In the book of Daniel (Chap. 12) the pious Jew was assured that he would be rewarded in the life to come for stubborn adherence to the faith in this life. Good deeds were not forgotten; fidelity would be rewarded. Evil was remembered. Names were recorded in the book of life, and woe to those whose names were omitted.

Christian mythology also emphasized rewards and punishments in the world to come and assured the believer of his personal worth. The Gospel of Luke informed readers that even the hairs of the head were numbered (12:6), and that when the apocalyptic end of the age came and endurance in persecution was called for among believers, not one of those numbered hairs would perish (21:18). According to Christian mythology, the individual counted for something.

There is another dimension in which the myth and the cult seem to have affected the individual. Successful social conditioning programmed the individual to experience tension and guilt when his personal aims, dreams, and needs conflicted with societal expectations, values, and demands. Guilt and fear produced psychic imbalance that could be rectified only through expiation rites and conformity to the norm. Through cultic ritual, individuals might experience moments of wholeness and self-unification in which inner tensions were resolved. Through ritual, the individual could experience a "high" when the existential "now" became all-important and the weight of the past and the uncertainty of the future did not intrude on the experience. Only a few records have been preserved which explain life-changing moments in the lives of hero figures. For example, the eighth century Judean prophet, Isaiah ben Amoz, had such an experience on the temple precincts during a festal rite that included purgation ceremonies (Isa. 6). Over a century later, another Judean prophet, Jeremiah ben Hilkiah, described in somewhat similar terms an experience that provided him with a sense of identity, destiny, and meaning (Jer. 1:4–10). Jesus' baptism may have been his moment of identity experience (Mark 1:9–15). The apostle Paul recorded his life-unifying and life-changing experience in rather vague terms in a letter to Galatian Christians written about the middle of the first century A.D. (Gal. 1:13–17). It is not possible to determine how accurately the slightly varying accounts in Acts record Paul's hallucinatory experiences (Acts 9:1–22, 22:4–16, 26:9–18).

Not all "high" moments necessarily resulted in reorientation of life. Some had value in themselves for what the individual felt at the moment plus whatever understanding, self-meaning, or identity he might acquire. Akhenaton of Egypt composed a hymn to Aton, the sun god, expressing joy in the miracle of life and in the beauty he observed in the world (fourteenth century B.C.). His awareness of personal intimacy with the god at the time of writing is clear from his statement, "You are in my heart," and from his claim that divine plans were revealed to him.[11] A hymn writer of a slightly later period wrote of being intoxicated with the beauty of the sun god Amon and exulted in the power and majesty of the deity.[12] The Nile also provoked jubilation among the people and received praise and adoration as a deity.[13] Egyptian hymns are marked by an all-pervading joy in living and in god-man relationships experienced by the worshiper. They appear to come from high experiential moments. Perhaps it can be assumed that those who sang the hymns shared the feelings of happiness and divine-human union experienced by the authors. The sun and the Nile sustained life; the poems express the exhilarating fullness the people felt when these natural factors provided Egypt with abundant harvests.

Ecstatic experiences were not uncommon among the Hebrews. King Saul was supposed to have entered into some sort of trance state when he encountered a band of prophets at Gibeath-elohim. The men carried musical instruments—harps, tambourines, flutes, and lyres—which may have been used to induce a high emotional reaction in Saul (1 Sam. 10:5ff). Traditions regarding Saul's volatile nature link his behavior to that of prophets who were accepted as having direct communication links to the deity. In Gibeah, the spirit of Elohim came upon Saul and transformed him into a raving individual who hacked his oxen to pieces to rouse his fellow Hebrews to come to the rescue of the beseiged city of Jabesh-gilead (1 Sam. 11:6ff). When Saul visited Samuel at Naioth, the spirit of Elohim seized him again. This time, he lay naked in a trance state for a day and a night (1 Sam. 19:23f). It is not possible to know what factors provoked the reactions in Saul, any more than it is possible to know what facets of cultic rites produced hallucinatory experiences in Isaiah of Jerusalem. In one instance, Saul was roused by music, in another against the Ammonites by reports of the seige, and in still another by whatever was occurring at Naioth. What factors contributed to prophetic ecstasy and how many "ordinary citizens" had similar experiences which were not recorded cannot be known. Early Christians also experienced moments of rapture, both as individuals and in groups. Stephen, an early preacher, envisioned the heavens opening, permitting him to see Jesus and God (Acts 7:56). In Jerusalem, a multitude from various parts of the Near Eastern world heard the preaching of early Christians in all of the languages represented by the crowd, a phenomenon said to have been occasioned by the action of the Holy Spirit (Acts 2:5ff). Hence, as individuals and in groups, early Christians had experiences that were uniquely personal and that linked the individual with the deity.

Whether intoxicants or hallucinatories were employed in worship to provide individuals with personal experiences of communication with the deities or to encourage visions cannot be known. Zoroaster's followers used the sacred intoxicant *Haoma* in their rites. Egyptian medical knowledge embraced herbs and various plants that had hallucinatory potential, but whether and how these were used in cultic rites is a matter for speculation. Sumerian, Babylonian, and Assyrian physicians also possessed information about the hallucinatory effects of certain plants, but to the best of our knowledge, these plants were used primarily for healing rather than to achieve experience of the sacred.

Those who have used mescaline and LSD to facilitate "mystical experiences" have not hesitated to compare those experiences with reports of mystics. Personal identity, new awareness of self, and often a feeling of ecstatic unity with the whole, with God, in which the individual retains awareness of personhood, are reported.[14] Does the biochemical structure of the human body contain something which could trigger reactions akin to those produced by hallucinogenics? If so, then the visionary experiences of mystics and others who have had hallucinations could be explained biochemically, without reference to myth. Such an explanation would by no means deny the reality of the experience, nor reject the new awareness discovered by the visionary. It would suggest that because of biochemical structure, some persons are more apt than others to have such experiences. On the other hand, ecstatic encounter experiences generally occur within the framework of religious organizations that *expect* their followers to enter mystic states, so that sociopsychological conditioning may also be involved.

There can be little doubt that certain rites gave individual worshipers a sense of intimate contact with the holy. The Canaanites used sexual intimacy as a rite of holy communion, and those who copulated with male or female sacred prostitutes not only entered into a divine-human relationship but contributed to the fecundity of the soil, flocks, and herds. These rites became part of the Hebrew cultic practice despite condemnation by the prophets (see 2 Kings 23:7; Amos 2:7f; Jer. 2:23ff). Because sacrificial offerings were believed to be received directly by the deity, it is not impossible that the worshiper sensed identity and communion when he made an offering (see 1 Sam. 1:3ff). However, as the cult became more and more institutionalized, the gap between the worshiper presenting an offering and the priest acting on behalf of the worshiper grew, and offering rites might easily have lacked personal identity. Tablets which have been found record that an individual brought an animal for sacrifice, it was received by such-and-such a priest, who put it in a stall and fed it, and it was later sacrificed by still another priest. Such arrangements could provide little personal satisfaction for the worshiper, other than knowing that he had fulfilled his obligations to the god.

Some modern religious groups provide their followers with experiences of intimate identification with the deity. After purgation rites have rendered them worthy, Roman Catholic believers partake of a holy wafer. Because of the mythic interpretation given to the rite and to the wafer, they often speak of experiencing newness of life. Conversion or life-changing experiences are anticipated among evangelical groups. Christian Scientists experience "healing," as do many who attend healing services conducted by popular preachers. The growth of groups "speaking in tongues" in Protestant and Catholic congregations that had been highly structured in worship patterns[15] and the introduction of the evangelistic fervor of groups like the so-called "Jesus people" may reflect the desire for some sort of personal divine-human breakthrough that was felt to be absent. Some who participated in these "encounter" rites claim to have felt the power of the holy in a personal way never experienced before and with an intensity that lifted them from the dull routine of daily existence. To move from religious ritual in which prayer is, in the words of one young person, "like talking into a telephone mouthpiece without being sure that the person at the other end has lifted up his receiver" to an assurance that prayer is heard and answered and that life is divinely guided is to move from life (as mere existence) to LIFE (with meaning and purpose). The power of the myth to transform existence into dynamic experience is, in the twentieth century, directly related to individual experiences which, when gathered together, provide the basis for a movement. As the movement becomes organized, individuals seeking membership are programmed to expect certain kinds of experiences. Out of the conditioning comes the reality of the experience, and the mythic claim is proved. To fail to have the experience demonstrates that there is something "wrong" with the individual; persons are made to feel inadequate, are continually urged to keep reaching (trying), or simply drop out because of feelings of rejection.

Throughout the ancient Near East, hymns of praise and adoration were addressed to the gods. In Mesopotamia, many hymns were concerned with the alleviation of suffering and other human problems. Often there were overtones of personal relationships with the gods. Perhaps it is reading too much into the incantation of an individual offering a lamb to nocturnal deities in a divination service to suggest that when he asks the gods to "put truth for me" into the rite, he is not merely reciting a formula but is reaching for an intimate response.[16] The hymn to the moon god Sin, found in the library of Ashurbanipal (seventh century B.C.), requested forgiveness for sins but also stated that the worshiper sought and wished to faithfully serve the deity.[17] Again, the phrases may be formalities, but they may also be genuine requests for personal divine-human relationships desired by the originator of the prayer and echoed by those who repeated it.

Hebrew psalms, used in the liturgy of the temple, contain hymns praising Yahweh, lamentation and thanksgiving songs for both public and private occasions, and other thematic poems. What individuals who used laments and thanksgiving psalms in personal worship may have felt is not known. Analysis of the structure of these poems determined that they follow somewhat fixed patterns.[18] For example, laments usually opened with a cry for help followed by an explanation of the worshiper's unhappy situation. Faith and trust in Yahweh were expressed and the deity was called on to hear and respond. Next, the petitioner stated his assurance of Yahweh's intention to act. The hymns closed with promises to praise Yahweh.[19] To the degree that the worshiper made the prayer his own, it is possible that some experience of personal relationship to the deity was involved and that emotions were evoked that transcended formal enactment of ritual. Records of Jewish mystics demonstrate that there has been a continuity of profound responses through the past two millennia.

Cultic ceremonies included thanksgiving rituals that, despite the danger of becoming perfunctory acts, called for joy in the recognition of what Yahweh had done for the people. As a great oratorio may stir the emotions of the individual participants and listeners today and rouse feelings of wholeness, beauty, and personal at-oneness, so the hymns of the past and the temple rituals may have produced similar reactions among some of the worshipers. For example, Psalm 33:2–3 is characterized by excitement, encouraging the worshiper to

> Praise Yahweh with the harp,
> make music to him on the ten-stringed lyre.
> Sing a new song to him,
> play skillfully on the strings with loud shouts.

Thanksgiving hymns have been found in all ancient Near Eastern religions. Although the hymns we know were used in structured ceremonial rites, the possibility of individual experiences of identity and joy during the singing of such hymns should not be negated.

The Deuteronomic tithing rite is a ritual of joy for survival and abundance. The worshiper who lived at a distance from Jerusalem was instructed to sell his agricultural tithe for silver, and having come to the sacred city, to

> ... spend the silver for anything you desire—oxen or sheep or wine or strong drink or anything your appetite fancies—and you will dine there before Yahweh your god and enjoy yourself—you and your household ... (Deut. 14:26)

Shouting, dancing, blowing the shofar, and sacrificial offerings accompanied the delivery of the sacred ark, the symbol of Yahweh's presence, into Jerusalem (2 Sam. 6:12–15). The ark was deposited within the sacred tent in Jerusalem, with joyous feasting (2 Sam. 6:19). The vigor of the dance is reflected in the scornful admonitions of David's wife Michal, who accused the king of indecent exposure during his ecstatic leaping (2 Sam. 6:20).

Zoroastrian prayers made specific requests for enlightenment and union with Good Mind.[20] Many prayers were anticipatory, calling for strength to do battle against evil. Although all believers were engaged in a constant struggle against the powers of Ahriman, only in individual lives could victory over the powers of darkness be experienced. Only the individual could atune life to cosmic good. Cultic rites served the community, but personal experience of divine-human relationships lay at the heart of the religion.

Christianity, with its inheritance of Zoroastrian concepts through Judaism, laid mythic importance upon the individual's personal relationship to the deity. Almsgiving, prayer, and fasting were private, not public, religious acts (Matt. 6). Even the ritualistic so-called Lord's Prayer was designed to be personal and meaning-filled, with overtones of personal responsibility to the deity and one's fellow humans (Matt. 6:9–15). The sermon on the mount addressed individuals and placed mythic emphasis on what each person must do. Nevertheless, there were those who experienced high moments of personal identity in the rites of the early church to such a degree that Paul found it necessary to play down the importance of experiences that tended to separate Christians in Corinth into rival camps, each exalting its own "spiritual gift" (1 Cor. 12).

It seems reasonable to suppose that most persons in the ancient past lived much as we do today, without too much questioning or discussing of identity issues. Individual living was composed of high and low points and a range of experiences between them. Happiness depended on an adequate supply of the basic needs for human survival: food, shelter, and love. Some people experienced well-being, joy, and a sense of integrity in work well done. Moments of wholeness and completeness were certainly found outside the cult in warm social and familial gatherings and in private acts of love. These personal moments, outside yet within the mythic structure, must have given ancient man some sense of personal identity. Truly, we live in moments, not in years, in brief and memorable experiences, not in the routine of daily existence.

King Shulgi, second king of the third dynasty of Ur (late third millennium), exulted in his role as monarch. He rejoiced in the blessings he received from the gods, in his supreme power, in his physical prowess, and in his undaunted courage. He reveled in his popularity and in the pleasures of food and drink. There is no question of his sense of fullness, meaning, and identity. He was truly a man in love with life, and as S. N. Kramer's translation of his joyous statement has been captioned, he was "King of the Road."[21]

Early Egyptian tomb paintings are alive with expressions of joy in action, pleasure in doing, and fulfillment through a variety of physical and social outlets. Delight in involvement in life and living carried over into the mythic projections of the nature of the afterlife. We can speculate that the Egyptians stressed enjoyment of the moment, found a sense of identity in accomplishments, and experienced fulfillment in the high glow and stimulation of the moment. Material rewards and physical well-being seem to merge in what has been recognized as a genuine zest for life. On the other hand, tombs from a much later date (first millennium B.C.) are more somber. Lists of magic spells enabled the deceased person to enter the world beyond death. In both cases, there was an expression of the worth of the individual and of self-identity. Although there was always a gap between the real and the ideal, the coffin texts contain a statement by the sun god of four divine acts expressing the equal worth of all men in the eyes of the god:

1. I created the four winds that each man might inhale them just like his fellow man during his time . . .
2. I created the overflow waters (of the Nile) so that the poor and the rich alike might use them . . .
3. I created each man like his fellow-man. I forbade evil. Their hearts disobeyed what I commanded . . .
4. I created their hearts not to forget the west (death) so that offerings might be made to the local gods . . .[22]

Egyptian workmen's songs, preserved in the eighteenth dynasty tomb of Paheri (sixteenth to fourteenth centuries B.C.), reflect joy in labor. Appreciation is expressed for the coolness of the day, the presence of the north wind, and the food the workers were harvesting.[23] Fourteenth century B.C. festal songs from the Luxor temple of the god Amon describe the joy of soldiers and sailors in the service of the god.[24]

Joy in victory is recorded several times in the Old Testament. The Hebrew women joined Miriam in a victory song and dance, using timbrels to beat time, when the Hebrews escaped from Egypt (Exod. 15:20–21). Timbrels and other instruments provided music for the victory dance and singing that greeted David when he returned flushed with victory over the Philistines (1 Sam. 18:6–7). Although Yahweh was recognized as the rescuer from Egypt and the power-giving source for David, the secular rites are given mythic overtones. In such moments of high ecstasy the individuals may be said to have experienced personal identity.

New Testament writers recognized the prevalence of those who experienced contentment and well-being in the abundance of good things to eat and enjoy, but the validity of such feelings was negated by the early church, which emphasized divine-human relationships and preparation for the rewards of the afterlife (see Luke 12:15–31). For the Christian, joy was to be found not in secular realms, but in the mythic realms where the individual was assured of identity, meaning, and future abundance. Paul could write:

> I will gladly boast about my weaknesses so that Christ's power may come upon me. For Christ's sake I am satisfied with weaknesses, insults, miseries, persecutions and hardships, for when I am weak, then I am strong. (2 Cor. 12:9–10)

In the proclamation of beatitudes, Jesus told his listeners that they should be happiest when they were reviled, persecuted, and lied about for the sake of Jesus, because they could be assured that their reward in heaven would be great (Matt. 5:11f). The otherworldly emphasis of the New Testament did not deny that there were others who found their fullness and meaning in the richness and happy experiences of the non-Christian way of life.

Although love between a man and a woman can hardly be said to have mythic significance, nevertheless love was given mythic importance in the ancient Near East in the love of gods and goddesses. In the cultic rites that celebrated divine love, every potential lover was introduced to the language of love and to its mythic significance.[25] What happened between Dumuzi and Inanna of Sumer in their most intimate associations, what developed between Isis and Osiris or Anat and Ba'al, was dramatized in ritual and became the possession of every participant and onlooker. To be loved by someone was to have identity, just as gods and goddesses had identity. To experience orgasmic explosion was to achieve completeness and to know simultaneously fullness and emptiness, ecstasy and relaxation.

Divine lovers in ancient Sumer experienced quarrels,[26] mutual physical attraction, courting and marriage, and intimate passionate love.[27] Egyptian love poems tell of a lover's desire to entrap his beloved, of joy in associations, and of the emptiness of separation.[28] An Egyptian poet stated that a woman's love made him "steady," and that a week's absence from her developed within him a sickness that no physician could cure. Only one thing would revive him—the announcement "She is here!"[29] Canaanite myths describe the intimate love-making of Ba'al and Anat.[30] In the Old Testament, what is surely a modified Canaanite poem of love between deities recites the love of a man for a woman and a woman for a man in antiphonal responses that are warm, intimate, and beautifully graphic.[31]

The sacred and the profane flowed together and blended into one. To know love was to know what gods and goddesses knew, to feel what they felt, and to experience identity and perhaps meaning. To know love was to discover to some degree one's personhood, and because love had divine overtones, it bestowed a mystical, mythical identity on those who shared it. The Judean tradition in Genesis announces the mythic new identity as "they become one flesh" (Gen. 2:24)—a psychic unity that conveyed new identity to both persons.

Human love assumed mythic qualities when Inanna and Ishtar, the love goddesses of ancient Mesopotamia, were in the underworld in the realm of death, and sexual love was dead among mortals. A Sumerian poet wrote that when a city or a people rejected Inanna, the women of that locale did not speak in love or whisper tenderly to their husbands, and did not reveal to them the "holiness" of their hearts.[32]

Modern love poetry echoes the feelings of ancient love poems. Individuals in love discover new depths in themselves, acquire new ways of looking at life, and achieve new identities. Perhaps some of the mythic overtones remain. Marriages are made "in heaven." Love is "divine," and the beloved is perfect.

Another dimension to the identity question often haunts those who are outside current mythic patterns and even troubles some who accept the myths. The question is usually phrased in terms of meaning, or ultimate meaning: What is it that gives meaning to life? The question is personal, for the query does not necessarily pertain to human life in general, but to individual lives. Obviously, then, each answer will be individual. Some are convinced that without some kind of mythic implications, life can be interpreted only as the period of existence between conception and death. That time span may be marked equally well by joy, success, beauty, and a sense of fullness, or by misery, failure, ugliness, and a feeling of emptiness. Meaningfulness is primarily an individual assessment, although some hero figures may acquire meaning beyond themselves. For many today, life is little more than existence—a series of good or bad sensations—mere survival.

For nine months during 1971, television crews documented all phases of the lives of the members of a California household. The edited video-tapes were presented to the public in a series called "The American Family," a continuum of utter tedium, for what came through was the empty routine of the family's existence, along with a frightening recognition that this was a rather clear depiction of the "average" American life-style. The lack of meaning in much that we do and worry about had been noted earlier in a song which asked, "Is that all there is?" It concluded, "Let's break out the booze and have a ball . . . if that's all there is." The question and the answer are not new; both have been explored by the writer of Ecclesiastes. The song, the television series, and Ecclesiastes retained the mythic assumption of something beyond the here and now, but life remained trapped in little routines. As we have noted earlier, we live in moments, not years, and certainly not in lifetimes. The moments may be strung together to suggest a pattern of the intrusion of the divine into the realm of the secular, or they may be examined to demonstrate that this *is* "all there is." The difference is one of personal outlook, of commitment to a myth of meaning or of commitment to secularism.

Within the lives of those who reject mythic implications for life, as well as in the lives of many who tacitly accept mythic implications, there is often a desperate search for something to give meaning to life, for moments that "put it all together." Life is fragmented. Moments pile upon moments, years upon years. Life is not smooth, but like a series of movements under strobe lights—jerky and uncoordinated. How does one maintain balance, discover harmony, find peace and wholeness? For some, the answer lies in the myth that ties all life together through faith. For others, it lies in certain experiences that appear to reach depths and heights beyond the ups and downs of daily life. For still others, the question is simply not to be asked.

NOTES

[1]John A. Wilson, *The Culture of Ancient Egypt* (Chicago: University of Chicago Press, 1956), p. 225.

[2]In the Genesis story of Cain and Abel, Cain was condemned to be a wanderer because he had murdered his brother. He complained that anyone who met him would kill him (Gen. 4:14). An individual without communal identification was a target for all.

[3] Gen. 12:1–3, 13:14ff, 28:10–17, 35:9–15; Deut. 7:6–9.

[4]Gen. 17:9–14; Exod. 19–20; Deut. 6:1–25, 27.

[5]Rom. 4:1–11; Matt. 2:15 (see also Exod. 4:22); Matt. 25:31–46 (see also Gen. 12:3); Rev. 5:9–10 (see also Exod. 19:5f); Heb. 7.

[6]Rom. 3:21ff; John 3:16–21, 6:35ff; Heb. 8:1–10:39.

[7]Conversations with those who have lived in communities dominated by one religion reveal that ostracism is one of the harshest penalties inflicted on the

outsider. School children do not associate with or speak to the newcomer. To walk past schoolmates who return silence for greetings becomes almost unbearable for children so isolated.

[8]I can recall that when I was a child in Canada, it was not uncommon for pupils from the Catholic and public schools to group on opposite corners of an intersection and shout "Potlicker" and "Catlicker" at one another. Societal myths thrive on denigration.

[9]For example, the Jonathan Club of Los Angeles has not permitted turtleneck sweaters on the third floor of the club since August 1968, with the exception of formal turtleneck garments at black-tie affairs. Turtlenecks obviously represent or suggest a life-style not in keeping with that approved of by club members. On the other hand, the exclusive Clift Hotel in San Francisco will provide service (registration, dining room, and bar) to men in turtleneck shirts (provided they are wearing coats), but bar males with "unconventional hair styling," that is, hair that falls beneath the top of the collar, no matter how well groomed. Clearly, long hair is out of keeping with the Clift Hotel's advertised conservatism.

[10]When I was a child in Alberta, Canada, my family moved into a neighborhood in Calgary where the youth were organized into gangs. Not to belong was to be subject to bullying by gang members wherever one went. For mutual protection, a number of us who had recently entered the community organized our own gang; after a few battles, persecution ceased.

[11]"The Hymn to Aton," *ANET,* pp. 369ff.

[12]"Hymns to the Gods as a Single God," *ANET,* pp. 371f.

[13]"Hymn to the Nile," *ANET,* p. 372.

[14]See G. Ray Jordan, "LSD and Mystical Experience," *Journal of Bible and Religion,* XXXI (1963), 114–23.

[15]Twenty thousand persons are reported to have attended the meeting of Roman Catholic Pentacostals held at Notre Dame University in June 1973. It is estimated that at least thirty-five thousand Catholic Pentacostals took part in weekly prayer groups around the United States as of January 1, 1973.

[16]*ANET,* p. 391.

[17]Ibid., p. 386.

[18]For a brief analysis, see Gerald A. Larue, *Old Testament Life and Literature* (Boston: Allyn & Bacon, 1968), pp. 364ff and the sources cited on pp. 495f.

[19]Psalms of lament include Pss. 3, 6, 13, 17, 22, 26, 28, 31, 35, 38, 54, 55, 56, 57.

[20]See Jacques Duchesne-Guillemin, *The Hymns of Zarathustra* (London: John Murray, 1952; paperback reprint, Boston: Beacon Press, 1963), Yasna 28:4 (p. 86), 49:3 (p. 127).

[21]"The King of the Road: A Self-Laudatory Shulgi Hymn," *ANET,* pp. 584ff.

[22]James H. Breasted, *The Dawn of Conscience* (New York: Scribner's, 1933; paperback ed., 1968), p. 221.

[23]*ANET,* p. 469.

[24]Ibid.

[25]Helmer Ringgren, *Religions of the Ancient Near East* (Philadelphia: Westminster Press, 1973), pp. 24ff; S. N. Kramer, *The Sacred Marriage Rite, Aspects of Faith, Myth, and Ritual in Ancient Sumer* (Bloomington: Indiana University Press, 1969), pp. 49–133.

[26]*ANET,* pp. 637f.

[27]Ibid, pp. 638ff.

[28]Ibid, pp. 467f.

[29]Ibid, pp. 468f.

[30]The fragmented texts tell of Ba'al caressing Anat's vulva, of Anat holding Ba'al's testicles, and of the two lovers kissing and embracing sexually. See C. Gordon, *Ugaritic Literature* (Rome: Pontificum Institutum Biblicum, 1949), p. 53.

[31]The so-called "Song of Solomon."

[32]"Hymnal Prayer of Enheduanna: The Adoration of Inanna in Ur," *ANET*, pp. 579–82, lines 51–57.

seven

Future Myth

Any attempt to deal with the future is presumptuous. Tomorrows may be anticipated, but they can not be determined—at least, not yet; far too many factors alter intentions and invalidate predictions. Nevertheless, because there is potential for dramatic change in our lifetime, we may perhaps explore tentatively some aspects of the future.

We live simultaneously in past, present, and future: in the past as we now interpret what has happened, in the present as we experience life now, in the future as we anticipate or project life now. As we express our anticipation of the future, we in some measure determine it. Tomorrow's world is revealing itself today, and at the same time today is affected and conditioned by what has been. What will emerge is now emerging; if Alvin Toffler is correct, we are accelerating into the future at an ever-increasing rate.[1] Humans must learn to cope if they are to survive.

As in every other human period of which we have knowledge, there is now both resistance to and eager acceptance of change. Fear of the breakdown of accepted, proven patterns, fear as ancient as man himself, clashes with anticipation of the new. But the new is here, upon us, engulfing us as never before. It is not the purpose of this section of the book to discuss the future in terms of psycho-bio-social concepts; others far more competent to do so are engaged in these tasks. Rather, we will touch on some implications for mythic thought that may be involved in our anticipation of and uncertainty about the future.

PROBLEMS OF CHANGE

It seems unlikely that ancient mythic themes will disappear completely from human thought or cease to affect human life. Our mythic heritage cannot be lightly dismissed. What was conceived and believed in the past has in no small way determined our present. The flow of mythic concepts from the ancient Near East effected dramatic changes in attitudes and life-style in Europe and subsequently in America and the rest of the world. Ancient myths are alive today and therefore extend into the future, affecting its development. We have moved a long way into the intellectual revolutions sparked by the works of Copernicus and Darwin, and the impact of technological developments has dramatically changed our way of living. Myths that have been challenged are still alive and functioning —some having been adapted to conform to altered ideas and some in settings that seem to be relatively unaffected by scientific thought. Even the attempts in Russia to suppress religious mythology and to supplant it with political dogma have not been completely successful. Ancient myths are a part of our world and our society. For many they are integral in sustaining personal and social psychic health. In the Western world, the myth supports the "system" or the "establishment," and the establishment in turn sanctions the myth. Changes in social outlook and individual life-style do take place, but ancient myths continue to program and condition attitudes and to modify and sometimes control new and emerging patterns.

For some people, the exploration of the mythic origins of Western religious tradition has tended to render beliefs, creeds, and rituals invalid or illusory. Some experience mythic loss. Scientific and technological approaches to living have led to the rejection of the "mystery" in our world and our cosmos, and to the seeking of mechanistic causations for our environment. Mythic loss produces in some people a feeling of emptiness. Almost in reaction against the loss, there are those who attempt to embrace both worlds, clinging dogmatically to ancient statements or "truths" and boxing off these beliefs from the rest of life, or attempting to adapt the essence of ancient mythic concepts to our changing ideas.

Some who embrace the mythology have taken what has been called "the leap of faith" which transcends intellectual analysis. They point out that the results of their commitment are real, satisfying, and life-giving. The experience justifies the belief. Hence, one either accepts or rejects the traditions and the experience, for whatever reasons. In the future, there will no doubt be some people who will find personal identity through mythic tradition. Christians will recite the Lord's Prayer and the Apostles' Creed without analysis and will sense a unity with millions of other Christians who have spoken the same words through two thousand years of human history. Jews will repeat the *Sh'ma* in the awareness that this statement of identity and faith has been associated with joy and tragic sorrow extending back to the sacking of Jerusalem by the Babylonians. These creedal statements will be made by some who are fully aware that they are adapting ancient mythic themes to modern settings, and who will not be disturbed by the knowledge. They will live in the spirit of Wallace Stevens, who has written,

The final belief is to believe in a fiction, which you know to be a fiction, there being nothing else. The exquisite truth is to know that it is a fiction and that you believe in it willingly.[2]

To know to whom one belongs, to sense poetically a heritage, to be linked emotionally and perhaps physically to a tradition rooted in antiquity and marked by beauty and suffering, joy and heartache is to acquire psychic strength to meet the trauma of existence and to answer the absurdity of the human dilemma of man existing briefly in endless time and space.

The validity of holding onto ancient myth and permitting it to affect modern life has been upheld by some who argue that concepts that have proven themselves effective and valid through several thousand years of human history should not be discarded. There can be no question that the past exerts a stabilizing effect on the present and provides continuity and solid, tested foundations for action. Experience has taught humans many lessons, and to reject lightly what man has learned and cherished could be the height of folly. But there is another side to the mythic influence of the past, and it has discouraging and even frightening aspects. Emphasis on obedience to antiquated norms simply because they are old or have withstood "the test of time" too often has meant the subservience of innovative thought to revelatory mythology. Threats of divine punishment for disobedience to the revealed "truth," the promise of heavenly blessing, and even miraculous rewards for conformity have given ancient myths restricting authority and stifling power that has hindered full and open exploration of the varied dimensions of humanity. One need only recall the opposition of organized religion to changes in astronomical constructs in the sixteenth century and observe the continuing opposition to evolutionary hypotheses in the space age because ancient mythological ideas were and are affected. In California, the State Board of Education has been under pressure for years to include in public school science textbooks a "religious version" of the origin of the universe which would be given equal treatment to the scientific hypotheses. A group known as the Institution for Creation Research has pressed for the inclusion of their theory of "special creation" and has sought to link the Priestly creation myth of the Old Testament (Genesis 1:1–2:4a) to their interpretation of present-day scientific theories. Their opponents argue that mythic concepts do not belong in science textbooks, citing the backing of the National Academy of Science and other scientific organizations.

Because of their authority, supported as it is by the cultic organizations, ancient myths tend to limit the way in which humans may experience the phenomenal world. Culture heroes discourage outreach, for they become the ideal embodiment of attitudes and behavior enhanced by ancient myth, and sometimes they dramatize the futility of attempts to break

established, god-given bonds. Even such mundane matters as what foods
to eat and what persons to associate with or marry are affected by myths
that carry the weight of divine approval or disapproval. The rich variety
of foods now available and the social and personal expansion possible
through association with other regardless of their race or creed are automatically denied. Future myth may act as a freeing agent, opening doors
to new experiences by emphasizing the worth of individuals as individuals
and experiences as experiences.

From childhood, many of us are programmed to accept authority and
to respond to certain praise and criticism, and we find as adults that we
cannot exist outside a present pattern of controls. Those who chafe at the
restrictions generally do so at the edges, those peripheral areas where
societal pressure rubs against their wishes or intents. The heart of the
matter, which concerns the true freedom of the individual, rarely surfaces,
and when it does, it often provokes fear and uncertainty, anger and hostility. The chicken bred for egg-laying and raised in a pen two feet by two
feet by three feet is unable to cope when released into a large area without
restrictive fencing. Similarly, individuals programmed to live by rules fear
freedom. It is more comfortable to work within a system, to respond to
regulations and win approval, and to behave in acceptable ways.

Some people are troubled by the suggestion that categories such as right
and wrong, good and evil, moral and immoral be abolished and each act
be taken for what it is—simply an act. According to this viewpoint, if an
act hurts another, corrective or restrictive action can be taken, but the
performer of the act is freed from the burden of being a good or a bad
person, being in the right or in the wrong, doing something moral or
something immoral. In some parts of the world, the right of consenting
adults to relate to one another in any way that they wish as long as their
actions do not infringe the rights of or cause hurt to others is slowly being
recognized. Some individuals prefer nudity, others prefer to wear clothes:
neither pattern is in itself right or wrong, moral or immoral. Some people
practice cunnilingus, some are lesbians, some eschew sex, some prefer to
live alone. What difference does it make, so long as these individuals do
not hurt others? Some people argue that behavior outside the accepted
norm might have undue influence on others, particularly on children. The
more open the society, the more opportunity each individual will have to
choose a life-style that suits his or her desires. Many individuals do not
adopt the life-style of their parents; instead, they move away from "old
ways" and establish their own. The new ways may be similar or parallel
to many of the ways of their elders, but the new family has established
its own ground rules and found its own way.

It is condemnation that hurts, ostracism that destroys. In one case,
parents who were heart-broken because their son was a homosexual, and

who plagued the youth until he separated from his male lover and finally committed suicide, were not sure whether they had really "saved" their boy! They had added to his unhappiness feelings of shame, guilt, and unworthiness, and when they had finally separated him from someone he loved, they helped to bring about his death. In another case, a young woman from an orthodox Jewish family was pronounced "dead" by her relatives because she fell in love with a Gentile. She suffered the agony of rejection by and separation from those whom she loved dearly. We still have not learned to accept one another. We are controlled by our mythic memories of the past.

Some people have resisted change and will continue to resist it because they fear that all social values, mores, and standards are in danger of collapse, and that only anarchy can result.[3] Why retention of ancient structures or anarchy are the only alternatives is not clear. What could instead emerge may be a far more important social value: the freedom of the individual to choose the life-style best suited to his interests, provided that life-style does not interfere with another's freedom or safety. For example, any and all sexual relationships between consenting individuals would be acceptable, but forcible rape would be unacceptable because it violates the victim's security and personhood. To program individuals from childhood to think in terms of free expression and open exploration of the infinite possibilities and varied dimensions of living encourages variation without threat or fear. Educating, conditioning, and programming individuals to be aware of the right and freedom of others to differ —emphasizing the importance of nonviolation of another's personhood— can hardly produce chaos. Restrictive personal mores would be open to acceptance or rejection. What one person or group of persons did alone or together would be their business, insofar as their actions did not infringe the rights of others. The influence of one life-style on other patterns of living would be through example, invitation, and education, not through enforced conformity. Individuals would be free to choose.

But we cannot really let go the old attitudes. Far too many people fear release from ancient "proven" or divinely revealed values. During the 'sixties there was widespread rebellion among students. The sacred cult of knowledge came under fire. Ancient mottoes carved in stone on university buildings were challenged. "Know thyself"—how? Through the classroom? "Know the truth and the truth shall make you free"—what "truth"? How does one acquire the magic formula? The cultic center of knowledge became the battleground. To know had always meant to accumulate knowledge, as students in the ancient wisdom schools had done; but this is the computer age, and what student can or wants to compete with a machine? Let the machines serve the student! Data storage does not make one human. However, despite the attention it attracted, the rebellion died down. Minor changes were made. The cult of knowledge continued much as it had before.

Intellectually, we encourage change and innovation. We cherish the concept of pressing on to new patterns, of experimentation in new dimensions. Actually, however, we resist change and discourage innovation. Ancient Mesopotamia, Egypt, and Israel, with their admiration of established patterns, continue to hold us in check. Individuals are encouraged to "do their own thing," but if their "thing" deviates from the accepted norm, they are condemned. Tension exists between individual freedom and communal standards even when personal expression does not infringe others' rights and freedoms. Judgments reflect ancient mythic standards of good and bad, right and wrong, acceptable and unacceptable, blessed and sinful. Clearly, the future holds promise of more conflict.

As the potential for mythic change continues to develop and become more apparent, those who desire stability tend to experience neurotic insecurity. But life has always been beset by uncertainties, and myths often touch on the factor of unpredictability. Moreover, in some ways each of us is unpredictable: we do what is not expected of us, we break the pattern. The fear associated with mythic change, however, is larger and more encompassing than minor aberrations; it relates to the ancient terror experienced in the face of potential chaos. Of course, chaos has always been present, held in check only by the power of mythic regulations. The mythic structure produced rewards in the form of a feeling of security among those who believed in it—at least they believed they knew what to expect of their fellow men. The same mythic structure produced frustration in those who desired or attempted to deviate from the established norms but were held in check. Now, change is upon us. The present age may be viewed as a period of estrangement and disintegration—estrangement because many individuals have become acutely aware of their aloneness, of the unique personal identity that separates them from their fellow man in the vast abyss of the universe: disintegration because mythically sustained values are in the process of being broken down.

The real issue lies elsewhere, with those who, like their forefathers, become so blindly committed to a particular mythology that they are willing to do battle over the acceptance or rejection of it by others. It is the epitome of insecurity to be so threatened by alternative mythic assumptions that violence is the only acceptable response. Hopefully, the future will be open to viable alternatives that can be calmly discussed and accepted or rejected by each individual without threats or compulsion to conform. The alternative to openness can only be suppression, enforced compromise, tension, and perhaps violence. There should be no need for attempts to reconcile differences in mythic outlook, or for any effort to compromise or modify another's mythic concepts.

There is condescension in the cliché, "I too am critical of the establishment or institution, yet I support it," when the speaker is actually deeply committed to the principles used by the dominant organization to inhibit the freedom of others. To be critical implies the development of a variant mythology without fear of rejection or condemnation. To be continually critical yet remain in the system is compromise. There are also those who are entrapped by the system for survival reasons and who feel compelled to live with the frustration of the limits it imposes.[4] The choices for the future are apparent: openness to and acceptance of our differences, or control in one form or another by the dominant group.

Then what of the future? In some ways the development of future myths involves the denegation of the validity of presently held myths. Only thus will the established power of ancient myths be broken. For example, the liberation of women involves the destruction of neat stereotypes that have been enhanced by ancient myth: men's work and women's work, the strong male and the weak female, controlled emotions in men and uncontrolled emotions in women, and so on. Women are now demanding equal work, responsibilities, wages, and sexual roles. Ancient sexual divisions are slowly disappearing; they will probably collapse even further in the future. As men and women, considered alike as "people" or "humans," share equal responsibilities and receive equal rewards, perhaps the liberation of sex will permit each person to live as he or she wishes, without guilt or frustrating social tensions.

COSMOLOGICAL MYTHS AND THE FUTURE

To talk about the future is to become involved with the potentials of the space age. One day, man will no doubt establish colonies on other planets and their satellites, in which groups of humans will live in controlled environments under massive protective domes. Food will be produced chemically and hydroponically. At first, animal products may be shipped in compressed, dehydrated form from the earth, but utimately, animals will be raised for food in a section of the space colony—if animals are still eaten at that time. Because the colony will be composed of highly skilled technicians, the loss of one such person will affect the balance of the community. The ancient concept of corporate personality, changed in emphasis and significance, may once again become a reality. The individual will be vitally linked to the group, and the group to the individual, with no loss of personal identity.

Outside the controlled environment, ancient forces of chaos and destruction will lurk. The boundaries of the colony will be the dividing line between safety and danger, security and insecurity, life and death; to move beyond them will be to enter hostile, alien territory. Portable life-support systems will permit exploration and exploitation of planetary potentials, but mutual concern and support and constant intercommunication will be essential for survival.

Cosmic terror, the fears lurking in outer space, will consist not of the angry faces of gods whose realms have been violated, but of technological failure and (as science fiction writers constantly remind us) creatures from other worlds. Science fiction fantasies are never removed from the realms of human concern—survival in an alien environment and encounter with those whose power or ways we do not know or understand.[5]

Different attitudes will develop in the space colony about the earth and the cosmos. The alien planet will become home to those who dwell there. In time, earth will become a foreign land, just as Europe, Asia, and Africa became foreign lands to inhabitants of the New World. Other parts of the solar system will become familiar. No longer will the planets be physical masses to be surveyed through telescopes or landed on by robots. Men will view them from close proximity and will personally explore the life-enhancing potential of the various parts of the solar system. Unmanned probes of other solar systems will prepare for the launching of manned space probes. The concepts of "heaven" and "earth" will probably remain in the earth inhabitants' vocabulary because they are convenient, but their ancient mythical significance will have forever faded. If gods are to have a dwelling place in space, the new heaven will have to be removed by millions of light years from man's new space habitations.

The image of a God in heaven has faded, and the need to demythologize ancient myths that continue to encourage such portrayals has been recognized. Too often, myths robbed of their supernatural qualities become ethical structures or moral imperatives. The flow of ideas from the Far East has been added to the flow from the ancient Near East. Meditation and contemplative groups, augmented by research into extrasensory perception and alpha brain waves, modify traditional approaches to the search for meaning. Electronic gear is employed to map and probe the mind, replacing ancient techniques of self-searching and self-control. Far Eastern myths are being interpreted in the light of Western experience; perhaps new myths which will become the myths of the future are emerging. As the world shrinks and travel facilitates communication among peoples, it is possible that from the intermixture of ancient and modern, from the fusion of Far Eastern, Near Eastern, and Western thought patterns, there will emerge new myths that incorporate aspects of the past with facets of the new and modern. New cosmic "gods" will emerge—or old images may appear in new form.

Another, and what may be for mythology a more devastating, concept has arisen from modern cosmological research: that the so-called "order," "system," or "laws" of the universe are the result of happenstance. Basically, there is no order, there is only chaos; what has evolved and is evolving from chaos is simply continuing chaos. The continuing interaction of cosmic particles throughout the five-thousand-million-year history of our galaxy produced life on earth about two thousand million years ago. What survives of those life forms today is simply a matter of happenstance. Some forms made it, others did not. Those that have survived have done so by adapting themselves to the chaos of their earthly environment and by making use of whatever is available for food, shelter, and protection. The so-called laws are patterns that happened to have evolved from aeons of chaos. But recognizing how a solar system operates is simply imposing on chaos a man-made order that may be important for human survival.

Moreover, if scientists' reading of the operation of the solar system is correct, the sun will burn out in another five thousand million years, and the earth will become as cold and lifeless as the moon. This fact may be of little importance for those of us who occupy the earth today—we won't be around to be involved, and we will be so far removed from whoever is around that we will not matter. So far, no myths have emerged to suggest how man may cope mythologically with this concept. The gods of order are, so far as this kind of thinking is concerned, absent, and chaos reigns. But this form of thinking has affected painting, poetry, music, novels, film, and almost every other kind of human expression, voicing awareness of the continuation of primeval chaos.[6] Like the people of the ancient Near East, we in our little world exist within chaos—the waters of Nun, the abyss, are all about us. Only as we remain within the security of the protective shell of our mythic world can we be safe and separate from the impacting power of chaos. As we dissolve the mythic shell, chaos impinges on us: we realize that we are part of the cosmic chaos and that order has emerged from the mythopoeic mind.

SOCIETAL MYTHS AND THE FUTURE

It seems probable that the most dramatic alterations of societal patterns will result from life in the space age. Space colonies will be composed of technicians chosen not only for their skills but also for their ability to live and work with others with minimum friction in circumstances that might ordinarily produce extreme tensions. Psychological tests will help eliminate those who would most easily become disaffected, but despite care in selection, the possibility remains that some persons in a colony will have problems adapting to space life and will have to be returned to earth. Communal harmony, balance of relationships, mutual concern, respect, and help will be of utmost importance. Perhaps those who have lived in communes on earth will be able to provide helpful guidance.

It is possible that persons designated to live in space will be specially bred on earth. Scientists can now freeze and store sperm; sperm from eminent thinkers, scientists, and creative geniuses might conceivably be stored and implanted in selected brilliant females to breed men and women of superior intellect. Ova can also be stored; thus, ova from brilliant women might be stored, fertilized artificially with sperm from the superior male storage bank, and implanted in healthy women, who would then bear the children. Offspring of such "parentage" would be carefully nurtured, educated, and conditoned in environments that would prepare them for life in space colonies.

Some aspects of this issue are already operative in our society. In Buenos Aires, Argentina, an ovary transplant was performed in 1972. The woman who received the ovary became pregnant by her husband. Their child has the characteristics of the donor of the ovary, rather than those of the woman who bore the child. What are the implications of births by implanting for the concept of the family? Donors of both ova and sperm might be dead. The "mother" who bears the child is not in reality its parent. The child might be of a different racial extraction from the "mother" who carries it in her womb. For these children, the terms *mother* and *father* would have little real significance, and the concept of family would probably assume the meaning of "living group," even as it has in some communal situations today.

Experiments with *cloning,* a word derived from a Greek term meaning "twig" or "shoot," suggest that in the future it may be possible to reproduce identical "copies" of any given individual. Cloning consists of the reproduction of cells that are precise duplicates of the parent cell; such cells can be reproduced in any quantity. Thus, from human cells from an individual such as Albert Einstein, innumerable Einsteins could theoretically be produced. Because such individuals would possess the same biochemical structure, there might be deep understanding between them, as there often is between identical twins. Such persons would tend to be ideally suited for settlement in space communities. Of course, there is no certainty that such techniques will be developed for humans or that they will be widespread.[7]

No doubt couples will continue to marry, but today's high divorce rate may accelerate even more in the future. We live in a throw-away world. Garbage dumps are filled with disposable "no deposit, no return" items. We have been programmed by mass advertising into discarding last year's model for this year's, all the while anticipating next year's innovations. Many persons do not buy homes or cars, but lease them on long- or short-term contracts. We have learned to live in the present in terms of our possessions, and to some extent also in terms of human relationships. A world with new patterns of human relationships is emerging, and there are no new myths to guide us, and so far there has been no suitable reinterpretation of old myths. There is no reason why friendships must extend throughout a lifetime unless they are comfortable and meaningful. Nor is there any reason why marriages should be continued for life, unless by mutual consent of the participants. The stigma attached to persons who have married and divorced several times is lessening, just as there is now no denigration of someone who changes homes or moves from city to city, state to state, or country to country. The new mobility, which will amost certainly increase in the future, is contributing to fluidity in human associations. One's friends may not be one's neighbors, and both neighbors and friends may change from year to year. The structure of one's family may also undergo change.

The most important societal issue pertaining to the future is the overall structure of society. Some people project a highly organized, controlled world.[8] The possibility that such a society will develop cannot be dismissed, nor can its form be determined now. Rigid societal controls may be more essential for survival in space than on earth, but with the burgeoning of survival problems such as overcrowding, pollution, and limited energy resources, it is not difficult to imagine severe restrictions being enacted for earth people, too. The implications for human freedom are important. How much restriction can be imposed to protect individuals and guarantee survival without smothering the tremendous potential within the human mind? What form of society will provide the greatest variety of alternatives and open the greatest number of potential avenues for exploration of life and living? Structuring implies predetermining roles, attitudes, and acceptable responses. Modern probes into the human mind indicate that the mind can be manipulated and controlled so that the individual will experience pleasure in doing the very things that would ordinarily be repugnant. Who, then, determines who does what? Who governs? For those committed to humanistic concerns, the potentials are frightening. In 1972, the Veterans Administration admitted performing since 1961 at least sixteen brain operations in what has been called "psychosurgery," aimed at correcting what was labeled "abnormal behavior" in cases where the patient failed to respond to traditional medical or psychiatric treatments and was in danger of harming himself or others. The issues of individual rights and freedoms versus communal survival become paramount. There will be continuing struggle until the question is settled.

During the past thousands of years, societal patterns have changed very slowly. Alteration in patterns occurs when established forms no longer satisfy or meet the prevailing mood or mind-set; when differing attitudes begin to predominate; when enforcement is weakened; when protesters are no longer silenced by death, ostracism, persecution and rejection; when the protest of some echoes what is deeply felt by others. Where the established structure is rigid, there may be revolution. Where options are possible, there may be coexistence—peaceful, or marked by friction.

We live in such a time. New social patterns continue to emerge; more are developing. Many people are willing to experiment with different life-styles. Enforced behavioral codes are failing. Church-promoted "blue laws" that restricted Sunday activities are almost extinct. The sale and distribution of alcoholic beverages is still severely regulated by government controls in some areas, but in ever-increasing numbers, communities are relaxing older rules and regulations and permitting individuals to make decisions about their purchase and use of such beverages without guilt or punishment. Attitudes toward the use of marijuana have undergone change as more and more youths who used it and enjoyed its effects without fear reach the age where their influence and their votes will eventually change the law.

Simultaneously, the emphasis on structure and order, on laws that regulate and control behavior, and on teaching that conforms to societal norms is being increased. The future is emerging from the present; it is not possible to stipulate the result. Some prophesy an ordered, controlled, structured society; others press for less structure and greater individual freedom. How can the two come together?

APOCALYPTIC MYTHS AND THE FUTURE

Our blue planet, floating and spinning endlessly in space, is, so far as anyone can tell, a freak. We may be the only form of intelligent life in the universe. Apart from the myths that seek to answer man's deep need to matter, there is really no reason to believe that our individual or collective lives matter to anything or anyone except ourselves. Our only meaning is the meaning we give to our being. Should we destroy ourselves by one means or another, it is impossible to imagine that the evolutionary process will begin again and that similar intelligent life forms will emerge over billions of years. The myth of meaning will cease, as will all other myths. The universe will absorb our existence and demise, just as it did that of the dinosaur. What mythology can be developed to enable humans to cope with the immensity of their nonexistence? Or as we move into space, what myths will enable man to maintian his psychic identity as he becomes increasingly aware of the immensity of the cosmos and his individual insignificance? As old myths lose their relevance, what myths can be projected to replace them? Can we accept the myth of meaninglessness?

One negative response involves the possibility of a future holocaust, self-destruction through the nuclear weaponry we are developing. Man and other forms of life do not matter anyway. If a global nuclear war breaks out, everyone will be eliminated, without exception. We cannot discount this possibility. One need only recall that after the explosion of the first atom bomb, American nuclear scientists admitted that they had contemplated the possibility that a nuclear chain reaction might be triggered that would annihilate all life on earth, but they were 99 percent sure that it would not happen. On the basis of one percentage, they were willing to risk the life of the world.[9]

A positive response might be the acceptance of our meaninglessness, and an individual commitment to whatever makes life full, sweet, and good for the years each of us has to to live. Psychic survival will continue to be important. New myths will have to work within our imaginations, opening channels for individual self-awareness and sensitivity to others. New myths may open the way to greater dimensions in love, understanding, and helpfulness, by which we gain intellectual and emotional depth. Perhaps the new myths will only rediscover the essence of old myths that emphasized the acceptance of mortality as the lot of all men. Perhaps they will emphasize the way of love as the most meaning-filled way of survival—love not in the sense of "Christian love," which demands the acceptance of a particularistic mythology, but simply human love in its manifold dimensions and expressions. Peace, wholeness, and identity would thus be mythically associated as products of our concern for others. Joy can be experienced in the pursuit of knowledge and the sharing of insights—in love—with others. It will be taught, as it has been in the past, that it is through others that we discover ourselves and achieve personal identity. From the probing of life and life processes, from the raising of questions about life and living, we may develop understanding and acceptance of our universe and our short-term relationship to it.

LIVING WITH THE ABSURD

Because man was not prepared to live with the absurd, he developed myths. Because he did not know *how* to live with the absurd, he canonized his myths. The myths echoed human hopes and dreams, repeating time and again in ritual drama and cultic ceremonies that the world had meaning, order, and purpose, and that man had meaning, direction, and purpose.

Old myths die hard, but for some of us they do die and the absurdity of life obtrudes. Man must learn to live with the absurd, with something beyond meaninglessness. Life itself is an absurdity if it has no meaning. What can man do? Myths themselves become absurdities.

For some, one answer lies in laughter, in the recognition of the meaning-less stupidity of all things and of the humor in the serious human effort to act as though there were some ultimate reality. A literature of black humor has sprung about this theme. Black humor is a kind of mythic substitute. It says, in effect, "There is no meaning in existence, but god [*sic*], isn't it funny!" Within the laughter there is a pathos, a deep sadness for the sickness of humans in their attempts to find themselves through the maze of living, a deep hurt at men's failures to achieve their human potential. The black humorist does not argue for ultimate meaning in life, but into the humor of his writing, weaves quiet tears for the wasted efforts of humans to achieve artificial goals, measure up to meaningless standards, live according to values set by others.[10] Among the scribes of this nonmyth approach are William Faulkner,[11] Donald Barthelme,[12] and Kurt Von-negut.[13]

Black humor has also been expressed in film, enabling all the world to consider the absurdities of that with which man occupies himself. Some viewers who shook with laughter at *Catch 22, Mash,* and *The Hospital* may have seen only the situation comedy; others recognized the humor as a response to existential meaninglessness. In *The Hospital,* men and women dedicated to the healing arts die and cause death in ludicrous situations: death becomes hilarious. The hospital as an institution is transformed into a slaughterhouse, with doctors and nurses as butchers. Days are marked by a series of life-destroying incidents perpetrated by serious people who seek to heal. And the audience roars with laughter.

For some people, to laugh is to cop out. The alternative is to enter into serious dialogue, a continual wrestling bout with the absurd—not to read meaning into existential nothingness, but to grapple with what it means to be human in a meaningless universe, to confront human suffering, misery, and hopelessness in grim determination to heal, to alleviate, to comfort. The absurdity may remain, but concerned involvement—and we return to the much abused term *love*—is one way of living with the absurd. One commits oneself to doing, to reaching out, to touching, to empathetic involvement with the tragedies of existence and their absurdities. One lives in moments, seeking bright interludes that compensate for the long, dull stretches and enrich life. Humans are not transformed by eschatologi-cal or apocalyptic myths that link them to a mythic future, but are strengthened by concern and lifted through doing.

For other people, the impossibility of fighting the hurricane becomes apparent, and they do what humans have done again and again in the long struggle for survival—adapt, accept the absurdity, recognize the limits of their understanding, and cease to question. Perhaps they simply accept some mythic interpretation "on faith" as the best way to make sense of the absurd. They perform their jobs and fulfill their other responsibilities.

Like the frustrated Gilgamesh, they build their "walls of Uruk" and "do their own thing," continuing to provide a solid social foundation. They live from day to day, not asking much and perhaps not even seeking to know. They may simply echo the words of Cardinal Newman, "I do not ask to see / The distant scene—one step enough for me."[14]

MYTHS OF DEATH AND DYING

Belief in an afterlife will probably continue to be important for the future, whether the mythology emphasizes individual immortality, absorption into a "world soul," or reincarnation. Some people may cling to the myth of the resurrection of the body when the messianic age arrives. Meanwhile, people will die and bodies will be turned over to morticians for burial or cremation.

New medicines and better understanding of the aging processes are prolonging life (too long, in the opinion of some).[15] For both legal and humanistic reasons, medical practitioners hesitate to relieve patients from prolonged suffering by administering lethal doses of life-destroying "medicine," or to bring about the death of persons whose brains have been destroyed and who have been reduced to "vegetable" status. Even though such a person experiences or makes no communication and though the valuable time of nurses, doctors, and orderlies is taken up by intravenous feeding, cleaning and caring for the inert patient, and pumping antibiotics into his senseless body, no one seems ready to "pull out the tubes" and let the person die or to administer a lethal poison. It has been argued that animals receive better treatment than humans: they are relieved of suffering, not permitted to "rot away." Although to permit the individual to die from lack of nutrition constitutes barbaric treatment, there are reports that this has been done. The most intelligent and humane response would seem to be to administer poison. Now voices are being raised in demand for death with the dignity befitting personhood. Some persons are drawing up legal permission for the physician or some other person to take such action in the event of incurable painful illness or irreparable destruction of the brain. The legal implications are, of course, enormous, and not many physicians would be willing to rely on a patient's written permission in a court of law to justify terminating a life.

That mythical overtones can be read into the death-with-dignity cause is clear from the efforts of several hundred residents of Pilgrim Place, a retirement home for full-time Christian workers, who in 1972 submitted a petition for death with dignity to the State Bar of California, the California Medical Association, and members of the California legislature. The petition requested the Bar

to instruct its legislative committee to hold hearings to ascertain the advisability of intro-
ducing legislation in the State Assembly for the purpose of protecting physicians from civil
suits or criminal prosecution if they fail to use surgical, medical or mechanical procedures
for the prolongation of life in those who are terminally ill, permitting them to die with
dignity, according to the will of God, with confidence in eternal life.

"Immortality" in the form of resuscitation of the dead body is assuming
new dimensions with the development of cryonic suspension of bodies.[16]
Bodies are stored in liquid nitrogen at minus 320 degrees Fahrenheit in
stainless steel storage capsules in underground cryonic vaults. Every three
months, the supply of liquid nitrogen is replenished. A number of bodies
have been preserved by this method, in the hope that at some future date,
cures will be found for whatever ailment caused their death. Physician-
scientists will then thaw and revive the body and administer the cure.
When the individual will be "awakened" cannot be foretold, but the
preservation of the body will be continued (financed by an insurance
policy) until the proper moment. No one has been able to say whether the
experiment will work, but Cryonic Societies have sprung up in major cities
in the United States, and a number of bodies have been placed in cryonic
suspension in California, where the necessary equipment is located.

THE FUTURE AND IMPLICATIONS FOR PERSONAL IDENTITY

What alternatives are open?
For those who can accept the mythic answers of Judaism and Christianity, life will continue to have meaning, purpose, and destiny as defined
by those faiths. Myths will continue to function, bringing dreams to the
dreamless, identity to those lost in the vastness of the universe, and hope
to those who are overcome by the meaninglessness of their existence.
There will be ongoing struggle of the relationship of faith and work, of
mythic principles for life as it is lived away from cult centers. The depth
and breadth of the gap that can develop was amply demonstrated by the
so-called "Watergate affair," where men of high office, ostensibly committed to high principles of the cult, engaged in activities that denied the
mythic values they openly espoused.

Some people will continue the struggle to give meaning to what is,
ultimately, a meaningless life. Some find fulfillment in experimentation
with the rich variety of life-styles available—awareness of beauty in a
multitude of forms, open friendship with peoples of different backgrounds
and outlooks, and enjoyment of food, drink, touch, and feeling. Such
activists seek to keep life open to enriching possibilities. Other people
prefer quiet, uncritical acceptance of whatever life may bring, refusing to

push with determination in any particular direction, but attempting to remain open to potential experiences. Still others dedicate themselves to humanitarian causes, committed to binding the wounds and healing the ills of society. Others, like Gilgamesh in the earlier stages of his growth, engage in aggressive attack on life as if trying to wrench from it what it has to offer.

Ancient myths programmed persons to think in terms of right and wrong, good and bad, and thus provided a basis for judgment. Future myth may emphasize the actualizing of the individual self and may make persons aware of the ways in which environment and education program thought and response. Future myth may emphasize individual self-acceptance without feelings of inadequacy or guilt, free from the effort to be what others suggest one "ought" to be, released from such values as "goodness" and acceptance. If a rose is a rose is a rose, and nothing else, then a self is a self is a self, and nothing else.

Ancient myth solved the problem of individual loneliness and isolation by guiding followers into paths of obedience to certain norms. Hebrew mythologists wrote of the *derek Yahweh*—the way of Yahweh, the way of righteousness and justice (Gen. 18:19). Christian mythographers had Jesus state that he was *the* way, *the* truth, *the* life, and that no one could attain salvation except through him (John 14:6). Routes to wholeness, personal identity, and security were exclusively within the fold of the faithful. For many, these mythic promises have been fulfilled. For others, they are not the way; hopefully, future myth will present viable alternatives wherein individuals may find personal fulfillment without condemnation from those who accept different mythic answers.

Future myths may continue to emphasize the deity and the relationship between the divine and the human. If societal patterns move toward restrictive stratification, then the mythic image may project a god who favors and blesses organizational patterns that control life-style. On the other hand, if societal patterns move toward viability, then the divine image may be of a god who provides choices for mankind and who is not hostile if individuals or groups make the poorer or poorest of choices. Such a deity will be opposed to constriction of opportunities. The new myth might celebrate man as master or determiner of his existence, an existence haunted neither by ghosts of ancient gods nor by specters of deities that dimly threaten what may develop out of human experimentation in living. The new emphasis might well be on a god who encourages man to rejoice in the "now," in being and becoming, in feeling, responding, and existing without lurking insecurity about evaluation, judgment, and rewards or punishments in some distant afterworld.

Future myth may encourage humans to experiment with the variety of persons they can be. Why must one remain always the same? Why not change and become many things? Hermann Hesse's story of Piktor describes the sadness of being fixed and immovable while life metamorphoses all around.[17] We encourage specialization in education, expertise in some narrow field—and there can be no doubt that much human progress has been made by persons who have delved into specific problems, particularly in the sciences. But a scientist is also a person and need not be a scientist all the time. To escape from a mold, to touch other areas of life and living, to be open to new dimensions of feeling, experiencing, to be aware of the many facets of beauty is to be alive and involved in metamorphosis. The specialization remains; the experiences become kaleidoscopic.

NOTES

[1]Alvin Toffler, *Future Shock* (New York: Random House, 1970; Bantam paperback ed., 1971).

[2]Wallace Stevens, *Opus Posthumous* (New York: Alfred A. Knopf, 1957), p. 163. I am grateful to my colleague Donald E. Miller for this reference.

[3]Societal chaos is the theme of Anthony Burgess's vision of the future in *The Clockwork Orange* (New York: Norton, 1963), which has been made into a powerful motion picture.

[4]I have in mind a friend who teaches in an institution that requires teachers to sign a very conservative statement of faith each year. Throughout his years of service, my friend has moved away from some of the concepts included in the statement. But his whole life has been committed to work in the institution, he is approaching retirement, and it does not appear likely that he could find another teaching post. To refuse to sign would mean his dismissal and distress for his dependent family. His economic survival is involved. He assuages his conscience by stating each year that he is signing "under protest." Nothing changes, but at least he has "gone on record." He is not satisfied with the arrangement, and he experiences deep frustration and a sense of impotence. Some suggest that he has "copped out" because of cowardice, but he is caught between his developmental process and the system that supports him.

[5]The fear and insecurity associated with change are projected into the future when beings from other planets come into contact with earth creatures, in Robert A. Heinlein, *Stranger in a Strange Land* (New York: Putnam's, 1961). The Martian, Smith, felt threatened by his strange new environment among earth people.

[6]For example, see Jean Arp, *Arp on Arp: Poems, Essays, Memories,* ed. Marcel Jean, trans. Joachim Neuroschel (New York: Viking, 1970).

[7]Should laboratory reproductive techniques become a reality, then terms like *family, parents, mother, father, brother,* and *sister* will assume different connotations or will be limited in application to those who reproduce in the "old way."

[8]See B. F. Skinner, *Beyond Freedom and Dignity* (New York: Knopf, 1971; Bantam paperback ed., 1972). Skinner is one of the most recent of many writers foreseeing a structured society.

[9]See Robert Jungk, *Brighter Than a Thousand Suns* (Harmondsworth, Middlesex: Penguin, 1960), chap. 6.

[10]See Benjamin DeMott, "Vonnegut's Otherworldly Laugher," *Saturday Review: Books* (1 May 1971).

[11]William Faulkner, *As I Lay Dying* (New York: Random House, 1964).

[12]Donald Barthelme, "The Piano Player," in *Come Back, Dr. Caligari* (Garden City, N.Y.: Doubleday, 1965), a collection of black humor short stories.

[13]Kurt Vonnegut, Jr., *Cat's Cradle* (New York: Dell, 1963), *God Bless you, Mr. Rosewater* (New York: Dell, 1965), and *Player Piano* (New York: Delacorte, 1952).

[14]John Henry Newman, "Lead Kindly Light" (1833).

[15]"100-Year Life Expectancy Predicted for 2000 A.D.," *Today's Health* (Jan. 1968).

[16]A. Michel Aron, "The New Ice Age," in *West Magazine,* supplement to *The Los Angeles Times* (11 June 1972). See also Robert C. W. Ettinger, *The Prospect of Immortality* (Garden City, N.Y.: Doubleday, 1964).

[17]Miguel Serrano, *C. G. Jung and Hermann Hesse,* trans. Frank MacShane (New York: Schocken, 1966), pp. 15ff.

Bibliography

ABBATE, FRANCESCO, ed., *Egyptian Art,* H. A. Fields, trans. New York: Octopus Books, 1972.

ALDRED, CYRIL, *Egypt to the End of the Old Kingdom.* New York: McGraw-Hill, 1965.

ALTIZER, THOMAS J. J., ed., *Toward a New Christianity: Readings in the Death of God Theology.* New York: Harcourt Brace Jovanovich, 1967.

ALTIZER, THOMAS J. J., WILLIAM A. BEARDSLEE, and J. HARVEY YOUNG, eds., *Truth, Myth and Symbol.* Englewood Cliffs, N.J.: Prentice-Hall, 1961.

BARR, JAMES, "The Meaning of 'Mythology' in Relation to the Old Testament," *Vetus Testamentum,* IX (1959), 1–10.

BAUMGARTEL, E. J., *The Cultures of Prehistoric Egypt.* London: Oxford University Press, 1955.

BRADEN, WILLIAM, *The Private Sea: LSD and the Search For God.* Chicago: Quadrangle Books, 1967. Bantam paperback ed., 1968.

BRANDON, S. G. F., *The Judgment of the Dead.* London: Weidenfeld & Nicolson, 1967.

———, *Religion in Ancient History.* New York: Scribner's, 1969.

BRATTON, FRED G., *Myths and Legends of the Ancient Near East.* New York: Thomas Y. Crowell, 1970.

BREASTED, JAMES H., *The Dawn of Conscience.* New York: Scribner's, 1933.

———, *Development of Religion and Thought in Ancient Egypt.* New York: Scribner's, 1912. Harper Torchbook ed., 1959.

———, *A History of Egypt.* New York: Scribner's, 1905. Bantam paperback ed., 1964.

BUDGE, E. A. WALLIS, *Amulets and Talismans.* New York: Macmillan, 1970. A reprint of *Amulets and Superstitions,* Oxford, Masters and Fellows of University College, 1930.

———, *The Book of the Dead.* New York: University Books, 1960. A reprint of the Medici Society version of 1913.

———, *Egyptian Magic.* London: Kegan Paul, Trench, Trubner, 1901. Dover paperback ed., 1971.

———, *The Gods of the Egyptians* (2 vols). Chicago: Open Court, 1904. Republished in 1969 by Dover Publications, New York.

———, *Osiris.* New York: University Books, 1961. Reprinted from the 1911 ed.

CAMPBELL, JOSEPH, *The Hero with a Thousand Faces.* New York: World, 1956.

———, *The Masks of God: Creative Mythology.* London: Secker & Warburg, 1968.

————, *The Masks of God: Occidental Mythology*. London: Secker & Warburg, 1965.

————, *Myths, Dreams and Religion*. New York: Dutton, 1970.

————, *Myths to Live By*. New York: Viking, 1972.

CERAM, C. W., *The Secret of the Hittites*. New York: Knopf, 1956.

CHILDS, BREVARD S., *Myth and Reality in the Old Testament*, Studies in Biblical Theology, 27. London: S. C. M. Press, 1960.

CLARK, R. T. RUNDLE, *Myth and Symbol in Ancient Egypt*. New York: Grove Press, 1960.

COLE, WILLIAM GRAHAM, *Sex and Love in the Bible*. New York: Association Press, 1959.

COTTRELL, LEONARD, *The Anvil of Civilization*. New York: New American Library, 1957 (Mentor paperback).

————, *The Lost Pharaohs*. New York: Grossett & Dunlap, 1961.

CROSS, FRANK MOORE, *Canaanite Myth and Hebrew Epic*. Cambridge, Mass.: Harvard University Press, 1973.

CUMONT, FRANZ, *Oriental Religions in Roman Paganism*. Chicago: University of Chicago Press, 1911. Reprinted in a paperback ed. by Dover Publications, New York, 1956.

DANIEL, GLYN, *The First Civilizations*. New York: Thomas Y. Crowell, 1968.

DAVIES, G. H., "An Approach to the Problem of Old Testament Mythology," *Palestine Exploration Quarterly*. London: Office of the Fund, 1956, pp. 83–91.

DRIVER, G. R., *Canaanite Myths and Legends*, Old Testament Studies, III. Edinburgh: T. & T. Clark, 1956.

EDWARDEES, ALLEN, *Erotica Judaica*. New York: Julian Press, 1967.

EDWARDS, I. E. S., *The Pyramids of Egypt*, rev. ed. Baltimore: Penguin 1961.

EISELEY, LOREN, *The Unexpected Universe*. New York: Harcourt Brace Jovanovich, 1969.

ELIADE, MIRCEA, *Cosmos and History*, W. R. Trask, trans. New York: Harper & Row 1959 (Harper Torchbook). First published by Pantheon Books, 1954.

————, *Cosmos and History: The Myth of the Eternal Return*. New York: Bollingen Foundation, 1954. Reprinted as a Harper Torchbook, 1959.

————, *Rites and Symbols of Initiation*, W. R. Trask, trans. New York: Harper & Row, 1965 (Harper Torchbook). First published as *Birth and Rebirth*, 1958.

ELIADE, MIRCEA, and JOSEPH M. KITAGAWA, eds., *The History of Religions: Essays in Methodology*. Chicago: University of Chicago Press, 1959.

————, *The Quest: History and Meanings in Religion*. Chicago: University of Chicago Press, 1968.

————, *The Sacred and the Profane*, W. R. Trask, trans. New York: Harcourt Brace Jovanovich, 1959.

EMERY, W. B., *Archaic Egypt*. Baltimore: Penguin, 1961.

ENGNELL, I., *Studies in Divine Kingship in the Ancient Near East*. Uppsala, Sweden: Appelbergs Boktryckeriaktiebolag, 1953.

ERMAN, ADOLF, *A Handbook of Egyptian Religion*. London: Archibald Constable, 1907.

————, *The Literature of the Ancient Egyptians*. London: Methuen, 1927. Republished as a Harper Torchbook, 1966.

EVERY, GEORGE, *Christian Mythology*. London: Hamlyn Publishing Group, 1970.

FABUN, DON, *The Dynamics of Change.* Englewood Cliffs, N.J. Prentice-Hall, 1967.

FAIRSERVIS, WALTER A., JR., *The Ancient Kingdoms of the Nile.* New York: Thomas Y. Crowell, 1962. Also in a Mentor paperback ed.

FEIFEL, HERMAN, ed., *The Meaning of Death.* New York: McGraw-Hill, 1959; paperback ed., 1965.

FERGUSON, JOHN, *Moral Values in the Ancient World.* London: Methuen, 1958.

FRANKFORT, HENRI, *Ancient Egyptian Religion,* New York: Harper and Brothers, 1948. Harper Torchbook edition, 1961.

_____, *The Birth of Civilization in the Near East.* Bloomington: Indiana University Press, 1951. Reprinted as an Anchor paperback.

FRANKFORT, HENRI, et. al, *Before Philosophy.* Baltimore: Penguin, 1959.

FROMM, ERICH, *Psychoanalysis and Religion.* New Haven, Conn: Yale University Press, 1950. Bantam paperback ed., 1967.

GARDINER, ALAN, *Egypt of the Pharaohs.* New York: Oxford University Press, 1961. Paperback ed., 1972.

GASTER, THEODOR H., *Festivals of the Jewish Year.* New York: William Sloane Associates, 1952.

_____, ed., *The New Golden Bough.* New York: Criterion Books, 1959.

_____, *The Oldest Stories in the World.* New York: Viking, 1952. Republished as a Beacon paperback, 1958.

_____, "The Religion of the Canaanites," in *Forgotten Religions,* V. Ferm, ed. New York: The Philosophical Library, 1950, pp. 113–143.

_____, *Thespis: Ritual, Myth, and Drama in the Ancient Near East.* New York: Schuman, 1950. Rev. ed. by Doubleday, 1961. Harper Torchbook ed., 1961.

GHIRSHMAN, R., *Iran.* Baltimore: Penguin, 1954.

GILLISPIE, CHARLES COULSTON, *Genesis and Geology.* Cambridge, Mass.: Harvard University Press, 1951. Harper Torchbook, 1959.

GORDON, CYRUS H., *The Loves and Wars of Baal and Anat, and Other Poems from Ugarit.* Princeton, N.J.: Princeton University Press, 1943.

_____, *Ugaritic Literature.* Rome: Pontificium Institum Biblicum, 1949.

GRAY, JOHN, *The Canaanites.* London: Thames & Hudson, 1964.

_____, *The KRT Text in the Literature of Ras Shamra.* Documenta et Monumenta Orientis Orientis Antiqui. Leiden: E. J. Brill, 1964.

_____, *The Legacy of Canaan.* Leiden: E. J. Brill, 1957.

_____, *Near Eastern Mythology.* Feltham, Middlesex: Hamlyn Publishing Group, 1969.

GUNKEL, H., *The Legends of Genesis.* Chicago: Open Court, 1901; New York: Schocken, 1964.

GURNEY, O. R., *The Hittites.* Baltimore: Penguin, 1954.

GUTHRIE, HARVEY H., JR., *God and History in the Old Testament.* London: SPCK, 1961.

HABEL, NORMAN C., *Yahweh Versus Baal: A Conflict of Religious Cultures.* New York: Bookman Associates, 1964.

HADAS, MOSES, and MORTON SMITH, *Heroes and Gods.* New York: Harper & Row, 1965.

HAPPOLD, F. C., *Religious Faith and Twentieth-Century Man.* Baltimore: Penguin, 1966.

HARDEN, DONALD, *The Phoenicians: Ancient People and Places.* London: Thames & Hudson, 1963.

HAYES, WILLIAM C., "Most Ancient Egypt," *Journal of Near Eastern Studies,* XXIII (1964), 74–114, 145–92, 217–74.

HEIDEL, ALEXANDER, *The Babylonian Genesis,* 2nd ed. Chicago: University of Chicago Press, 1951. Phoenix paperback ed., 1963.

_____, *The Gilgamesh Epic and Old Testament Parallels.* Chicago: University of Chicago Press, 1946. Phoenix paperback ed., 1963.

HERNTON, CALVIN C., *Coming Together.* New York: Random House, 1971.

HOOKE, S. H., ed., *The Labyrinth.* London: SPCK, 1935.

_____, *Middle Eastern Mythology.* Baltimore: Penguin, 1963.

_____, *Myth, Ritual, and Kingship.* Oxford: Clarendon Press, 1958.

_____, *The Origins of Early Semitic Ritual.* The Schweich Lectures, 1935. London: Oxford University Press, 1938.

HUFFMAN, HERBERT B., "Prophecy in the Mari Letters," *The Biblical Archaeologist,* XXI, 4 (December 1963), 1110–21. Reprinted in *The Biblical Archaeologist Reader: 3,* New York: Doubleday, 1970, Anchor ed.

ILLICH, IVAN D., *Celebration of Awareness.* New York; Doubleday, 1970.

IONS, VERONICA, *Egyptian Mythology.* Feltham, Middlesex: Hamlyn Publishing Group, 1968.

JACOBSEN, THORKILD, "Primitive Democracy in Ancient Mesopotamia," *Journal of Near Eastern Studies,* II (1943), 159–72.

JACK, J. W., *The Ras Shamra Tablets: Their Bearing on the Old Testament.* Old Testament Studies No. 1. Edinburgh: T. & T. Clark, 1935.

JAMES, E. O., *The Ancient Gods.* London: Weidenfeld & Nicolson, 1960.

_____, *From Cave to Cathedral.* London: Thames & Hudson, n.d.

_____, *The Nature and Function of the Priesthood.* New York: Vanguard, 1955.

_____, *Marriage and Society.* New York: John de Graff, 1955.

_____, *Sacrifice and Sacrament.* New York: Barnes & Noble, 1962.

_____, *Seasonal Feasts and Festivals.* New York: Barnes & Noble, 1961.

JAMES, T. R., *Myths and Legends of Ancient Egypt.* New York: Grosset & Dunlap, 1971. Bantam paperback ed., 1972.

JUNG, CARL G., *Man and His Symbols.* Garden City, N.Y.: Doubleday, 1964.

JUNG, C. J., and KERENYI, C., *Essays on a Science of Mythology.* trans. R. F. C. Hull. New York: Harper & Row, 1963.

JUNGK, ROBERT, *Brighter Than 1000 Suns.* Harmondsworth, Middlesex: Penguin, 1960.

KAPELRUD, ARVID S., *Ba'al in the Ras Shamra Texts.* Copenhagen: G. E. C. Gadd, 1952.

_____, *The Ras Shamra Discoveries and the Old Testament,* trans. G. W. Anderson. Norman: University of Oklahoma Press, 1963.

KASTER, JOSEPH, *Wings of the Falcon.* New York: Holt, Rinehart and Winston, 1968.

KENYON, KATHLEEN, *Amorites and Canaanites.* The Schweich Lectures, 1963. London: Oxford University Press, 1966.

KEY, ANDREW F., "The Concept of Death in Early Israelite Religion," *Journal of Bible and Religion,* XXXII (1964), 239–47.

KITAGAWA, JOSEPH, M., and CHARLES H. LONG, eds., *Myths and Symbols.* Chicago: University of Chicago Press, 1969.

KLIEVER, LONNIE D., and JOHN H. HAYES, *Radical Christianity.* Anderson, S.C.: Droke House, 1968.

KRAMER, SAMUEL NOAH, ed., *Mythologies of the Ancient World.* Chicago: Quadrangle, 1961.

————, *The Sacred Marriage Rite.* Bloomington: Indiana University Press, 1969.

————, *Sumerian Mythology.* Philadelphia: American Philosophical Society, 1944. Rev. Torchbook ed., 1961.

————, *The Sumerians: Their History, Culture, and Character.* Chicago: University of Chicago Press, 1963.

LAMBERT, W. G., *Babylonian Wisdom Literature.* Oxford: Clarendon Press, 1960.

LAMBERT, W. G., and A. R. MILLARD, *Atra-Hasis, The Babylonian Story of the Flood.* Oxford: Clarendon Press, 1969.

LANGER, SUSANNE K., ed., *Reflections on Art.* Baltimore: Johns Hopkins Press, 1958.

LARUE, GERALD A., *Old Testament Life and Literature.* Boston, Mass: Allyn & Bacon, 1968.

LEWIS, I. M., *Ecstatic Religion.* Baltimore: Penguin, 1971.

LLOYD, SETON, *The Art of the Ancient Near East.* London: Thames & Hudson, 1961. Praeger paperback ed., 1965.

LOEW, CORNELIUS, *Myth, Sacred History and Philosophy.* New York: Harcourt Brace Jovanovich, 1967.

LOHMEYER, E., *Lord of the Temple,* trans. S. Todd. London: Oliver & Boyd, 1961, pp. 1–23.

LORENZ, KONRAD, *On Aggression.* New York: Harcourt Brace Jovanovich, 1966. Bantam ed., 1967.

MCKENZIE, JOHN L., "Myth and the Old Testament," *The Catholic Biblical Quarterly,* XXI (1959), 265–82.

————, *Myths and Realities: Studies in Biblical Theology.* Milwaukee: Bruce, 1963.

MASPERO, GASTON C. C., *Life in Ancient Egypt and Assyria,* rpt. 1892. English ed., New York: Ungar, 1971.

MAY, H. G., "Pattern and Myth in the Old Testament," *The Journal of Religion,* XXI (1938), 285–99.

MAY, ROLLO, ed., *Symbolism in Religion and Literature.* New York: Braziller, 1960.

MELLAART, JAMES, *Earliest Civilizations of the Near East.* London: Thames & Hudson, 1965.

MERCER, S. A. B., "The Religion of Ancient Egypt," in *Forgotten Religions,* ed. V. Ferm. New York: Philosophical Library, 1950.

————, *Tutankhamen and Egyptology.* London: A. R. Mowbray, 1923.

MERTZ, BARBARA, *Temples, Tombs, and Hieroglyphs.* New York: Coward-McCann, 1964.

MIDDLETON, JOHN, ed., *Myth and Cosmos.* Garden City, N.Y.: Natural History Press, 1967.

MILLER, ARTHUR R., *The Assault on Privacy.* Ann Arbor: University of Michigan Press, 1970 (now in a Mentor paperback ed).

MITCHELL, ROGER S., *The Homosexual and the Law.* New York: Arco, 1969.

MONTAGU, ASHLEY, *Sex, Man and Society.* New York: Putnam's, 1969.

MONTET, PIERRE, *Eternal Egypt.* trans. Doreen Weightman. London: Weidenfeld & Nicolson, 1964.

MOSCATI, SABATINO, *Ancient Semitic Civilizations.* New York: Putnam's, 1958.

———, *The Face of the Ancient Orient.* New York: Quadrangle, 1960. Anchor paperback ed., 1960.

MURRAY, HENRY A., ed., *Myth and Mythmaking.* New York: Braziller, 1960.

MURRAY, MARGARET A., *The Splendor That Was Egypt.* New York: Hawthorn, 1963.

NOBLECOURT, CHRISTIANE DESROCHES, *Ancient Egypt.* Greenwich, Conn.: New York Graphic Society, 1960.

OBERMANN, JULIAN, *Ugaritic Mythology: A Study of Its Leading Motif.* New Haven, Conn.: Yale University Press, 1948.

OGLETREE, THOMAS W., *The Death of God Controversy.* Nashville, Tenn.: Abingdon, 1966.

OLMSTEAD, A. T., *History of the Persian Empire.* Chicago: University of Chicago Press, 1948.

OPPENHEIM, A. LEO, *Ancient Mesopotamia.* Chicago: University of Chicago Press, 1964.

OSTBORN, GUNNAR, *Yahweh and Baal.* Arsskrift: Lunds Universitets, 1956.

OTTO, EBERHARD, *Ancient Egyptian Art.* New York: Abrams, 1967.

OTTO, WALTER, *Dionysus: Myth and Cult.* Bloomington: Indiana University Press, 1965.

PATAI, RAPHAEL, *Myth and Modern Man.* Englewood Cliffs, N.J.: Prentice-Hall, 1972.

———, *Sex and Family in the Bible.* New York: Doubleday, 1959.

———, "What Is Hebrew Mythology?" *Transactions of the New York Academy of Sciences,* Nov. 1964, pp. 73–81.

PEDERSEN, JOHS, "Canaanite and Israelite Cultus," *Acta Orientalia,* XVIII (1939), 1–14.

PEPIN, JEAN, *Myth et Allegorie.* Paris: Montaigne, 1957.

PERRY, JOHN WEIR, *Lord of the Four Quarters.* New York: Braziller, 1966. Collier paperback ed., 1970.

PIANKOFF, ALEXANDRE, *The Shrines of Tut-Ankh-Amon.* New York: Bollingen Foundation, 1955. Harper Torchbook ed., 1962.

PIGGOT, STUART, ed., *The Dawn of Civilization.* New York: McGraw-Hill, 1961.

POPE, M. H., *El in the Ugaritic Texts.* Vetus Testamentum Supplement II, 1955.

POULSEN, VAGN, *Egyptian Art.* Greenwich, Conn.: New York Graphic Society, 1968.

PYLE, LEO, ed., *Pope and Pill.* Baltimore: Helicon, 1969.

RAGLAN, LORD, *The Hero.* New York: Random House, 1956.

———, *The Temple and the House.* New York: Norton, 1964.

RANK, OTTO, *The Myth of the Birth of the Hero.* New York: Random House, 1959.

REIK, THEODOR, *Myth and Guilt.* New York: Grosset & Dunlap, 1970. Reprint of the 1957 ed.

The Report of the Commission on Obscenity and Pornography. New York: Random House, 1970. Bantam ed., 1970.

REYMOND, E. A. E., *The Mythical Origin of the Egyptian Temple.* New York: Barnes & Noble, 1969.

RINGGREN, HELMER, *Religions of the Ancient Near East,* trans. John Sturdy. Philadelphia: Westminster, 1973.

ROUX, GEORGES, *Ancient Iraq.* New York: World, 1965.

SAGGS, H. W. F., *The Greatness That Was Babylon.* New York: Hawthorn, 1962.

SANDARS, N. K., *The Epic of Gilgamesh.* Baltimore: Penguin, 1962.

SAUNERON, SERGE, *The Priests of Ancient Egypt.* New York: Grove, 1959.

SCHUTZ, WILLIAM C., *Joy.* New York: Grove, 1967.

SEBEOK, THOMAS A., *Myth, A Symposium.* New York: American Folklore Society, 1955; Bloomington: Indiana University Press, 1958. Paperback (Midland Book) ed., 1965.

SELLERS, JAMES, *Theological Ethics.* New York: Macmillan, 1966. Paperback ed., 1968.

Sex and the College Student. New York: Atheneum, 1965.

SEZNEC, JEAN, *The Survival of the Pagan Gods.* New York: Pantheon, 1953. Harper torchbook ed., 1961.

SIMPSON, WILLIAM KELLEY, ed., *The Literature of Ancient Egypt.* New Haven, Conn.: Yale University Press, 1972.

STEINDORFF, GEORGE, and KEITH C. SEELE, *When Egypt Ruled the East,* 2nd ed. Chicago: University of Chicago Press, 1957.

STEVENSON, W. TAYLOR, *History as Myth.* New York: Seabury, 1969.

TAYLOR, GORDON RATTRAY, *The Biological Time Bomb.* New York: New American Library, 1968 (now in a Mentor paperback ed.).

THOMAS, D. WINTON, ed., *Documents From Old Testament Times.* London: Thomas Nelson & Sons, 1958. Reprinted as a Harper Torchbook, 1961.

THORWALD, JÜRGEN, *Science and the Secrets of Early Medicine.* London: Thames & Hudson, 1962.

TODRANK, GUSTAVE H., *The Secular Search for a New Christ.* Philadelphia: Westminster, 1969.

TOFFLER, ALVIN, *Future Shock.* New York: Random House, 1970. Bantam ed., 1970.

TOOMBS, LAWRENCE E., "The Formation of Myth Patterns in the Old Testament," *The Journal of Bible and Religion,* XXIX (1961), 108–12.

VAHANIAN, GABRIEL, *The Death of God.* New York: Braziller, 1961.

VAN DER LEEUW, G., *Religion in Essence and Manifestation,* trans. J. E. Turner (2 vols.). London: Allen & Unwin, 1938. Reprinted as a Harper Torchbook, 1963.

VAN GENNUP, ARNOLD, *The Rites of Passage,* trans. Monika B. Vizedom and Gabrielle L. Caffee. Chicago: University of Chicago Press, 1960. Phoenix paperback ed., 1961.

VAN ZYL, A. H., *The Moabites,* Pretoria Oriental Series, III. Leiden: E. J. Brill, 1960.

VAUX, KENNETH, ed., *Who Shall Live?* Philadelphia: Fortress, 1970.

WALKER, Brooks R., *The New Immorality.* New York: Doubleday, 1968.

WHITE, J. E. MANCHIP, *Ancient Egypt.* New York: Thomas Y. Crowell, 1952. Dover paperback ed., 1970.

WHITELEY, C. H., and WHITELEY, WINIFRED, *Sex and Morals.* New York: Basic Books, 1967.

WILSON, JOHN A., *The Burden of Egypt.* Chicago: University of Chicago Press, 1951. Also available in a Phoenix paperback titled *The Culture of Ancient Egypt.*

WOOLLEY, C. LEONARD, *The Sumerians.* New York: Norton, 1965.

ZANDEE, JAN, *Death as an Enemy.* #5 Suppl. Leiden: E. J. Brill, 1960.

Index